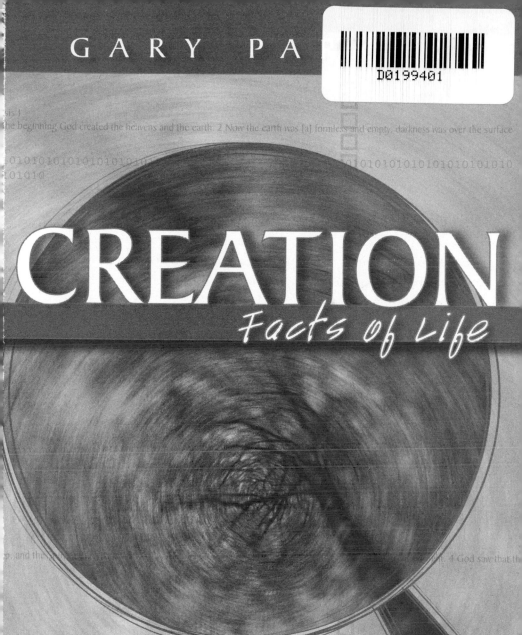

GARY PA

D0199401

CREATION
Facts of Life

How **Real Science**
Reveals the **Hand of God**

First printing: 1980
Tenth printing (revised): May 2006
Fifteenth printing: February 2013

ISBN: 978-0-89051-492-4
Library of Congress Number: 2006929843

Please consider requesting that a copy of this volume be purchased by your local library system.

Printed in the United States of America

Please visit our website for other great titles:
www.masterbooks.net

For information regarding author interviews, please contact the publicity department at (870) 438-5288

Master
Books®
A Division of New Leaf Publishing Group
www.masterbooks.net

Dedicated to

Charles Signorino, Allen Davis,
Henry M. Morris, and John C. Whitcomb,
men of science and men of God
who introduced me to the wonders of God's creation,
sorrow for my self-righteous sin,
the glorious joy of new life in Christ,
and the exhilarating freedom to build
my life and my science on the eternal foundation
of the written and Living Word
(John 1:1–3, 14).

CONTENTS

Chapter 1 — Evidence of Creation? 7

Where to Begin? 7

Tools for Inquiry: Logic and Observation 16

The Origin of Life: DNA and Protein 20

Comparative Similarities: Homology 43

Embryonic Development.. 54

Adaptation and Ecology: The Marvelous Fit
    of Organisms to Their Environments..................... 63

Think About It! 68

Chapter 2 — Darwin and Biologic Change 75

Design without a Designer 75

Natural Selection 76

Change, Yes; Evolution, No 80

Natural Selection, Yes; Evolution, No......................... 84

Mutation, Yes; Evolution, No 108

Variation, Yes; Evolution, No 126

Speciation, Yes; Evolution, No 133

Mutation-Selection in Biblical Perspective 138

Chapter 3 — The Fossil Evidence............................ 149

Introduction 149

I. WHAT KINDS? 153

Invertebrates: Animals Without Backbones 154

Fossil Plants 163

Vertebrates: Animals With Backbones 166

Human Beings 174

Summary: Fossil Kinds 186

II. HOW FAST? 191

The Grand Canyon 213

Index... 236

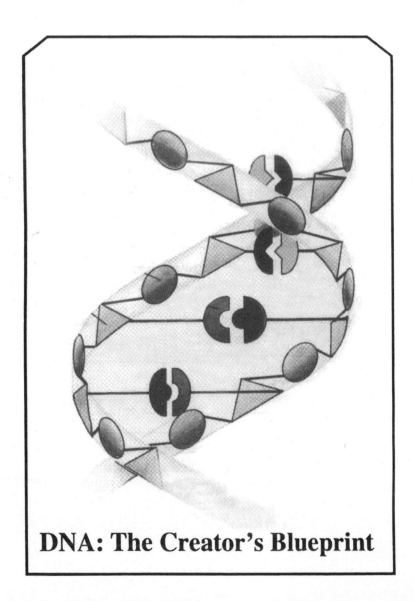

DNA: The Creator's Blueprint

Chapter 1

Evidence of Creation?

WHERE TO BEGIN?

"Evolution's just a theory. We don't have to believe it, do we?" Every year at least one of my students would bring up the "evolution's just a theory" argument, but I was ready. Feeling my heart starting to race, I would respond enthusiastically, "Oh, no. Evolution's a fact, perhaps the best established fact in all of science. It's the cornerstone of modern biology, and the basis for all of our thinking about the origin, meaning, and destiny of life!"

"It's easy to prove evolution," I'd say. "Just imagine you're on a cruise around the world (all expenses paid!) with a young man named Charles Darwin." Darwin had received college training in theology, but didn't really care for Bible study. He tried medical school, but didn't do well. He did enjoy nature study, and was an avid beetle collector. Both his interest in nature and his birth into a wealthy family helped make it possible for young Charles to travel as ship's naturalist aboard the HMS *Beagle* on its five-year circumnavigation of the globe, 1831–1836 (not bad work, if you can get it!).

Sailing through the Atlantic and around South America, Darwin arrived at the now-famous Galapagos Islands, on the equator about 600 miles (960 km) west of Ecuador. While there he saw sea turtles hatch out of the eggs that had been laid in beach sand above high tide. As they scrambled toward the sea, most of the hatchlings were gobbled up by predators. Perhaps only three in a hundred of the tiny turtles made it to saltwater, and perhaps two of those were eaten up by predators beneath the waves! Maybe only one in a hundred of the turtle hatchlings survived to grow and perpetuate the species.

This cruel, wasteful, and inefficient struggle for survival made a powerful impression on young Darwin. He found it increasingly difficult to reconcile his scientific observations of deadly struggle with biblical teachings about an all-powerful, all-loving God.

On the positive side, the young man who grew up in England had been astounded by the astonishing variety and beauty of life forms he'd seen where the *Beagle* stopped for study of tropical rain forests. On the Galapagos, his attention was drawn to a fascinating group of small birds now called Darwin's finches. Some with big beaks crushed seeds to eat; some with small beaks ate insects; one variety even used spines or thorns from plants to pry insects out of their burrows in bark.

Two dozen years after his fantastic voyage, an older Darwin made his observations of variety and struggle on the Galapagos Islands the basis of an evolutionary theory that shook the world. Some have called Darwin's *Origin of Species* (1859) second only to the Bible in its influence on human history; others would put it first.

Despite the profound impact of Darwinian evolution, his theory is based, simply and convincingly I'd tell my classes, on two irrefutable observations leading to one inescapable conclusion. First, living things exist in incredible variety, and each new generation expresses a wide range of traits. Second, all living things experience an intense struggle for existence, and only a few of each generation survive to reproduce and pass on their traits. Since there is variation and only some in each generation survive, the obvious and unmistakable conclusion is that some varieties are more likely to survive than others: **survival of the fittest!** In short form:

1. hereditary variation
+2. struggle for survival

=3. survival of the fittest

As I told my students, "Evolution is a fact; we see it going on around us every day. Does anyone doubt variation? Just look around the room, think of your parents and grandparents, or picture the many breeds of dogs, cats, horses, roses, oranges, etc. Does anyone doubt there's a struggle for survival? Think about lions pouncing on zebras, cats chasing mice, or kudzu vines destroying a forest (or getting out of bed Monday mornings). Add it up for yourself: nature 'selects' some varieties for survival rather than others. This **natural selection** of the fittest leads to evolutionary progress over time."

There is a price for this progress, however. Natural selection is based on a **struggle** to the **death,** what Darwin called the "**war of nature.**" *Hereditary variability can improve only if large numbers of the less fit die in each generation.* The horrific struggle and death Darwin saw in the Galapagos had caused him to begin doubting the existence of a loving God. But, in a complete about-face, Darwin came to see death in one generation as opening doors of opportunity for the next. *What had been ascribed to the creative power of God, Darwin credited instead to the creative power of struggle and death.* In concluding the book that changed the world's world view, Darwin wrote:

Thus, from the war of nature
from famine and death,
the production of higher animals
directly follows.

Darwin included mankind among the "higher animals" produced by the evolutionary **"war of nature,"** and so did I. Rejecting the biblical teaching that mankind was a special creation made in the image of some "God," I taught that we (like microbes, plants, and "other animals") were a result of *millions of years of struggle and death.*

Nothing supernatural was required for human origins, I emphasized, but only the ordinary **process of evolution — time, chance, struggle, and death.** Time and chance produce hereditary variation **(mutations)**; struggle and death **(natural selection)** determine which variations survive. I stressed time, chance, struggle, and death (mutation-selection) so much that my students began to abbreviate it **TCSD.**

Believing it was a consequence of millions of years of struggle and death, I summarized the classic sequence and significance of molecules-to-mankind evolution as follows:

> In the beginning, the earth was quite different from what it is now. Lightning flashed back and forth in an atmosphere of methane and ammonia for perhaps a billion years, producing molecules that rained down into the ancient oceans. Then, just by chance, a group of molecules got together that could reproduce, and life on earth began.
>
> About 500 million years ago, fossils first began to form, in abundance, of those early, simple kinds of life, forms like the trilobites. About 400 million years ago, the first land plants and animals appeared in the sequence. About four million years ago, certain ape-like animals took those first upright steps toward becoming human beings.
>
> People are the first animals able to look back over the history of their own evolution. As we do so, we learn things that help us understand ourselves and our nature. Why do we do things harmful to our own kind? It's that

"jungle fight for survival" that brought us into being in the first place.

But we're not without hope. We're already beginning to take control of that molecule of heredity, DNA. Using the techniques of genetic engineering, we can re-make ourselves into our own image of what mankind really ought to be. We're already reaching for the stars. There's simply no limit to what human beings can do.

For me, "evolution" was much more than just a scientific theory. It was a total world-and-life view, an alternate religion, a substitute for God. It gave me a feeling of my place in the universe, and a sense of my relationship to others, to society, and to the world of nature that had ultimately given me life. I knew where I came from and where I was going.

I had heard Christians and other "religious fanatics" talk about "back to God, back to the Bible, back to this, or back to that." But for me as an evolutionist, the best was yet to come. And, as a scientist and professor of biology, I could help make it happen. By contributing to advances in science and technology, both directly and through my students, I could be part of the process of bringing "heaven on earth."

Let's face it. Evolution is an exciting and appealing idea! A lot of scientific evidence can be used to support it. Perhaps most importantly for me and many others, evolution means there is no God, no "Creator" who sets the rules. Human beings are the top. Each of us is his or her own boss. We set our own rules, our own goals. We decide what's best for us.

I didn't just believe evolution; I embraced it enthusiastically! And I taught it enthusiastically. I considered it one of my major missions as a science professor to help my students rid themselves completely of old, "pre-scientific" superstitions, such as Christianity. In fact, I was almost fired once for teaching evolution so vigorously that I had Christian students crying in my class!

Once in a while Christian students would say something like, "You don't have to be that hard on the Bible or the Christian faith. After all, you can believe in the Bible and evolution at the same time." Thinking I had them in a trap, I would respond something like this: "Who wants to pray to a god that used millions of years of struggle and death to create things? Aren't time and chance the logical opposites of plan and purpose? What kind of god would wipe out 99 percent of all the species he/she/it created, and bury the mistakes in fossil graveyards? Besides that, don't you Christians believe God sent His Son, Jesus, to conquer death and give us new life? If God had been using millions of years of struggle and death to create things, Jesus would be opposing God's plan! You don't really understand evolution or the Bible either one!"

Although I thought I was "open-minded" and didn't mean to be mean, my remarks must have been offensive to many Christian students. Since Christians, Jews, and Muslims share the same basic account of creation and the earth's early history, my evolutionist exuberance would have been offensive to Jewish and Islamic students as well. Actually, I was more than willing to let students believe in whatever God they wanted to — so long as their religious belief did not dispute the "scientific fact of evolution."

Then I got invited to a Bible study. How silly, I thought, that educated people in this age of science would still study a dusty old outmoded book like the Bible, but the Bible study was led by the chemistry professor where I was teaching. More importantly, I was promised free coffee and donuts for coming. Now those are three of my favorite words: free . . . coffee . . . donuts! So, for less than honorable motives, my wife, Mary, and I set off for that Bible study. Besides, I thought, by pointing out all the obvious errors in the Bible, maybe I could convince them to study something more relevant, like evolution, for instance!

Most of the errors I tried to point out turned out to be my errors. The chemistry professor, Dr. Charles Signorino, was a

□ □ □ □ □ □ □ □ □ □ □ □ □

superb Bible teacher, and that got to be irritating, but the free coffee and donuts kept us coming back anyway. I soon learned, much to my amazement at first, that the Bible describes the origin and history of life on earth in a way dramatically different from evolution's story:

> In the beginning was God. With plan, purpose, and special acts of creation, God stretched out the heavens and clothed the earth with plants both "pleasant to the sight and good for food." He created our first parents (Adam and Eve) in His own "image," mandated that they care for and cultivate the earth as a "garden of delight" (Eden), and asked only for their love and trust.

> Unfortunately, our first parents sinned — rejected God's love and put their trust in their own opinions rather than God's Word. That self-centered arrogance ruined the world God had created "all very good," and brought death, disease, and disaster to the earth — a "bondage to decay."

> The early earth became so filled with violence and corruption that God destroyed it in a global flood to give the world a fresh start with Noah and those with him on the ark. Sadly, human evil has again polluted God's world, and the present world is destined for cleansing by fire. We might summarize the sad history of our planet so far as 3 Cs: creation, corruption, and catastrophe.

> We're not without hope. There is a fourth "C." The same God who created us, the same God who daily cares for us, is the same God who sent His Son, Jesus Christ, to conquer sin and death and to raise us to new life, rich and abundant, now and forever. As "new creations in Christ," we wait for a "new heaven and new earth," where "the wolf and the lamb will lie down together," there will be no more pain, tears, or death, and peace and paradise will be perfectly restored.

The evolutionary world view can be abbreviated TCSD for time, chance, struggle, and death. The biblical view can be represented as 7 Cs (say "Seven Seas"), but I'll focus on just 4 Cs: God's perfect world (creation), ruined by man (corruption), destroyed by Noah's flood (catastrophe), restored to a new life in Christ — *creation, corruption, catastrophe, Christ.*[1]

What a difference! In evolutionary thinking, time, chance, struggle, and death produce "new and improved" forms of life. In biblical thinking, chance and struggle produce disease, decline, and death. Evolution begins with dead things; living things — including us — are temporary intruders in the universe, and when the sun burns out, death wins at last. The Bible begins with the life of God; death is a temporary intruder, and eternal life wins at Christ's return.

Most people agree that it's the Bible that has the happy ending: life triumphs over death. During an interview, a famous evolutionist and anti-creationist admitted that it would be nice to believe that we were especially created by a loving God who put us here to superintend the earth. Then he quickly added that it isn't right. During a television program in which I also appeared, another leading evolutionist told how he had grown up in a religious household and had heard the "wonderful story" of a beautiful creation, ruined by man's sin, restored by Christ's love. Then he went on to say that the whole of his scientific training, indeed the whole development of science during the last 200 years, had convinced him the "wonderful story" was wrong.

That's the way I looked at it, too; the Bible was just a story with a happy ending — like all those other fairy tales. My strong belief in evolution was a huge stumbling block to my accepting the good news of new life in Christ. I thought evolution had proved the Bible was wrong, and that there was no God out there to keep all its wonderful promises.

Dr. Signorino, an excellent Bible teacher, was also a top-notch scientist. He challenged me to look again at the scientific evidence I thought I knew so well. Then Allen Davis, a biologist newly hired at the college, began to share creationist evidences and resources with me, including the famous (or infamous) book by John C. Whitcomb and Henry M. Morris, *The Genesis Flood*. For three years we argued creation/evolution. For three years I used all the evolutionary arguments I knew so well. For three years I lost every scientific argument. Reluctant and surprised, I finally concluded that what we read in God's Word is the surest guide to understanding what we see in God's world.

Now I'd like to invite you to consider some of the evidences that suggest the "wonderful story" is true after all! And it's not just me. Thousands of scientists are sharing the scientific evidences in God's world that encourage us to believe all the wonderful promises and principles in God's Word, the Bible.

How can that be? How can *scientists* — *all using the same evidence* — come up with such different ideas about what that evidence means? Hasn't "science" proved the Bible wrong? Don't we "know" that man created "God" in his image when he reached the stage of abstract thought in evolution? Wouldn't going back to believing God created man in His image bring back other superstitions and destroy the very fabric of society in our scientific age? Isn't it unconscionable (and unconstitutional) to mix religion, like the Bible, with science, like evolution?

People do get "fired up" about creation/evolution. There really are important issues at stake here, both personal and social. That's all the more reason to hold our emotions in check and to examine our beliefs calmly and thoughtfully. After all, it's important to know not only what we believe but *why we believe it.* Being comfortable and confident with our beliefs means that we have honestly considered the merits of beliefs different from ours, and understanding another's beliefs helps to generate *respect* and *compassion*, even if the disagreement is deep, profound, and absolute.

I love science. This book is especially for those who love and/or respect science. In it I'd like to share with you some of the *scientific* evidence that helped to change me, as a biology professor, from an enthusiastic (even "evangelical") belief in evolution to a belief instead that the Bible is the best guide to understanding God's world and our place in His plan. The Bible contains no *explicit* references to DNA, mutations, fossils, or the Grand Canyon, so my scientific *applications* of biblical truths are no better than the evidence I use to support them.

I also want you to understand evolution clearly and thoroughly, so I'll also be going over with you — as I still do with my students — all the standard textbook arguments used in favor of evolution.

Take your time. Be critical. Think it through. It took me three years of re-examining the evidence before I gave up my deep-seated belief in evolution and concluded, like thousands of other scientists in recent times, that the 4 C biblical outline of earth history is the more logical inference from our scientific observations.

TOOLS FOR INQUIRY: LOGIC AND OBSERVATION

Science is both a fabulous body of knowledge and a fantastic method of investigation. Most people just assume evolution can be studied scientifically — but not creation. According to a slogan popular these days, "Evolution is science, and creation is religion," and that's supposed to stop the discussion even before it starts. Let's start, then, with the most basic question of all: Is it really possible to talk honestly and fairly about *scientific* evidence of *creation*??

For many people, that question is a major stumbling block. Some even use it as an excuse to throw creation out of the courtroom or classroom without even hearing the evidence, but nothing is really easier for scientists and just "ordinary people" than finding and recognizing evidence of creation.

To illustrate, let me borrow your imagination for a moment. Imagine that you are walking along a creek on a lazy summer afternoon, idly kicking at the pebbles along the bank. Occasionally you reach down to pick up a pebble that has an unusual shape. One

□□□□□□□□□□□□□□□

pebble reminds you of a cowboy boot (Figure 1). As you roll the pebble around in your hand, you notice that the softer parts of the rock are more worn away than the harder parts, and that lines of wear follow lines of weakness in the rock. Despite some appearance of design, the boot shape of the tumbled pebble is clearly the result of time, chance, and the processes of weathering and erosion.

But then your eye spots an arrowhead lying among the pebbles (Figure 1). Immediately it stands out as different. In the arrowhead, chip marks cut through the hard and soft parts of the rock equally, and the chip lines go both with and across lines of weakness in the rock. In the arrowhead, we see matter shaped and molded according to a plan that gives the rocky material a special purpose.

You have just done what many people dismiss as impossible. In comparing the pebble and arrowhead, you were easily able to recognize evidence of creation. I am speaking here only of human creation, of course. The arrowhead might have been carved by one of my ancestors (a Cherokee), for example, but the same approach can be used even when we don't know who or what the creative agent might have been.[2]

What does it take to recognize evidence of creation? Just the ordinary tools of science: logic and observation.

Using your knowledge of erosional processes and your observations of hard and soft rock, you were able to distinguish a result of time and chance (the tumbled pebble) from an object created with plan and purpose (the arrowhead). If we had found such objects as arrowheads on Mars, all scientists would have recognized them immediately as the products of creation, even though in that case we would have no idea who made them or how. The late Carl Sagan, the evolutionist of *Cosmos* television fame, spent millions of dollars listening for signals from outer space, because he knew full well that we can tell the difference between wave patterns produced by time and chance and those sent with design and purpose.

Pebble
Time and Chance:
Properties of Matter

Arrowhead
Design and Creation:
Properties of Organization

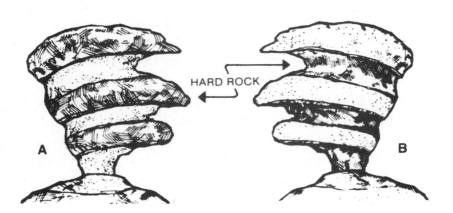

HARD ROCK

A

B

Figure 1. Try your hand at recognizing scientific evidence of creation. Both rock formations above resemble a man's head, but examine the relationship between hard and soft rock in each. Which (A or B) is more likely the result, like the tumbled pebble, of *time and chance* acting on the properties of hard and soft rock? Which is more likely the result, like the arrowhead, of plan and purpose? Can you recognize *evidence of creation* without seeing either the creator or the creative act?

I was in a friendly mini-debate at a California college when the evolutionist interrupted me: "But creation can't be scientific. Science deals only with things you can see and touch. Take energy, for example. . . ." Then he stopped. "Whoops! Made a mistake, didn't I?" I hastened to agree. He, his students, and I all knew that there are forms of energy, like gravity, that you can't see or touch or put in a bottle. Yet you know "gravity" is there (whatever it is!) because you can see the effects it has on matter. Similarly, God is a Spirit and can't be seen — but you can see His effects on matter. Even the Bible tells us that "the invisible things of God are clearly seen in all the things that have been made" (Rom. 1:20).

Note: You don't have to see the Creator, and you don't have to see the creative act, to recognize evidence of creation. Even when we don't know who or what the creative agent is, there are cases where "creation" is simply the most logical inference from our scientific observations.

Although the pebble and the arrowhead are made of the same substance, they reflect two radically different kinds of order. The tumbled pebble has the kind of order that results from time and chance operating through weathering and erosion on the inherent properties of matter. Those same factors will eventually destroy not only the pebble, but also the arrowhead, which has the kind of order clearly brought into being by plan and purpose, mind acting on matter.

In a way, the tumbled pebble represents the idea of *evolution.* As I once believed and taught, evolutionists believe that life itself is the result, like the tumbled pebble, of *time, chance, and the inherent properties of matter.* The arrowhead represents the *creation* idea, that living systems have *irreducible properties of organization* that were produced, like the arrowhead, by *plan, purpose, and special acts of creation.*

In our daily experience, all of us can differentiate these two kinds of order (inherent and *"exherent"*). On the basis of logic and observation, for example, we recognize that wind-worn rock formations are the products of time, chance, and the inherent properties of matter. Those same techniques (logical inference from scientific observations) convince us that pottery fragments and rock carvings must be the products of plan, purpose, and acts of creation giving matter irreducible properties of organization.

Let's suppose for a moment you are willing to agree, even tentatively and reluctantly, that "creation" (the model, the process, and the products) *can* be studied scientifically. Does that mean you have to be (shudder) a "creationist?" Not at all! Indeed, there were a couple of teachers at a California university convinced, as I am, that creationist ideas can be tested scientifically — but they thought that scientific tests proved them false! So we can agree ahead of time that both classic models of origin, creation and evolution, can be compared on the basis of scientific merit, but that still leaves it up to me to convince you that the bulk of scientific evidence available supports the Bible, not evolution.

So far, we've only agreed to discuss, to "reason together." Now, let's apply these ordinary scientific techniques to the study of living systems. When it comes to the origin of life, which view is the more logical inference from our scientific observations? Time, chance, and the evolution of matter? Or plan, purpose, and special acts of creation?

THE ORIGIN OF LIFE: DNA AND PROTEIN

The two basic parts of the tumbled pebble and the arrowhead we considered are hard and soft rock. Two basic parts of every living system are DNA and protein.

DNA is the famous molecule of heredity. It's a focus of crime scene investigations, and we often hear news stories about it. This is the molecule that gets passed down from one generation to the next. Each of us starts off as a tiny little ball about the size of a period on a printed page. In that tiny ball, there are over six feet (2m) of DNA all coiled up. All of our physical characteristics (height, skin color, etc.) are "spelled out" in that DNA.

What are proteins? Proteins are the molecules of structure and function. Hair is mostly protein; skin cells are packed full of proteins; the enzymes that break down food and build it up are proteins; the filaments that slide together to make muscles work are proteins.

So DNA and protein are two basic "parts" of every living system. When you get down to a virus, that's all you find — DNA and protein. (In some viruses, RNA substitutes for DNA.) The DNA molecules code for the protein molecules that make us what we are. That same principle applies to all life forms: viruses, plants, and animals, as well as human beings.

My students study all of the details,[3] but DNA and protein molecules are really quite simple in their basic structure. If you can picture a string of pearls, you can picture DNA: it is a chain of repeating units. Figure 2-A is a diagram of a DNA molecule. The parts that look like railroad boxcars are sugar and phosphate groups, and the parts that stick out from each boxcar in the chain are groups called *bases*.

Proteins are built in about the same way. Proteins are also chains of repeated units. As shown in Figure 2-B, the links in protein chains are called *amino acids*. In all living things, inherited chains of DNA bases are used to line up chains of amino acids. These amino acid chains are the protein molecules responsible for structure and function. For example, chains of several hundred DNA bases tell the cell how to make a protein called hemoglobin, and that protein functions as the oxygen carrier in red blood cells. In short form, *DNA → protein → trait*, and that relationship is the physical basis of all life on earth.

Now, what about that relationship between DNA and protein? How did it get started? Evolutionists picture a time long ago when the earth might have been quite different. They imagine that fragments of DNA and fragments of protein are produced. These molecules are supposed to "do what comes naturally" over vast periods of time. What's going to happen? Will time, chance,

Figure 2-A. *DNA* is built like a string of pearls, whose links (specifically the *bases* G, C, A, and T) act like alphabet letters that "spell out" hereditary instructions.

Figure 2-B. *Proteins* are chains of *amino acids*. Each chain coils into a special shape that has some special function: muscle contraction, digestion, oxygen transport, holding skin together, etc.

and chemical reactions between DNA and protein automatically produce life?

At first, you might think so. After all, nothing is more natural than a reaction between acids and bases. Perhaps you've used soda (a base) to clean acid from a battery. The fizz is an acid-base reaction. So is using "Tums" to neutralize stomach acid. Nothing is more common than reactions between acids and bases. If you just wait long enough, acid-base reactions will get DNA and protein working together, and life will appear — right? Wrong! Just the opposite.

The problem is that the properties of bases and acids produce the *wrong* relationship for living systems. Acid-base reactions would "scramble up" DNA and protein units in all sorts of "deadly" combinations. These reactions would prevent, not promote, the use of DNA to code protein production. Since use of DNA to code protein production is the basis of all life on earth, these acid-base reactions would *prevent,* not promote, the evolution of life by chemical processes based on the inherent properties of matter.

These wrong reactions have produced serious problems for Stanley Miller, Sidney Fox, and other scientists trying to do experiments to support chemical evolution. Almost all biology books have a picture of Miller's famous spark chamber (Figure 3). In it, Miller used simple raw materials and electric sparks to produce amino acids and other simple molecules — the so-called "building blocks of life." Some newspapers reported that Miller had practically made "life in a test tube."

Miller's experiment was brilliant, and I loved to tell my students about it. Then I came to see there were just three little problems: he had the wrong starting materials, used the wrong conditions, and got the wrong results.

What do I mean by "wrong starting materials"? Miller left out oxygen. Why? Because of the scientific evidence? No. He left it out because he knew oxygen would destroy the very molecules he

Labels in figure:
Electrodes
Spark discharge
Gases
CH₄
NH₃
H₂O
H₂
Condenser
Water containing organic compounds
Trap
WRONG MOLECULES AND RIGHT MOLECULES IN THE WRONG PLACES
Base – Acid

Figure 3. Left to time, chance, and their chemical properties, the bases of DNA and amino acids of proteins would react in ways that would prevent, not promote, the evolution of life. In the same way, reactions among molecules in Miller's famous "spark chamber" would destroy any hope of producing life. Living systems must constantly repair the chemical damage done to them, and when biological order loses out to inherent chemical processes, death results — even though a dead body has all the right molecules in the right places in the right amounts at the right times (almost!).

was trying to produce. It's hard for us to realize how "corrosive" oxygen is, since most modern living things depend on it. But oxygen is so valuable to life precisely because it's so chemically reactive, and aerobic living things today have systems to protect themselves against the harmful effects of oxygen, while using its chemical power to their advantage. (Anaerobic organisms and some viruses are quickly destroyed by contact with oxygen.)

A.I. Oparin, the Russian biochemist who "fathered" modern views of spontaneous generation or chemical evolution, knew oxygen in the atmosphere would prevent evolution. He also "knew," by faith in Engels' materialistic philosophy (the view that matter is the only reality), that creation was impossible (there was no spiritual dimension). As an act of faith, then, Oparin believed evolution must have occurred, and as a concession to his faith, he left oxygen out. Science has not been kind to that belief. We find oxidized rocks, suggesting an oxygen atmosphere, as deep as we can dig.

Furthermore, methane (CH_4) and ammonia (NH_3), two prime gases in the Miller spark chamber, could *not* have been present in large amounts. The ammonia would be dissolved in the oceans, and the methane should be found stuck to ancient (deep) sedimentary clays. It's not there! Those who still believe in chemical evolution are aware of these problems (as is Miller himself), so they are simply trying (as yet unsuccessfully) to simulate the origin of life using different starting materials. (Carbon monoxide and hydrogen cyanide are two popular, if unlikely, gases being used today.)

Wrong conditions? Miller used an electric spark to get the gas molecules to combine, and that works. Problem: The same electric spark that puts amino acids together also tears them apart, and it's much better at destroying them than making them, meaning that few, if any, amino acids would actually accumulate in the spark chamber. Miller, a good biochemist, knew that, of course, so he used a common chemist's trick. He drew the products out of the spark chamber and into a "trap" that would save the amino acids from destruction by the same electric spark that made them. Using product removal (the principle of LeChatelier or law of mass action) to increase yield is ordinary chemical practice, but it depends on intervention by informed intelligence. Miller was supposed to be demonstrating that the gases could make the "building blocks of life" all by themselves without any outside help, yet *his* outside, intelligent help was necessary to save the molecules from their destructive chemical fate. (Moreover, creating life in a test tube as a consequence of intelligent design would offer more support to creation than to evolution.)

Wrong results? How could that be? Miller wanted to make amino acids, and he got amino acids (along with sugars and a few other things). How could those results be wrong?

The proteins in living cells are made of just *certain kinds* of amino acids: those that are "alpha" (short) and "left-handed." Miller's "primordial soup" contained many long (beta, gamma, delta) amino acids and equal numbers of both right- and left-handed forms. Problem: Just one long or right-handed amino acid inserted into a chain of short, left-handed amino acids would prevent the coiling and folding necessary for proper protein function. What Miller *actually* produced was a seething brew of potent poisons that would absolutely destroy any hope for the chemical evolution of life.

The "left-handed amino acid problem" is particularly well-known to evolutionists, and several have been trying to solve it. One brilliant researcher, after working unsuccessfully for years on the problem, just smiled and chuckled when asked about it: "Perhaps God is left-handed." He may have been closer to the truth than he realized. From what we know about the chemistry of the molecules involved, it really looks like the molecules could never put themselves together into living cells apart from the careful selection, engineering genius, and deliberate design of the transcendent, creative intelligence we call God![4]

Chemistry, then, is not our ancestor; it's our problem. When cells lose their biological order and their molecules start reacting in chemical ways, we die. A dead body contains all the molecules necessary for life and approximately the right amount of each, but we never see a "road kill" get up and walk off because sunlight energy shining on the carcass made all the molecules of life start working together again. What's lost at death are balance and biological order that otherwise use food to put us together faster than chemistry tears us apart! (See Bliss and Parker[5]; Illustra Media[6]; and Thaxton, Bradley, and Olsen[7] for details.)

Time and chance are no help to the evolutionist either, since time and chance can only act on inherent chemical properties. *Trying to throw "life" on a roll of molecular dice is like trying to throw a "13" on a pair of gaming dice.* It just won't work. The possibility is not there, so the probability is just plain *zero*.

The relationship between DNA and protein required for life is one that no chemist would ever suspect. It's using a series of bases (actually taken three at a time) to line up a series of R-groups (Figure 4). R-groups are the parts of each amino acid that "stick out" along the protein chain. "R" stands for the "variable radical," and variable it is! An R-group can be acid; it can be a base; it can be a single hydrogen atom, a short chain, a long chain, a single ring, a double ring, fat-soluble, or water-soluble!

The point is this: There is no inherent chemical tendency for a series of bases (three at a time) to line up a series of R-groups in the orderly way required for life. The base/R-group relationship has to be *imposed on* matter; it has *no basis within* matter.

The relationship between hard and soft rock in the arrowhead in Figure 1 had to be imposed from the outside. All of us could recognize that matter had been shaped and molded according to a *design* that could not be produced by time, chance, and weathering processes acting on the hard and soft rock involved. In the same way, our *knowledge* of DNA, protein, and their chemical

Time and Chance:
Properties and Matter

BASE-ACID, ETC!

BASES → R

Design and Creation:
Properties of Organization

3 BASES → 1 R

Figure 4. All living cells use groups of three DNA bases as code names for amino acid R-groups. But all known chemical reactions between these molecules (e.g., base-acid) would prevent, not promote, development of this coding relationship. Is the hereditary code, then, the logical result of time, chance, and the inherent properties of matter (like the water-worn pebble), or does it have the irreducible properties of organization (like the arrowhead) that scientists ordinarily associate with plan, purpose, and creative acts?

properties should lead us to infer that *life also is the result of plan, purpose, and special acts of creation.*

Let me use a simpler example of the same kind of reasoning. Suppose I asked you this question: Can aluminum fly? Think a moment. Can aluminum fly? I'm sure that sounds like a trick question. By itself, of course, aluminum can't fly. Aluminum ore in rock just sits there. A volcano may throw it, but it doesn't fly. If you pour gasoline on it, does that make it fly? If you pour a little rubber on it, that doesn't make it fly, either. Suppose you take that aluminum, stretch it out in a nice long tube with wings, a tail, and a few other parts. Then it flies; we call it an airplane.

Did you ever wonder what makes an airplane fly? Try a few thought experiments. Take the wings off and study them; they don't fly. Take the engines off, study them; they don't fly. Take the pilot out of the cockpit; the pilot doesn't fly. Don't dwell on this the next time you're on an airplane, but an airplane is a collection of non-flying parts! Not a single part of it flies!

What does it take to make an airplane fly? The answer is something every scientist can understand and appreciate, something every scientist can work with and use to frame hypotheses and conduct experiments. What does it take to make an airplane fly? *Creative design and organization.*

Take a look at the features of a living cell diagrammed in Figure 5. Don't worry; I am not going to say much about this diagram. Just notice the DNA molecule in the upper left circle and the protein in the lower right. What are all the rest of those strange looking things diagrammed in the cell? Those represent just a few of the molecules that a cell needs to make just one protein according to the instructions of just one DNA molecule. A cell needs over 75 "helper molecules," all working together *in harmony,* to make one protein (R-group series) as instructed by one DNA base series. A few of these molecules are RNA (messenger, transfer, and ribosomal RNA); most are highly specific proteins.[8]

Figure 5. Living cells use over 75 special kinds of protein and RNA molecules to make one protein following DNA's instructions. What we know about airplanes convinces us that their flight is the result of creative design. What scientists know about the way living cells make protein suggests, just as clearly, that life also is the result of creative design. The real "heroes," the molecules that establish the non-chemical, grammatical/linguistic coding relationship between triplet base codons and amino acid R-groups are the set of specific activating enzymes I call "translases." (Drawing from Bliss and Parker, *Origin of Life* [Green Forest, AR: Master Books, 1979]).

Contrary to popular impression, DNA does not even possess the genetic *code* for making protein, but only the genetic *alphabet*. The "alphabet letters" of DNA (the four bases, abbreviated GCAT) are used in groups of three (triplet codons) as code names for the 20 different amino acids of proteins. But bases are equally spaced along DNA; there's nothing in the structure or chemistry that even hints why or which bases should be grouped as triplet codons. Three letter groupings are *not inherent* in base sequences; they are *imposed on* the base series by huge cellular particles called ribosomes.

Ribosomes don't act directly on DNA, but on expendable "base pair copies" of DNA called messenger RNA, or mRNA. The production of mRNA, and of more DNA for reproduction, is magnificently profound, but it's a simple consequence of interlocking base shapes and ordinary chemical attraction (mediated by enzymes). The way ribosomes establish the genetic coding system, however, completely transcends the inherent properties of DNA bases.

Ribosomes are "molecular machines" each consisting of about 50 specific proteins and three large RNA molecules. Its overall 3-D shape gives a ribosome two adjacent slots each precisely shaped to hold three and only three bases, thus establishing the triplet coding system. This coding system is not based on time, chance, and the properties of the bases, but on plan, purpose, and intelligent design. In the structure of the ribosome, however, as in the arrowhead, nothing supernatural, complex, or even unusual is involved, and the function of the ribosome is easy to understand and explain. In both the ribosome and the arrowhead, the evidence of creation is not in what we can't see and don't know; it's in the pattern of order ("exherent") that we do see and can explain: matter shaped and molded to accomplish the purpose of its Creator, not to satisfy inherent chemical properties.

Besides the above, the ribosomes which establish the amino acid code names for making proteins are themselves made of

50 or more specific proteins. It takes specific proteins to establish the code for making specific proteins, so how did the system get started? Evolutionists admit that's a problem for them because they insist evolution based on time, chance, and the properties of matter is a blind process that can't plan ahead or work toward a goal. On the other hand, creationists see the goal-oriented function of ribosomes as another evidence of creation. Like batteries can be used to start car engines that then recharge the batteries, so proteins can be used to code for the production of proteins that can then "recharge" the coding proteins.

And there's more. Even after ribosomes establish triplet codon names for amino acids, the protein building blocks have no chemical way to recognize their code names! All sorts of wrong chemical reactions between amino acids and base triplets are possible, but these would destroy the code. It falls to transfer RNA (tRNA) molecules to pick up amino acids and base pair them with their codons on the ribosome slots. The base pairing of tRNA and mRNA triplets is based on interlocking shapes and ordinary chemical attraction, but the proper pairing of tRNAs with amino acids requires much more than ordinary chemistry.

When it comes to "translating" DNA's instructions for making proteins, the real "heroes" are the activating enzymes that unite specific tRNA/amino acid pairs. Enzymes are proteins with special slots for selecting and holding other molecules for speedy reaction. As shown in Figure 5 (circle 3), each activating enzyme has five slots: two for chemical coupling *(c, d)*, one for energy (ATP), and, most importantly, two to establish a *nonchemical* three-base "code name" for each different amino acid R-group *(a, b)*. You may find that awe-inspiring, and so do my cell biology students!

The living cell requires at least 20 of these activating enzymes I call **"translases,"** one for each of the specific R-group/code name (amino acid/tRNA) pairs. Even so, the whole set of translases (100 specific active sites) would be (1) *worthless* without ribosomes (50 proteins plus rRNA) to break the base-coded message of heredity into three-letter code names; (2) *destructive* without a continuously renewed supply of ATP energy to keep the translases from tearing up the pairs they are supposed to form; and (3) *vanishing* if it weren't for having translases and other specific proteins to re-make the translase proteins that are continuously and rapidly wearing out because of the destructive effects of time and chance on protein structure!

Most enzymes are proteins that select and speed up chemical reactions that would occur slowly without them. *Translases* are an entirely different category of enzymes. They *impose a relationship* that transcends the chemistry of base triplets and amino acids, *a code that would not occur at all, slowly or otherwise, in their absence.*

Let's forget about all the complexity of the DNA-protein relationship and just remember two simple points. First, it takes *specific* proteins to make *specific* proteins. That may remind you of the chicken-and-egg problem: how can you get one without the other? That problem is solved if the molecules needed for "DNA-protein translation" are produced by creation.

Second, among all the molecules that translate DNA into protein, there's not one molecule that is alive. There's not a single molecule in your body that's alive. There's not a single molecule in the living cell that's alive. A living cell is a collection of non-living molecules! What does it take to make a living cell alive? The answer is something every scientist recognizes and uses in a laboratory, something every scientist can logically infer from his observations of DNA and protein. What does it take to make a living cell alive? *Creative design and organization!*

Only creative acts could organize matter into the first living cells, *but once all the parts are in place, there is nothing "supernatural" or "mysterious" in the way cells make proteins. If* they are continually supplied with the right kind of energy and raw materials, and *if all* 75-plus of the RNA and protein molecules required for

DNA-protein "translation" are present in the *right* places at the *right* times in the *right* amounts with the *right* structure, *then* cells make proteins by using DNA's base series (quite indirectly!) to line up amino acids at the rate of about two per second. *In ways scientists understand rather well,* it takes a living cell only about four minutes to "crank out" an average protein (500 amino acids) according to DNA specifications.

Scientists also understand how airplanes fly. For that very reason, no scientist believes that airplanes are the result of time, chance, and the properties of aluminum and other materials that make up the airplane. Flying is a property of organization, not of substance. A Boeing 747, for example, is a collection of 4.5 million non-flying parts, but thanks to design and creation (and a continuous supply of energy and of repair services!), it flies.

Similarly, "life" is a property of *organization,* not of *substance.* A living cell is a collection of several billion non-living molecules, and death results when a shortage of energy or a flaw in the operational or repair mechanisms allows inherent chemical processes to destroy its biological order.

It's what we *do know* and *can explain* about aluminum and the laws of physics that would convince us that airplanes are the products of creation, even if we never saw the acts of creation. In the same way, it's what we *do know* and *can explain* about DNA and protein and the laws of chemistry which suggests that life itself is the result of special creation.

My point is not based on design *per se,* but on the *kind of design* we observe. As creationists point out, some kinds of design, such as snowflakes and wind-worn rock formations, *do* result from time and chance — *given* the properties of the materials involved. Even complex relationships, such as the oxygen-carbon dioxide balance in a sealed aquarium, can result from organisms "doing what comes naturally," *given* the properties of living things. But just as clearly, other kinds of design, e.g., arrowheads and airplanes, are the direct result of creative design and organization giving matter properties it doesn't have and can't develop on its own. What *we know* about the DNA-protein relationship suggests that living cells have the *created kind* of design. It's not so much the molecular complexity as it is the *transcendent simplicity*.

In the well-known *Scientific American* book, *Evolution*, Dickerson[9] seems to support my point (without meaning to, I'm sure). After describing the problems in producing the right kinds of molecules for living systems, he says that those droplets that by "sheer chance" contained the right molecules survived longer. He continues, "This is not life, but it is getting close to it. The missing ingredient is. . . ."

What will he say here? The "missing ingredient" is . . . one more protein? . . . a little more DNA? . . . an energy supply? . . . the right acid-base balance? No, he says: "The missing ingredient is an orderly mechanism. . . ." *An orderly mechanism!* That's what's missing — but that's what life is all about! As I stated before, life is not a property of substance; it's a property of organization. The same kind of reasoning applies to the pyramids in Egypt, for example. The pyramids are made of stone, but studying the stone does not even begin to explain how the pyramids were built. Similarly, until evolutionists begin to explain the origin of the "orderly mechanism," they have not even *begun* to talk about the origin of life.

When it comes to the evolutionary origin of that orderly mechanism, Dickerson adds, we have "no laboratory models; hence one can speculate endlessly, unfettered by inconvenient facts." With "no laboratory models" to provide data, the case for the *evolution* of life must be based on *imagination*. But, as Dickerson admits, "We [evolutionists] can only imagine what probably existed, and our imagination so far has not been very helpful."

The case for *creation*, however, is not based on imagination. Creation is based instead on *logical inference* from our *scientific observations*, and on simple acknowledgment that everyone, scientists and laymen alike, recognize that certain kinds of order imply creation.

Let me give you another example of the same sort of reasoning. Imagine that you have just finished reading a fabulous novel. Wanting to read another book like it, you exclaim to a friend, "Wow! That was quite a book. I wonder where I can get a bottle of that ink?" Of course not! You wouldn't give the ink and paper credit for writing the book. You'd praise the author, and look for another book by the same writer. By some twist of logic, though, many who read the fabulous DNA script want to give credit to the "ink (DNA base code) and paper (proteins)" for composing the code.

In a novel, the ink and paper are merely the means the author uses to express his or her thoughts. In the genetic code, the DNA bases and proteins are merely the means God uses to express His thoughts. The real credit for the message in a novel goes to the author, not the ink and paper, and the real credit for the genetic message in DNA goes to the Author of life, the Creator, not to the creature (Rom. 1:25).

The message conveyed by DNA is the kind called "*specified complexity*" in contrast to randomness or "mere" order. It takes only a simple program or algorithm, for example, to generate a random sequence of letters: (1) Print any letter; (2) Repeat step 1. An ordered, repeat pattern, such as ABCABCABC, could be generated by an algorithm nearly as simple: (1) Print ABC; (2) Repeat step 1. A program ENORMOUSLY larger and more sophisticated would be required to specify, for example, the letter sequence in the first volume of an encyclopedia set! The letter sequence is complex and specific ("specified complexity"), like the base letter sequence in human DNA — except that the DNA contains more information than a thousand volumes of literary works![10]

Occasionally, naïve evolutionists argue that crystal formation demonstrates that order can appear spontaneously, without "supernatural" help. *Crystal order, yes; specified complexity, no.* A crystal is a beautiful but simple repeat pattern produced by the shape and charge of its constituents. At 32°F (0°C), for example, the areas of partial plus and minus charges on water molecules attract them with a force greater than the thermal motion that keeps them apart at higher temperatures. The exquisite shape of the ice crystal is an automatic consequence of the shape and charge distribution ("design features") of the water molecules. (Incidentally, ice crystal formation is driven by decreasing electrostatic potential, an illustration — not a contradiction — of the famed second law of thermodynamics.)

The "specified complexity" in a DNA sequence is nothing like the "ordered simplicity" or repeat pattern in the ice crystal. Breaking a big ice crystal produces little ice crystals, each with structures and properties like the original. Breaking a DNA chain produces fragments that are dissimilar in structure and lose their function entirely. A child at home can make ice crystals; it takes a team of chemists using expensive equipment to produce a specific DNA sequence from scratch.

The *specified complexity* in a DNA gene sequence has very *high information content*. Scientists know two things about information. First, information is independent of the material that carries it. The phrase "In God We Trust" can be written in pen or pencil, typed onto paper or a computer screen, embroidered in lace, etched in stone, impressed on American coins, etc. The message is the same in any case, and it is obviously not produced by the material that conveys it. In other words, informational messages — including genetic messages — have the "exherent" kind of design, reflecting plan, purpose, and special acts of creation. Thus, the *meaning of a message lies with its Creator, not its carrier*.

Second, information comes only from pre-existing information. Much more information on information can be found in the landmark[11] book by internationally respected information theorist Werner Gitt, *In the Beginning Was Information*. Biblically, that concept is expressed as "In the beginning, God . . ."

(Gen. 1:1) and as "In the beginning was the Word" (John 1:1). The word "Word," identified as Jesus Christ in John 1:14, is the Greek word "*Logos.*" Logos is a grand word in Greek, connoting divine plan, reason for being, etc., and means "study of" as the suffix "ology" attached to the various academic disciplines. Wow! Our DNA ties us back to the ultimate source of meaning and purpose for the whole universe!

Creation thus stands between the classic extremes of mechanism and vitalism. Mechanists, including evolutionists, believe that both the *operation* and *origin* of living things are the result of the laws of chemistry which reflect the inherent properties of matter. Vitalists believe that both the operation and origin of living systems depend on mysterious forces that lie beyond scientific description. According to creation, living things, including their DNA codes, *operate* in understandable ways that can be described in terms of scientific laws, but such observations include properties of organization that logically imply a created origin of life.

In this sense, the Bible proved to be, as it often has, far ahead of its time. Into the 1800s, most scientists and philosophers believed living things were made of something fundamentally different from non-living. Genesis 1–2 tells us living things, human beings included, were just made of "dust of the ground." Indeed, scientists now recognize that living cells are composed of only a few simple elements. It's not the stuff ("dust") we're made of that makes us special; it's the *way* we're put together. It's not the metal and glass that make an airplane fly, nor the ink and paper that write a novel. Similarly, it's not the "dust" that makes life, but the way it's put together with creative design and organization. When that organization is lost, we return to "dust," the simple elements that we are made of, just as other created objects break down into their simpler parts when left to the ravages of time, chance, and chemistry.

The creationist, then, recognizes the orderliness that the vitalist doesn't see, but he doesn't limit himself to only those kinds of order that result from time, chance, and the properties of matter, as the evolutionist does. Creation introduces levels of order and organization that greatly enrich the range of explorable hypotheses and turn the study of life into a *scientist's delight*. Science requires an orderliness in nature. One of the real emotional thrills of my changing from evolution to creation was realizing both that there are many more levels of order than I had once imagined and that order in nature, and a mind in tune with it, were guaranteed by God himself. It's no wonder that explicit biblical faith gave initial success to the founding fathers of modern experimental science (a couple of centuries before evolution came along to shift the basis toward time and chance).

If the evidence for the creation of life is as clear as I say it is, then other scientists, even those who are evolutionists, ought to see it — and they do.

I once took my students to hear Francis Crick, who shared a Nobel Prize for the discovery of DNA's structure. After explaining why life could not and did not evolve on earth, he argued instead for "directed panspermia," his belief that life reached earth in a rocket fired by intelligent life on some other planet. Crick admitted that his view only moved the creation-evolution question back to another time and place, but he argued that different conditions (which he did *not* specify) might have given life a chance to evolve that it did not have on earth.[12]

Creationists are pleased that Crick recognized the same fatal flaws in chemical evolution that they have cited for years, but creationists also point out that the differences between "chemical chemistry" and "biological chemistry" are wrapped up with the fundamental nature of matter and energy and would apply on other planets as well as on earth. [13]

That opinion seems to be shared in part by famed astronomer Sir Fred Hoyle,[14] who made the news under the heading: "There *must* be a God." Hoyle and his colleague, Chandra Wickramasinghe, independently reached that conclusion after their mathematical analyses showed that believing that life could result from time, chance, and the properties of matter was like believing that "a tornado sweeping through a junkyard might assemble a Boeing 747 from the materials therein."

Drawing the logical inference from our scientific knowledge, both scientists concluded that "it becomes sensible to think that the favorable properties of physics on which life depends are in every respect *deliberate*" (emphasis Hoyle's). Both were surprised by their results. Hoyle called himself an agnostic, and, in the same article, Wickramasinghe said he was an atheistic Buddhist who "was very strongly brainwashed to believe that science cannot be consistent with any kind of deliberate creation."

My purpose in quoting these scientists (and others later on) is not, of course, to suggest that they are creationists who would endorse all my views.[15] Rather, it is simply to show that experts in the field, even when they have no preference for creationist thinking, at least agree with the creationists on the facts, and when people with different viewpoints agree, we can be pretty sure what the facts are. I also want to show that scientists who are not creationists are able to see that creation is a legitimate scientific concept, whose merits deserve to be compared with those of evolution.

In that light, I'd like to call your attention to a fascinating and revolutionary book, *Evolution: A Theory in Crisis,* by a prominent molecular biologist, Dr. Michael Denton.[16] In a television program we did together, and in our extensive personal conversations, Dr. Denton describes himself as a child of the secular age who desires naturalistic explanations when he can find them. When it comes to the origin of life, Dr. Denton explains with authority and stark clarity that evolutionists are nowhere near a *naturalistic* explanation at present. After comparing the genetic programs in living things to a library of a thousand volumes encoding a billion bits of information and all the mathematically intricate algorithms for coordinating them, Dr. Denton refers to the chemical evolution scenario as "simply an affront to reason," i.e., an insult to the intelligence! (p. 351).

He openly and frankly states that the thesis of his book is "anti-evolutionary" (p. 353), but it seems to me that he is cautiously taking a step even further. The first chapter of his book is titled "Genesis Rejected," and he would react very strongly against being called a creationist, but in his honest analysis of the creation-evolution controversy through history, Dr. Denton freely admits that many of the scientific views of the early creationists have been vindicated by modern discoveries in science.

Take William Paley's classic argument that design in living things implies a Designer just as clearly as design in a watch implies a watchmaker. In *The Blind Watchmaker*,[17] discussed later, Richard Dawkins argues — incorrectly — that Paley was wrong. Denton states, "Paley was not only *right* in asserting an analogy between life and a machine, but also *remarkably prophetic* in guessing that the technological ingenuity realized in living systems is vastly in excess of anything yet accomplished by man" (emphasis added). Then Denton goes on to summarize his thinking on life's origin (p. 341) as follows:

> The almost irresistible force of the analogy has completely undermined the complacent assumption, prevalent in biological circles over most of the past century, that the design hypothesis can be excluded on the grounds that the notion is fundamentally a metaphysical *a priori* concept and therefore scientifically unsound. *On the contrary, the inference to design is a purely* a posteriori *induction based on a ruthlessly consistent application of the logic of analogy.* The conclusion may have religious implications, but *it does not depend on religious presuppositions* (emphasis added).

Now that's quite an admission! Even though he would deny any leaning toward a Christian concept of creation, this leading molecular biologist sees quite plainly that a scientific concept of creation can be constructed, just as I've said, using the ordinary tools of science, logic, and observation. In fact, Denton intimates that creation scientists have shown more respect than evolutionists for empirical evidence and a "ruthlessly consistent" application of logic!

It's also true, as Denton concludes, that creation may have religious implications, but so does evolution, and that should not prevent our evaluating their scientific merits on the basis of logic and observation alone.

In a short but thought-provoking article, British physicist H.S. Lipson[18] reached the same conclusion. First he expressed his interest in life's origin, then his feeling — quite apart from any preference for creation — that, "In fact, evolution became in a sense a scientific religion; almost all scientists have accepted it and many are prepared to 'bend' their observations to fit with it."

After wondering how well evolution has stood up to scientific testing, Lipson continues: "To my mind, the theory [evolution] does not stand up at all." Then he comes to the heart of the issue: "If living matter is not, then, caused by the interplay of atoms, natural forces, and radiation [i.e., time, chance, and chemistry], how has it come into being?" After dismissing a sort of directed evolution, Lipson concludes: "I think, however, that we must go further than this and admit that the only acceptable explanation is *creation*" (emphasis his).

Like Hoyle and Wickramasinghe, Lipson is a bit surprised and unhappy with his own conclusion. He writes, "I know that this [creation] is anathema to physicists, as indeed it is to me." But his sense of honesty and scientific integrity forces him to conclude his sentence thus: ". . . but we must not reject a theory that we do not like if the experimental evidence supports it."

By the way, let me assure you that not *all* who see the evidence of creation are unhappy about it! Witness Dr. Dean Kenyon. Dr. Kenyon is a molecular biologist whose area of research interest is specifically the origin of life. His book on life's origin, *Biochemical Predestination,* opened with praises for Darwinian evolution, and he taught evolution at San Francisco State University for many years.

A couple of students in Dr. Kenyon's class once asked him to read a book by Dr. Duane Gish on creation science. He didn't want to, but thanks to their polite persistence (1 Pet. 3:15), he resolved to read it and refute it, but, as I heard him tell it, he read it and *couldn't* refute it. Instead, Dr. Kenyon got interested in creation science and began a long re-evaluation of the scientific evidence, which finally led him to the *happy* conclusion that life, including his, is here as a result of creation, the deliberate plan and purpose of a personal Creator God![19]

COMPARATIVE SIMILARITIES: HOMOLOGY

If God made people as people, why are we full of "animal parts"? Look at your arm for a moment and try to picture the bones inside. There's one bone attached to the body, two bones in the forearm, a little group of wrist bones, and bones that extend out into the fingers. As it turns out, there are many other living things that have forelimbs with a similar pattern: the foreleg of a horse or dog, the wing of a bat, and the flipper of a penguin, for example, as shown in Figure 6. Biologists use the term "homology" for such similarities in basic structure.

Why should there be that kind of similarity? Why should a person's arm have the same kind of bone pattern as the leg of a dog and the wing of a bat? There are two basic ideas. One of these is the evolutionary idea of *descent from a common ancestor.* That idea seems to make sense, since that's the way we explain such similarities as brothers and sisters looking more alike than cousins do. They have parents closer in common.

Using descent from a common ancestor to explain similarities is probably the most logical and appealing idea that evolutionists have. Some think that our ability to classify plants and animals on a groups-within-groups hierarchical basis virtually forces

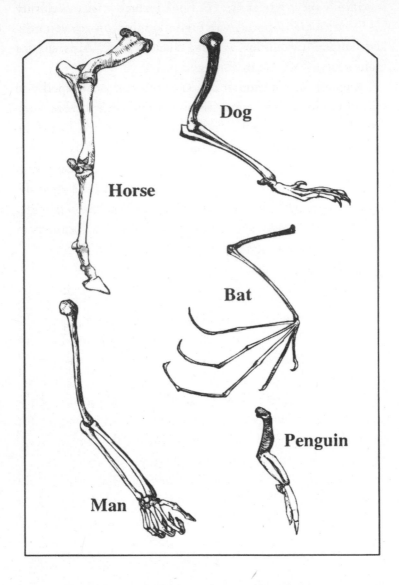

Figure 6. Bones in the human arm, the forelimbs of horses and dogs, a bat's wing, and a penguin's flipper all share a similarity in basic structural pattern called *homology*. What does this similarity (homology) mean: descent from a *common ancestor* (evolution), or creation according to a *common plan* (creation)?

scientists to treat evolution as a "fact." However, we can classify kitchen utensils on a groups-within-groups basis, but that hardly forces anyone to believe that knives evolved into spoons, spoons into forks, or saucers into cups and plates.

After all, there's another reason in our common experience why things look alike. It's *creation according to a common plan.* That's why Fords and Chevrolets have more in common than Fords and sailboats. They share more design features in common.

What's the more logical inference from our observation of bone patterns and other examples of homology: descent from a common ancestor, or creation according to a common plan? In many cases, either explanation will work, and we can't really tell which is more reasonable. But there seems to be times when the only thing that works is creation according to a common design.

I get support for my claim again from Denton,[20] in his chapter titled "The Failure of Homology." Dr. Denton is not only a research scientist with a Ph.D. in molecular biology, but also an M.D. with an intimate knowledge of comparative anatomy and embryology. He admits his desire to find naturalistic explanations for patterns of similarity among organisms (homology), but he also admits the failure of evolutionary explanations.

Like every other scientist, Denton recognizes the striking similarity in bone pattern evident between vertebrate fore- and hindlimbs. Yet no evolutionist, he says, claims that the hindlimb evolved from the forelimb, or that hindlimbs and forelimbs evolved from a common source. I was once taught to refer to corresponding parts of the male and female reproductive systems as "sexual homology." Homology, in that case, could not possibly be explained by descent from a common ancestor; that would mean that males evolved from females, or vice versa, or that human beings evolved from some animal that had only one sex.

Worse yet for evolution, structures that appear homologous often develop under the control of genes that are *not* homologous. In such cases, the thesis that similar structures developed from genes modified during evolutionary descent is precisely falsified.

In frogs, for example, the five digits on each limb grow out from buds on the embryonic paddle; in human embryos, the digits form as the tissue between them is resorbed. Here quite *different* gene-enzyme mechanisms produce *similar* (homologous) patterns. Structures in adult lobsters and crayfish are so similar (homologous) that the same lab instructions can be used for dissecting either, yet the crayfish egg develops directly into the adult form while the lobster egg reaches the homologous pattern through a free-swimming larval stage.

Our observation of similarity or homology is real enough, but that's true, Denton points out, "whether the causal mechanism was Darwinian, Lamarckian, vitalistic, *or even creationist*" (emphasis added). Although the evidence is not as spectacular and compelling as the biomolecular data, I would say the weight of our present knowledge of homology favors Denton's final alternative: creation according to a common design.

Perhaps the clearest anatomical evidence of creation is "convergence." The classic example is the similarity between the eyes of humans and vertebrates and the eyes of squids and octopuses. Evolutionists recognize the similarity between the eyes easily enough, but they've never been able to find or even imagine a common ancestor with traits that would explain these similarities. So, instead of calling these eyes homologous organs, they call them examples of "convergent evolution." Rather than evolution, however, we have *another* example of similarity in structure that cannot be explained as evolutionary descent from a common ancestor.

Convergence, in the sense of similar structures designed to meet similar needs, would be expected, of course, on the basis of creation according to a common design. As we'll see later, both the octopus eye and the vertebrate eye are complete, complex, and totally distinct from one another right from their first appearance in the fossil sequence. Biologist Michael Land[21] sounds like a creationist when he mentions in passing that the vertebrate eye "shares design features but not evolution" with the eye of the cephalopod mollusks such as the octopus.

The real focus of Land's article, however, is "divergence," the occurrence of quite distinct structures in plants and animals that otherwise are supposed to be close evolutionary relatives. Certain shrimp-like animals that live in deep ocean darkness, he says, have compound eyes with lenses all arranged to focus light at a common point (rather than forming multiple images, as most compound eyes do). But, he continues, some members of the group have "lens cylinders" that smoothly bend the incoming light (because of smoothly varied refractive indices), whereas others have square facets with a "mirror system" for focus (utilizing even a double-corner bounce). Ingenious use of physics and geometry should be evidence enough of creation it seems to me — but there's more.

Comparing the mirrors with the lens cylinder system, Land says, "Both are successful and very sophisticated image-forming devices, but I cannot imagine an intermediate form [or common ancestral type] that would work at all." The kind of design in these eyes, he says, seems impossible to explain as a result of evolutionary relationship. So Land goes on to suggest that the shrimp-like animals with different systems should not be classified as evolutionary relatives, even though they are otherwise quite similar.

Even more interesting is Land's statement about how he felt when he was trying to figure out the mirror system. He said he was "trying not to come to the conclusion that these eyes had been put there by God to confuse scientists." They may confuse evolutionists, but may I suggest instead that these eyes were put there by God to *inform* scientists. As such cases show, a mind open to examples of created order can hasten and enrich the scientific search for understanding.

Some evolutionists admit they have failed to find good evidence of evolution in comparing large structures, so they are looking instead for homology among molecules. In a foundational book basically describing the three-dimensional structures first known for proteins, Dickerson and Geis[22] state that "from the perfection of protein sequence and structure analysis. . . . We can pin down with great precision the relationships between the species and how the proteins evolved." Then, with every example they give, they proceed to *disprove* that evolutionary prediction.

Consider hemoglobin, for example, the protein that carries oxygen in red blood cells. Dickerson says that hemoglobins pose "a puzzling problem. Hemoglobins occur sporadically among the invertebrate phyla [the animals without backbones] in no obvious pattern." That is, they don't occur in an evolutionary *branching* pattern. I would suggest that they *do* occur in a creationist *mosaic* or *modular* pattern, like bits of blue-colored stone in an artist's mosaic. We find hemoglobin in nearly all vertebrates, but we also find it in some annelids (the earthworm group), some echinoderms (the starfish group), some mollusks (the clam group), some arthropods (the insect group), and even in some bacteria! In all these cases, we find the same kind of molecule — complete and fully functional. As Dickerson observes, "It is hard to see a common line of descent snaking in so unsystematic a way through so many different phyla. . . ."

If evolution were true, we ought to be able to trace how hemoglobin evolved. But we can't. Could it be *repeated* evolution, the spontaneous appearance of hemoglobin in all these different groups independently, asks Dickerson? He answers that repeated evolution seemed plausible only as long as hemoglobin was considered just red stuff that held oxygen. It does *not* seem possible, he says, that the entire eight-helix folded pattern appeared repeatedly by time and chance. As far as creationists are concerned, hemoglobin occurs, complete and fully functional, wherever it is appropriate in the Creator's plan, somewhat like a blue-colored tile in an artist's mosaic.

Mosaic refers here to a picture or mural formed of many little bits of colored stone. According to the **mosaic concept of kind,** God used several different genes or gene sets over and over again in different combinations and proportions to make a variety of life forms, somewhat like an artist might use several different kinds of colored stones over and over in different proportions and arrangements to make a variety of artistic designs. The different bits of stone in the artist's mosaic would correspond to the many different genes or gene sets in God's "mosaics," which are the various forms of living things.

According to this *mosaic* concept, also called *modular* or *matrix,* God used a basic plan in making living creatures, somewhat similar to the plan He used in making different non-living substances. All the countless chemical substances in the universe are made from different combinations and proportions of only about a hundred different elements, usually displayed in a "chemistry mosaic" called the periodic table. Each kind of chemical compound can be represented by a formula expressing the number, kind, and arrangement of elements within it.

Perhaps God used genes as "elements" in making the various kinds of life, so that conceivably each different kind of life could be represented by a *"formula"* representing the number, kind, and arrangement of different genes in its chromosomes. Such formulas would, of course, be much larger and much more complex than those for the most complicated chemical substances. Nevertheless, the mosaic concept does suggest that all the incredible variety and diversity of life forms we see about us may be constructed using only the information in a few thousand DNA segments, compared to about 100 chemical elements. Even more exciting, creationists might be able to use a mosaic pattern (or mathematical matrix) to predict the existence of unknown organisms and their features, like Mendeleev used his periodic table to predict the existence and properties of elements before their discovery.

The mosaic, non-branching (non-evolutionary) pattern of trait distribution produces practical problems for the biologist. Algae are usually classified into major groups on the basis of their pigment (greens, reds, browns, goldens, etc.), for example. But then both their structural complexity (unicellular, colonial, multicellular) and type of sexuality (iso-, hetero-, or oo-gamy) must be re-evolved independently ("convergently") on different branches of the evolutionary tree based on color. If they are classified by level of structural complexity, then neither the color pattern nor type of sexuality can be traced back to one common ancestor. Similarly, the evolutionary tree based on type of sexuality contradicts the branching trees predicted by pigment and structural complexity.

While he was yet the internationally respected senior paleontologist at the British Museum, Colin Patterson[23] stunned the scientific world by calling evolution an "anti-theory" that generates "anti-knowledge" — a concept full of explanatory vocabulary that actually explains nothing and that even generates a false impression of what the facts are.

Patterson said that he finally awoke, after having been duped into taking evolutionism as revealed truth all his life, to find that evolutionary theory makes bad systematics (the science of classification). He then proceeded to examine the data as a creationist would, in simple recognition that creationists produce testable hypotheses, and that he could understand and explain what inferences creationists would draw from the data, without either agreeing or disagreeing with them. What a superb example of healthy scientific skepticism! Patterson was able to see the data regarding homology in their wholeness, and experience the unbridled freedom to wonder not only *how* but *whether* evolution occurred!

Some are hoping that DNA comparisons and gene sequencing ("molecular homology") can somehow salvage evolutionary classification.[24] Is there anyone who hasn't heard that DNA comparison suggests something like 98 percent similarity between man and chimpanzee? The evidence so convinced one evolutionist debater that he told the audience if a chimp asked to take his daughter out on a date, he was not sure he could say "No." (I hope the daughter would be allowed to say "No.") There are even some groups pushing for the extension of U.N. human rights protection to chimps and orangutans!

It only takes a trip to the zoo, of course, to convince us that man and ape share many features, and there are unseen similarities in bone, muscle, nerve and sense organs, circulatory and digestive systems, hair, milk, etc. It should be equally obvious, however, that creatures designed by the same Creator to move, eat, breathe, etc. in similar ways would have many molecular similarities in common.

An article on "The 2% Difference" (*Discover*, April 2006) praises evolution and puts down intelligent design, but the author (Sapolsky) actually admits and describes key evidences noted by creation scientists over the past two decades.[25] "Regulation is everything," he says. A sidewalk, fence, patio, and house may be made of bricks that are 100 percent identical, for example, but they are arranged in different ways to serve dramatically different purposes. Sapolsky points out that the brains of man and chimp operate using "the same basic building blocks" while they achieve "vastly different outcomes," so that in his opinion "there's not the tiniest bit of scientific evidence that chimps have aesthetics, spirituality, or a capacity for irony or poignancy." These awesome gaps or "qualitative distinctions" between the brains of chimps and people Sapolsky credits to a "relatively few" genes that regulate the number of brain cells (neurons) produced. Sapolsky seems to forget, of course, that a dysfunctional or diseased brain has just as many neurons as the ones we call normal, and stuffing more chips into a computer does not automatically improve it. It's not just the number of parts that produce the great gulf between human and chimp; it's how the parts are connected. As creation scientists have long noted, and the Bible implies, living things (and their functioning parts) are not a product of substance, but of organization. At the atomic level ("dust of the ground"), all organisms are essentially 100 percent identical; if the 2 percent difference in DNA presumed for man and chimp told the other 98 percent how to organize, the differences would be at least as vast and unbridgeable as we observe.

And there's more. The April 2006 *Discover* article finally admitted what creation scientists have stressed for over 20 years: "a tiny 2% difference translates into tens of millions of AGCT differences." Indeed, a 2 percent difference among three billion base pairs would mean about *60 million* code letter differences between man and chimp. So, as creationists pointed out long ago and Sapolsky admits, "There are likely to be nucleotide differences in every single gene." In fact, reported in 2004 studies comparing chimp chromosome 22 with its presumed counterpart on human chromosome 21 showed a DNA difference of about 1.5 percent resulted in differences of more than 80 percent among the proteins produced by those genes.[26] That did not surprise creation scientists, but shocked evolutionists.

Actually, studies of molecular homology have produced major controversies within the evolutionists' camp, since DNA trees frequently disagree with evolutionary trees based on fossils and/or on comparative anatomy. The evolutionist split is greatest when it comes to conflicting attempts (based on dubious, compounded assumptions) to use molecular homology as some sort of "evolutionary clock." After documenting the misfit of molecular data with both of two competing evolutionary views, Michael Denton[27] writes this summary (p. 306):

> The difficulties associated with attempting to explain how a family of homologous proteins could have evolved at constant rates has created chaos in evolutionary

□□□□□□□□□□□□□□

thought. *The evolutionary community has divided into two camps — those still adhering to the selectionist* position, and those rejecting it in favor of the *neutralist*. The devastating aspect of this controversy is that neither side can adequately account for the constancy of the rate of molecular evolution; yet *each side fatally weakens the other.* The selectionists wound the neutralists' position by pointing to the disparity in the rates of mutation per unit time, while the neutralists destroy the selectionists' position by showing how ludicrous it is to believe that selection would have caused equal rates of divergence in "junk" proteins or along phylogenetic lines so dissimilar as those of man and carp. Both sides win valid points, but in the process the credibility of the molecular clock hypothesis is severely strained and with it the *whole paradigm of evolution itself is endangered* (emphasis added).

Denton doesn't stop with these devastating anti-evolutionary comments (and a comparison of belief in molecular clocks with belief in medieval astrology!). He also describes data from molecular homology as a "biochemical echo of typology," where typology is the pre-evolutionary view of classification developed by scientists on the basis of creationist thinking.

Although partial data fit too easily into conflicting branching patterns, comparative similarities and homologies don't fit well at all onto evolutionary trees. They fit instead into hierarchical (groups within groups) categories, perhaps suggesting a multidimensional matrix (a "cube of cubes" in more than three dimensions). When Mendeleev discovered the pattern God used in creating the chemical elements, he was able to predict the existence and properties of elements not then known to science. Creationists may one day discover predictive patterns of trait distribution among living things, and prediction is the real measure of merit among scientific theories.

EMBRYONIC DEVELOPMENT

Some see the birth of a child as the most personal expression of God's creativity, but evolutionists say, "Look, if you're talking about creation, then surely the Creator must not be very good at it, or else there wouldn't be all those mistakes in human embryonic development."

Figure 7 shows an early stage in human development. Consider it your first "baby picture." You start off as a little round ball of unformed substance. Then gradually arms, legs, eyes, and all your other parts appear. At one month, you're not quite as charming as you're going to be, and here's where the evolutionist says, "There's no evidence of creation in the human embryo. Otherwise, why would a human being have a yolk sac like a chicken, a tail like a monkey, and gill slits like a fish? An intelligent Creator should have known that human beings don't need those things."

Well, there they are, "gill slits, yolk sac, and a tail." Why are they there? What's a creationist going to say? The evolutionist believes these structures are there only as useless leftovers or "vestiges" of our evolutionary ancestry, reminders of the times when our ancestors were only fish, reptiles, and apes.

The concept of vestigial organs even resulted in cases of "evolutionary medical malpractice." Young children once had their healthy (and helpful, disease-fighting) tonsils removed because of the widespread belief that they were only useless vestiges. That idea actually slowed down scientific research for many years. If you believe something is a useless, non-functional leftover of evolution, then you don't bother to find out what it *does*. Fortunately, other scientists didn't take that view. Sure enough, studies have shown that essentially all 180 organs once listed as evolutionary vestiges have significant functions in human beings.

Take the yolk sac, for instance. In chickens, the yolk contains much of the food that the chick depends on for growth. But we, on the other hand, grow attached to our mothers, and they

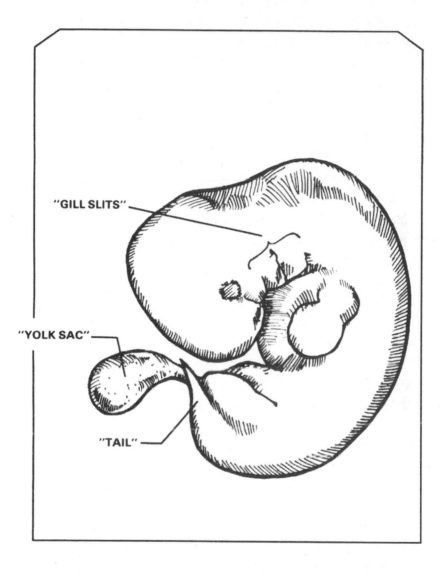

"GILL SLITS"

"YOLK SAC"

"TAIL"

Figure 7. The marvelous development of the human embryo should make everyone a creationist, it seems to me, but evolutionists say that the so-called "gill slits, yolk sac, and tail" are useless evolutionary leftovers (vestiges) that virtually "prove" we evolved from fish, reptiles, and apes. How does a creationist respond?

nourish us. Does that mean the yolk sac can be cut off from the human embryo because it isn't needed? Not at all. The so-called "yolk sac" is the source of the human embryo's first blood cells, and death would result without it!

Now here's an engineering problem for you. In the adult, you want to have the blood cells formed inside the bone marrow. That makes good sense, because the blood cells are very sensitive to radiation damage, and bone would offer them some protection. You need blood in order to form the bone marrow that *later on* is going to form blood. So, where do you get the blood first? Why not use a structure similar to the yolk sac in chickens? The DNA and protein for making it are "common stock" building materials. Since it lies conveniently outside the embryo, it can easily be discarded after it has served its temporary — but vital — function.

Notice, this is exactly what we would expect as evidence of good creative design and engineering practice. Suppose you were in the bridge-building business, and you were interviewing a couple of engineers to determine whom you wanted to hire. One person says, "Each bridge I build will be entirely different from all others." Proudly he tells you, "Each bridge will be made using different materials and different processes so that no one will ever be able to see any similarity among the bridges I build." How does that sound?

Now the next person comes in and says, "Well, in your yard I saw a supply of I-beams and various sizes of heavy bolts and cables. We can use those to span either a river or the San Francisco Bay. I can adapt the same parts and processes to meet a wide variety of needs. You'll be able to see a theme and a variation in my bridge building, and others can see the stamp of authorship in our work." Which would you hire?

As A.E. Wilder-Smith[28] pointed out long ago, we normally recognize in human engineers the principles of creative economy and variations on a theme. That's what we see in human embryonic development. The same kind of structure that can provide food and blood cells to a chicken embryo can be used to supply blood cells (all that's needed) for a human embryo. Rather than reflecting time and chance, adapting similar structures to a variety of needs seems to reflect good principles of creative design.

The same is true of the so-called "gill slits." In the human embryo at one month, there are wrinkles in the skin where the "throat pouches" grow out. Once in a while, one of these pouches will break through, and a child will be born with a small hole in the neck. That's when we find out for sure that these structures are *not* gill slits. If the opening were really part of a gill, if it really were a "throwback to the fish stage," then there would be blood vessels all around it, as if it were going to absorb oxygen from water as a gill does. But there is no such structure in humans of any age. We simply don't have the DNA instructions for forming gills.

Unfortunately, some babies are born with three eyes or one eye. That doesn't mean, of course, that we evolved from something with one eye or three eyes. It's simply a mistake in the normal program for human development, and it emphasizes how perfect our design features and operation must be for normal life to continue.

The throat (or pharyngeal) grooves and pouches, *falsely* called "gill slits," are *not* mistakes in human development. They develop into absolutely essential parts of human anatomy. The first pouches form the palatine tonsils that help fight disease. The middle ear canals come from the second pouches, and the parathyroid and thymus glands come from the third and fourth. The thymus prepares T cells, the immune cells destroyed by the AIDS virus, so you know how important the thymus is for human life. Without the parathyroids, we would be unable to regulate calcium balance and could not even survive. Another pouch, thought to be vestigial by evolutionists until just recently, becomes a gland that assists in calcium balance. Far from being useless evolutionary vestiges, then, these so-called "gill slits" (pharyngeal pouches) are quite essential for distinctively human development.

As with "yolk sac," "gill slit" formation represents an ingenious and adaptable solution to a difficult engineering problem. How can a small, round egg cell be turned into an animal or human being with a digestive tube and various organs inside a body cavity? The answer is to have the little ball (or flat sheet in some organisms) "swallow itself," forming a tube which then "buds off" other tubes and pouches. The anterior pituitary, lungs, urinary bladder, and parts of the liver and pancreas develop in this way. In fish, gills develop from such processes, and in human beings, the ear canals, parathyroid, and thymus glands develop. Following DNA instructions in their respective egg cells, fish and human beings each use a similar process to develop their distinctive features (see Figure 8).

What about the "tail"? Some of you have heard that man has a "tail bone" (also called the sacrum and coccyx), and that the only reason we have it is to remind us that our ancestors had tails. You can test this idea yourself, although I don't recommend it. If you think the "tail bone" is useless, fall down the stairs and land on it. (Some of you may have actually done that — unintentionally, I'm sure!) What happens? You can't stand up; you can't sit down; you can't lie down; you can't roll over. You can hardly move without pain. In one sense, the sacrum and coccyx are among the most important bones in the whole body. They form a crucial point of muscle attachment required for our distinctive upright posture (and also for defecation, but I'll say no more about that).

So again, far from being a useless evolutionary leftover, the "tail bone" is quite important in human development. True, the end of the spine sticks out noticeably in a one-month embryo, but that's because muscles and limbs don't develop until stimulated by the spine (Figure 8). As the legs develop, they surround and envelop the "tail bone," and it ends up inside the body.

Once in a great while there are reports of a child born with a "tail." Since the parents were quite pleased, one such child born recently in India was featured prominently on TV news in 2005.

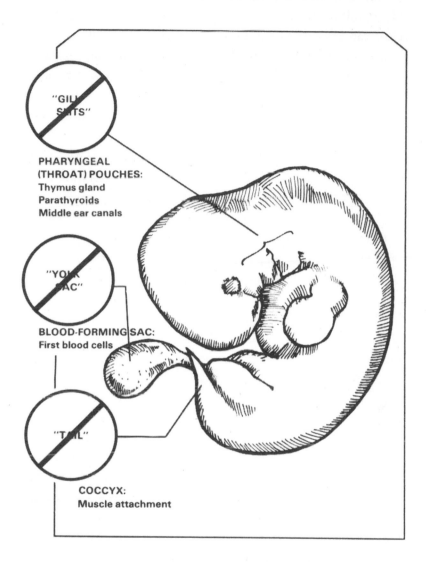

Figure 8. Far from being "useless evolutionary leftovers," the misnamed structures above are absolutely essential for normal human development. Similar structures are used for different functions in other embryos — and we normally consider variation on a theme and multiple uses for a part as evidence of good creative design.

But was it really a tail? No, it's just a bit of skin and fat that tells us, not about evolution, but about how our nervous systems develop. The nervous system starts stretched out open on the back. During development, it rises up in ridges and rolls shut. It starts to "zipper" shut in the middle first, then it zippers toward either end. Sometimes it doesn't go far enough down, and that produces a serious defect called *spina bifida*. Sometimes it rolls a little too far. Then the baby will be born, *not* with a tail, but with a fatty tumor. It's just skin and a little fatty tissue, so the doctor can just cut it off. It's not at all like the tail of a cat, dog, or monkey that has muscle, bones, and nerve, so cutting it off is not complicated. (So far as I know, no one claims that proves we evolved from an animal with a fatty tumor at the end of its spine.)

Unfortunately, evolution has such a hold on our thinking that doctors hate to tell a mother if she has a baby with a "tail." They can imagine the dismay: "Oh no; I've given birth to a throwback to the monkey stage in evolution!" Then the arguments begin: "It's your side of the family." "No, it's your side!" Fortunately, the extra skin and fat is not a tail at all. The details of human development are truly amazing. We really ought to stop, take a good look at each other, and congratulate each other that we turned out as well as we did!

There is an extremely rare but more serious defect in developmental regulation that can produce a "caudal appendage" with some muscle, nerve, blood, and cartilage or bone tissue. Defects in other embryonic regulator genes can result in too many or too few parts, failure of growth or of resorption, parts growing together that should remain separate, or parts remaining separate that should grow together, etc. *Hox gene errors* in insects can result in legs growing where antennae should be, and in flies with an extra but functionless set of wings. Such defects tell us nothing about evolutionary ancestry, but a lot about how normal development requires extreme precision in activating the right genes in the right places at the right times for the right duration.

There are a few famous cases of human beings with hair over most of their bodies (hypertrichosis universalis). Normal human beings have hair, of course, so *all* nucleated cells in the human body have the DNA instructions for producing hair. Regulators that turn genes on and off, therefore, may result in more or less hair than the normal amount in the usual places, but such people just have "people genes" and are NOT "throwbacks" to the supposed "ape stage" in evolution!

Evolutionists once said that human embryonic development retraced stages in our supposed evolutionary history. That idea, the now-defunct "biogenetic law," was summarized in the pithy phrase, "ontogeny recapitulates phylogeny." (Want to sound educated? Just memorize that phrase!) The phrase means that the development of the embryo is supposed to retrace the evolution of its group. Dr. Down named a syndrome "Mongoloid idiocy" because he thought it represented a "throwback" to the "Mongolian stage" in human evolution.

The "throwback concept" was based on faked diagrams that brought modest disgrace to "Germany's Darwin," Ernst Haeckel, in the 1860s.[29] Yet the embryo diagrams falsified to support evolution over 140 years ago were still in the 2005 lab manual used in a state college biology class where I spoke in 2006.

After a university talk on creation in which I didn't mention the embryo, a student asked, "If God created us, why do human embryos have a yolk sac, gill slits, and tail?" Before I could say anything, a local professor scolded emphatically: "Sit down! Hush. We don't believe that anymore!" In a debate at the University of New Brunswick, my opponent actually complimented what I had to say about the human embryo, stressing that the "throwback theory" (based on fudged diagrams!) had been disproved decades ago and desperately needed to be removed from textbooks.

It was even once believed that the fertilized egg represented our one-celled ancestors, sort of the "amoeba stage." Sure enough, we start as small, round single cells, but notice how superficial that argument is. The evolutionists were just looking at the outside appearance of the egg cell. If we look just on the *outside appearance,* then maybe we're related to a marble, a BB pellet, or a ball bearing — they're small, round things! An evolutionist (or anyone else) would respond, of course, "That's crazy. Those things are totally different on the *inside* from a human egg cell." That's exactly the point. If you take a look on the inside, the "dot" we each start from is totally different from the first cell of every other kind of life. A mouse, an elephant, and a human being are identical in size and shape at the moment of conception. Yet in terms of DNA and protein, right at conception each of these types of life is as totally different chemically as each will ever be structurally. Even by mistake, a human being can't produce gills or a tail, because we just don't have and never had those DNA instructions.

The human egg cell, furthermore, is not just human, but also a unique individual. Eye color, general body size, and perhaps even temperament are already present in DNA, ready to come to visible expression. *The baby before birth is not even a part of his or her mother's body.* From conception onward, we may have genes for a blood type or hair color different from that of our mother. We may be a sex different from that of our mother — about half of us are. Our uniqueness begins at conception, and blossoms continuously throughout life.

Embryonic development is not even analogous to evolution, which is meant to indicate a progressive increase in potential. The right Greek word instead would be *entelechy,* which means an unfolding of potential present right from the beginning. That's the kind of development that so clearly requires creative design. That's why evolutionists don't use the change from tadpole to frog as an example of evolution. Unlike the *supposed* evolution of fish to frog, all the genes necessary to change a tadpole into a frog are present right from the very beginning.

Again, the Bible proves to be far ahead of its time. Scientists once thought (and some claimed they saw) tiny, pre-formed people in either egg or sperm cells. But 3,000 years ago, the Psalmist David talked about how God beheld his "unformed substance" in the womb, and how he was "knit together," step by step, according to God's plan. His response in Psalm 139 should be ours: "I will praise You, for I am fearfully and wonderfully made."

ADAPTATION AND ECOLOGY: THE MARVELOUS FIT OF ORGANISMS TO THEIR ENVIRONMENTS

We've looked now at molecules, bone patterns, and embryonic development, but the clearest and simplest evidence of creation is "the marvelous fit of living things to their environment." In the *Scientific American* book *Evolution,* Harvard evolutionist Richard Lewontin[30] says that "the marvelous fit of organisms to their environment . . . was [and I say is] the chief evidence of a Supreme Designer." In fact, Lewontin says that organisms "appear to have been carefully and artfully designed." Lewontin himself sees it only as a tough case to be solved by evolutionary theory, but other scientists might logically infer from their observations that living things *were* "carefully and artfully designed."

There are literally thousands of examples of the unique adaptations that suit each type of organism for its special role in the web of life (Figure 9). The fantastic features of structure, function, and behavior that make the honeybee so wondrous, for example, are familiar to almost anyone. But then there's cleaning symbiosis; the explosive chemical defense system of the bombardier beetle; the navigational skills of migrating reptiles, birds, fish, and mammals, etc. Jobe Martin continues the list in a captivating series of videos called "Incredible Creatures That Defy Evolution."[31]

Let me single out one example for now. Take the woodpecker, for instance.[32] Here's a bird that makes its living banging its head into trees. Whatever gave it the idea to do that in the first place? Was it frustration over losing the worm to the early bird? How did banging its head into trees increase its likelihood for survival — until *after* it had accumulated (by chance?) a thick

Figure 9. As evolutionist Lewontin acknowledges, living things "appear to have been carefully and artfully designed." Each type possesses various features complete and well fitted into the whole, like the tiles in an artist's mosaic. Although other animals share such adaptations with the platypus as milk glands, a leathery egg, and electric-signal sensitivity, it seems to me that all these could be put together into a single fascinating, functioning whole only by plan, purpose, and special acts of creation.

skull with shock-absorbing tissues, muscles, etc.! What would be the survival value of all these features (and how could they build up in the population) until *after* the bird started banging its head into trees?

The woodpecker is a marvel of interdependent parts or "compound traits," now popularly called "irreducible complexity" — traits that depend on one another for *any* to have functional value. When a woodpecker slams its head into a tree, the deceleration experienced is many times gravity. The nerve and muscle coordination must produce a dead-on hit; a slip to one side or the other could virtually wrench the cover off the brain! The eyelids snap shut when the beak strikes its target. Some scientists say that's to keep wood chips out of the eyes; others say it's to keep the eyeballs from popping out of their sockets! Both may be right!

For such drilling, a woodpecker obviously needs a tough bill, heavy-duty skull, and shock-absorbing tissue between the two. But if the woodpecker were put together by time and chance, without any planning ahead, which part came first? Suppose, just by chance, a baby bird is born with a tough bill. It decides to try it out. WHACK! It throws its head into a tree. The bill is just fine, but it squishes in the front of its face. One dead bird, end of evolutionary story!

But maybe I got it backward. Maybe, just by chance, a baby bird was born with a heavy-duty skull. WHACK! It throws its head into a tree. This time its skull is okay, but its bill folds up like an accordion. There's no evolutionary future in that either!

In fact, neither the tough bill nor the heavy-duty skull would have any functional survival value until both occurred together — along with the shock-absorbing tissue, nerve and muscle coordination, etc.! That's no problem if the woodpecker were put together by plan, purpose, and a special act of creation. We expect drilling tools created by people to have interdependent parts that must all be completely assembled before the machine works. That's just good sense, and good science. We would surely expect no less from the perfect devices created by God!

There's more. At least since death entered the world, some woodpeckers are doing more than just drilling holes to store acorns. They're looking for bark beetles. The beetles hear all this pounding, of course, so they just crawl further down their tunnels. Some types of woodpeckers that are looking for bark beetles need more than just drilling tools; they need long, sticky tongues.

But if a bird gets a long, sticky tongue just by chance, what's it going to do with it? Dangling out of the bill, the tongue gets bit or even stepped on. As the bird is flying over a twig, the tongue could wrap around the twig and hang the hapless "pre-woodpecker." The answer for the woodpecker is to slip its tongue attachment into a muscular sheath that wraps around the skull *under* the scalp and inserts into the nostril! That makes good sense (and good science) if you're planning ahead, but poses real problems if your faith is in time and chance, trial and error. (Except in video games, you don't get another trial if the error is fatal!)

Evolutionists believe (like I once did) that all adaptations begin with time and chance, that is, with random changes in DNA and hereditary traits called mutations. In evolutionary theory, those chance mutations that suit an organism better to its environment are preserved by the process called natural selection. But natural selection can't act until the favored traits arise by mutation, i.e., by time and chance.

Well, what about mutations? Mutations certainly do occur, and they are responsible for perhaps 5,000 hereditary defects in human beings alone. Could mutations and selection working together (time, chance, struggle, and death, TCSD) produce the coordinated set of structural and behavioral adaptations necessary to originate the woodpecker? Let's see what two well-known biologists have to say about that.

Early creationists were primarily Christians, and that was often used as an excuse for ignoring their scientific arguments.

When Michael Denton exposed *Evolution: A Theory in Crisis* to the secular community, a number of scientists got interested in design evidences divorced from deity, and the influential movement called *Intelligent Design*, or *ID*, was born.

Biochemist Michael Behe coined the term *irreducible complexity*, which has become the watchword for ID. Before it can function to catch mice, he illustrates, a mousetrap must have several parts working together (e.g., platform, spring, holding bar, hammer, catch). Its function is "irreducibly complex," i.e., it can't function at all with parts fewer than these. The same is true for many "molecular machines" within living cells, as Behe argues persuasively with multiple detailed examples in *Darwin's Black Box* (and as I tried to illustrate with the woodpecker above). The Darwinian concept of step-by-step evolution by mutation-selection requires *survival rewards* AT EACH STEP, and Darwin said his theory would be falsified by any example of adaptation that could not be built one step at a time. Behe falsifies Darwinian evolution many times over, but then continues on to present the scientific support for intelligent design on a secular basis.[33]

Here's a brilliant scientist whose observations of the living world force him to postulate at least an *impersonal creative force*. Here's a scientist who recognizes that intelligent design can be logically inferred from observations of certain kinds of order, even when he does not say who or what the creative agent is.

Garrett Hardin,[34] a noted biologist and textbook author, seems to go even further than this in an old, but timeless, *Scientific American* book on adaptations and ecology, *39 Steps to Biology*. The first section, titled "Fearfully and Wonderfully Made" (a phrase from Psalm 139), describes several marvels of adaptation often used as evidence of creation. In the second section, "Nature's Challenges to Evolutionary Theory," Hardin discusses other remarkable relationships which, he says, "are only a few of the unsolved puzzles facing biologists who are committed to the Darwinian [evolutionary] theory." Then he openly wonders, "Is the [evolutionary] framework wrong?" That is, do our observations of the living world force us, at least for the present, to rule out evolution as an explanation for origins? (Figure 10).

Hardin doesn't stop there. He goes on to ask, "Was Paley right?" If you're like me, you never heard of William Paley, but Hardin explains. Paley was a thinker in the 18th century who argued that the kind of design we see in the living world points clearly to a Designer. Then the evolutionists came along in the 19th century and argued that they could explain design on the basis of time, chance, struggle, and death that did *not* require a Designer. Now, said Hardin in the 20th century, "Was Paley right" after all? Do the kinds of design features we see in living things point clearly to a Designer? Paley was not thinking of an "impersonal creative force"; he was thinking, instead, of a personal Creator God.

Hardin's conclusion? *"Think about it!"* (emphasis added).

THINK ABOUT IT!

"Think about it!" What a sane and yet sensational idea. What a rallying point for both creationists and evolutionists.

The Scopes trial showed it was foolish to teach only creation; is it any wiser to teach only evolution? A detailed doctoral study by Richard Bliss[35] demonstrated that students using a two-model (creation-evolution) approach to origins showed more improvement in inquiry skills than those using the now traditional evolution-only approach. (By the way, the two-model students learned evolution concepts better than those taught evolution only.) Furthermore, a two-model approach cannot be accused of indoctrination; can evolution only? Surely, the only way students can "think about it" is when they have access to *all* the relevant data and the true academic freedom to explore *both* models of origin.

As Garrett Hardin so perceptively observes, the challenge to evolution does not come simply from a few religious fanatics. The challenge to evolution comes from the study of nature itself: "Nature's Challenges to Evolutionary Theory," he calls it. Even

Figure 10. Marvels of adaptation are described under the heading "Nature's Challenges to Evolutionary Theory" in a *Scientific American* book edited by Garrett Hardin. Even though he's an evolutionist, Hardin asks, "Is the [evolutionary] framework wrong?" Then he goes on to ask, "Was Paley right?" when he said the kind of design we see in the living world requires a Designer. Then, in an expression of open-ended fairness that everyone can appreciate, Hardin concludes, "Think about it!" *Think about it.*

if various *pressure groups* (ironically operating under the guise of "academic freedom") succeed in *censoring* and *suppressing* all views except evolution, the case for creation will still be studied in science classes. The case for creation will be evident in sets of adaptations working together, such as we see in the woodpecker; in the growth and birth of a baby; and in the fantastic molecular integration within cells, such as the relationship between DNA and protein. Because of the way things have been made, the case for creation will always be present in the subject matter of science itself, especially in lab and field work.

We can differentiate the stone implements produced by human creative effort from those shaped by time, chance, and erosion. Similarly, we can distinguish created relationships among living things, such as those among the parts of a woodpecker, a growing baby, or a living cell.

One other special feature of creation is so obvious we often fail to notice it: its beauty. I once took my invertebrate zoology class to hear a lecture on marine life by a scientist who had just returned from a collecting trip to the Philippines. Toward the end of his lecture he described the brightly colored fish he had observed at a depth where all wavelengths of light were absorbed except for some blue. In their natural habitat, the fish could not even see their own bright colors, so what possible survival value could the genetic investment in this color have? Then he challenged the students to pose that question to their biology professors.

When my students asked me, I couldn't help thinking of Genesis 2:9, where God is described as creating plants both *"pleasant to the sight* and good for food." We normally expect to find aspects of beauty as well as usefulness in the artifacts of human creation; perhaps we should expect to find beauty in God's creation of life as well.

Remember, though, that I'm not trying to convince you of all these things in one short book. I used to teach evolution in university biology classes, and it took me several years to change my thinking from evolution to creation. Let's face it, there is much to be said for evolution. In fact, I still present the case for evolution to my classes, then let them bombard me with questions which I answer as an evolutionist. That certainly surprises some of my students, but it stimulates all of them to "think about it."

That's my purpose in this book: to stimulate your thinking. The case is not all one-sided in favor of creation, but it's certainly not one-sided in favor of evolution either. When it comes to origins, we can't appeal to direct observation, nor can we run experiments on the past. We're stuck with *circumstantial evidence,* i.e., evidence subject to more than one interpretation. Our goal must be to weigh *all* the relevant evidence, asking ourselves which is the more logical inference from the weight, on balance, of our scientific observations.

The case for creation I've presented so far is based on what we *do know* and *can explain* in the areas of molecular biology, homology, embryology, and adaptation. But what about Darwinian natural selection and the fossil evidence? Well, let's dig in. All you need is an inquiring mind, a sharp eye, and a willing heart. "Think about it!" What's the more logical inference from our scientific observations of genetics and the fossil evidence: time, chance, and the evolution of matter, *or* plan, purpose, and irreducible properties of organization pointing to special acts of creation?

Endnotes

1. The 4 Cs of biblical history can be expanded to 7 Cs by introducing *confusion* for the confusion of languages at Babel and/or *chill* for the Ice Age. For a college brochure in 1989, I used *creation, corruption, catastrophe, chill, confusion, Christ,* and *coming again* as the 7 Cs. Answers in Genesis uses *creation, corruption, catastrophe, confusion, Christ, Cross,* and *consummation.*

2. Gary E. Parker, "Clarifying Creation-Evolution," *American Biology Teacher,* letter to the editor (April 1977): p. 247.

3. Gary E. Parker, W. Ann Reynolds, and Rex Reynolds, *DNA: The Key to Life,* Rev. ed., Programmed Biology Series (Chicago, IL: Educational Methods, Inc., 1977).

4. Gary E. Parker, "The Origin of Life on Earth" *Creation Science Research Quarterly* (September 1970); Gary E. Parker and Thomas R. Mertens, *Life's Basis: Biomolecules* (New York: John Wiley and Sons, 1977), available in Spanish as *Biomoleculas: Basa de la Vida*.

5. Richard B. Bliss and Gary E. Parker, *Origin of Life*, Two Models Creation-Evolution Series (Green Forest, AR: Master Books, 1979).

6. Illustra Media, *Unlocking the Mystery of Life*, DVD/VHS, 2002.

7. Charles Thaxton, Walter Bradley, and Roger Olsen, *The Mystery of Life's Origin: Reassessing Current Theories* (New York: Philosophical Library, 1984).

8. Parker, Reynolds, and Reynolds, *DNA: The Key to Life;* Parker and Mertens, *Life's Basis: Biomolecules;* Bliss and Parker, *Origin of Life;* Thaxton, Bradley, and Olsen, *The Mystery of Life's Origin.*

9. Richard E. Dickerson, "Chemical Evolution and the Origin of Life," *Scientific American,* and Scientific American book *Evolution* (September 1978).

10. Jonathan Sarfati, *Refuting Evolution* (Green Forest, AR: Master Books, 1999).

11. Werner Gitt, *In the Beginning Was Information* (Green Forest, AR: Master Books, 2006).

12. Francis Crick, "The Seeds of Life," *Discover* (October 1981).

13. Michael Denton, *Nature's Destiny* (New York: The Free Press, 1998).

14. Sir Fred Hoyle and Chandra Wickramasinghe, as quoted in "There *Must* Be a God," *Daily Express* (August 14,1981); and "Hoyle on Evolution," *Nature* (November 12, 1981).

15. Duane T. Gish, *Creation Scientists Answer Their Critics* (Green Forest, AR: Master Books, 1993).

16. Michael Denton, *Evolution: A Theory in Crisis* (London: Burnctt Books, 1985).

17. Richard Dawkins, *The Blind Watchmaker* (New York: W.W. Norton, 1986).

18. H.S. Lipson, "A Physicist Looks at Evolution," *Physics Bulletin* (May 1980): page 138.

19. Percival Davis and Dean Kenyon, *Of Pandas and People*, 2nd edition (Dallas, TX: Haughton Pub. Co., 1999).

20. Denton, *Evolution: A Theory in Crisis*, chapter 7.

21. Michael Land, "Nature as an Optical Engineer," *New Scientist* (October 4, 1979).

22. Richard E. Dickerson and Irving Geis, *The Structure and Action of Proteins* (New York: Harper and Row, 1969).

23. Colin Patterson, address at American Museum of Natural History, New York, November 5, 1981 (summarized by Gary Parker and Luther

Sunderland in *Acts and Facts,* Impact No. 108, Institute for Creation Research, El Cajon, CA, December 1982).

24. Clete W. Knaub, *A Critique of Molecular Homology* (Santee, CA: Institute for Creation Research, 1983), master's thesis.

25. Robert Sapolsky, "The 2% Difference," *Discover* (April 2006).

26. The International Chimpanzee Chromosome 22 Consortium, "DNA Sequence and Comparative Analysis of Chimpanzee Chromosome 22," *Nature* (May 27, 2004).

27. Denton, *Evolution: A Theory in Crisis*, p. 306.

28. A.E. Wilder-Smith, *The Natural Sciences Know Nothing of Evolution* (Green Forest, AR: Master Books, 1981).

29. Jonathan Sarfati, *Refuting Evolution 2* (Green Forest, AR: Master Books, 2002).

30. Richard C. Lewontin, "Adaptation," *Scientific American,* and Scientific American book *Evolution* (September 1978).

31. Jobe Martin, *Incredible Creatures That Defy Evolution*, video series (Rockwall, TX: Real Productions, 2000).

32. Richard B. Bliss, *The Strange Case of the Woodpecker* (Green Forest, AR: Master Books Video, 1985).

33. Michael Behe, *Darwin's Black Box* (New York: The Free Press, 1996).

34. Garrett Hardin, *39 Steps to Biology,* a Scientific American book (San Francisco, CA: W.H. Freeman and Co., 1968).

35. Richard B. Bliss, *A Comparison of Two Approaches to the Teaching of Origins of Living Things to High School Biology Students in Racine, Wisconsin.* Dissertation, University of Sarasota (ERIC Ed 152568), 1979. See also, R. B. Bliss, "A Comparison of Students Studying the Origin of Life from a Two-Model Approach vs. Those Studying from a Single-Model Approach," *Acts and Facts,* Impact No. 60 (June 1978).

Chapter 2

Darwin and Biologic Change

Design without a Designer

"Wait a minute! Stop! Let's come to our senses! I just read through a whole bunch of evidence for 'creation,' evidence that's supposed to convince me that this world was created by the all-loving, all-powerful God of the Bible. But just look around. The world's a mess! People are starving, babies are born deformed, disease kills millions, and 'acts of God' like earthquakes, fires, and floods have killed millions more. This is supposed to convince me the world was made by an *all-wise Creator?*"

Have such troubling thoughts crossed your mind? They certainly troubled a young amateur naturalist as he sailed around the world on the *HMS Beagle* back in the 1830s, as described earlier. Charles Darwin was brought up in an England that at least paid lip service to the Bible and creationist thinking. Yet, everywhere he looked, as he collected specimens for the *Beagle*, he found only struggle and death.

How could such wholesale waste, violence, and death result from the plan, purpose, and direct creative acts of God? Darwin began to look for another explanation for the origin of life — and he found it. After years of thought, research, and self-doubt, Darwin was coaxed into publishing his revolutionary new theory in 1859: *On the Origin of Species by Means of Natural Selection, or The Preservation of Favoured Races in the Struggle for Life.*

Darwin's book *(Origin of Species* for short) revolutionized human thought. Many saw in natural selection a means to explain all appearance of design without any reference to a Designer, and many more seized on that as an excuse to disbelieve a "Creator God" and to get out from under the oppressive rules of organized religion. The old creationist argument from design, "the watch implies a watchmaker," was dead; long live the new "blind watchmaker," natural selection: evolution by time, chance, struggle, and death (TCSD).

After biologist Michael Denton identified himself on television[1] as a skeptic regarding *both* creation and evolution, the interviewer asked him what he thought the chief impact of Darwin's book had been. After a pause, Denton replied that its chief impact had been to make atheism possible, or at least respectable. The much-admired historian and philosopher Will Durant[2] said that we are now coming out of a pagan era that began in 1859 with Darwin's *Origin.* Darwin's book changed the whole course of history. Certainly, I can claim that scientific evidence supports the biblical account of origins *if and only if* I can deal fairly and honestly with natural selection.

NATURAL SELECTION

In spite of its revolutionary philosophic impact, Darwin's concept of natural selection is quite easy to understand *(and to misunderstand)*. It was based on observations of artificial selection, the results of selective breeding by farmers and animal fanciers. Darwin, for example, referred to all the different breeds of pigeons that had been produced by artificial selection.

The ordinary one in Figure 11A is the wild rock pigeon, the one you often find around city statues and country barns. But all the other birds pictured are just pigeons, too: the fan tail, the one with the neck pouch, etc. All these birds can be bred from the wild rock pigeon, and crossing among the different varieties can lead right back to the wild rock pigeon. Everyone knows, of course, about the results of selective breeding with dogs, cats, cattle, roses, and so on.

"So," Darwin said, in effect, "we see what artificial selection by man can do. I believe selection can also happen in nature. After all, there is a constant *struggle for survival'* because of population growth and limited resources, and certainly each kind can produce many *varieties.* Therefore, there will be *'survival of the fittest,'* or *natural selection,* of those varieties of a population that fit best into their environments. Given enough generations [time] and the right trait combinations [chance], organisms that seem designed for their environment will simply result from natural selection [struggle and death]."

Replacing the Creator God with what he called the "war of nature," Darwin claimed that all appearance of design in biology is the result of time, chance, struggle, and death — the process of "natural selection." Is there any evidence that Darwin was right? Can nature select as well as man? Answer: There is considerable evidence that Darwin was indeed *correct* about natural selection and the "war of nature."

For over 50 years, the prime example of natural selection used in textbooks, museum displays, and TV programs has been the peppered moths. Take a look first at the top photo in Figure 11B, which represents a camera close-up of tree bark with some moths on it. How many moths do you see? One is easy to see, and most people see two. (Some claim to see three, but I've never found the third!) At least we can agree that one moth stands out and one is camouflaged. Presumably, that's the way birds saw it, too, back in the 1850s. The darker moth stood out, but the lighter one

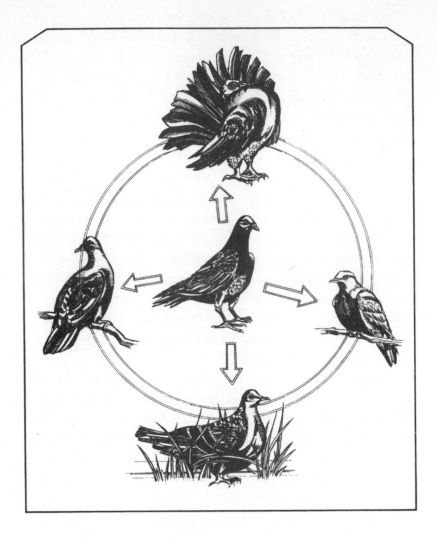

Figure 11A. By artificial selection, all the "fancy" varieties of pigeons above have been bred from the common wild rock pigeon, and they can be bred *back* to the wild rock pigeon (just as special varieties of dogs and cats can be bred from and to the "mongrel" types). Darwin used *artificial selection,* selective breeding by man, as a model for *natural selection,* survival of the fittest selected by nature in the struggle for life. But does natural selection lead to evolution, or point back to the biblical concept of a corrupted creation?

Figure 11B. Light moths so common in 1850 (well-camouflaged in the top photo) lost out in the struggle for life to the more "fit" variety (camouflaged by the dark, polluted background in the bottom photo). By 1950, most of the moths were the dark (melanic) variety.

NOTE: It was discovered recently, however, that these famous photographs show dead moths glued to tree trunks. Live peppered moths flying among the branches can recognize camouflaging backgrounds (a "habitat choice" instinct) and/or migrate out of the polluted area. Still, the peppered moth story as originally told *does* seem to provide at least logical evidence for natural selection. But, can it really be called "evolution going on today"?

was camouflaged against the mottled gray lichen that encrusted the trees back then. As a result, birds ate mostly dark moths, and light moths made up over 98 percent of the population.

But then pollution killed the lichen on the trees, revealing the dark color of the bark. As a result, the dark moths were more camouflaged than the light ones. Thus, the dark ones had a better chance of surviving and leaving more offspring to grow into dark moths in succeeding generations. Sure enough, just as Darwin would have predicted, the population shifted. The "dark environment" just *naturally selected* the dark moths as more likely to survive and reproduce. By the 1950s, the population was over 98 percent dark, proof positive of *"evolution going on today."* At least that's the way it's stated in many biology books, and that's what I used to tell my biology students.

CHANGE, YES; EVOLUTION, NO

When I "proved" natural selection to my classes (pages 7–11), I just assumed I was also proving evolution. Perhaps the most powerful argument for evolution is the word "change," and the most persuasive (and ambiguous) definition of evolution is *"change through time."* If I say "No" when asked if I believe in evolution, the likely response is an astonished look and the incredulous query, "What?? You don't believe in change?!"

To get the conversation started, I might reply, "Of course I believe in change; I've got some in my pocket." An evolutionist would counter, of course, "Not that kind of change!" Lots of examples of "change through time" would get the same response: the change from round to flat in an opossum run over by a truck; from athletic young runner to old man in a wheel chair; from seed to mighty oak; God making man from the dust of the ground; plants and animals successively buried during Noah's flood, etc. There are obviously all kinds of "change through time" that are not evolution, so evolution must be *only a particular kind* of change through time. Natural selection certainly produces change in populations, but is it the evolutionary kind of change?

Take a look again at the peppered moth example (Figure 11B). What did we start with? Dark and light varieties of the peppered moth, species *Biston betularia*. After 100 years of natural selection, what did we end up with? Dark and light varieties of the peppered moth, species *Biston betularia*. The moths themselves didn't change; there were always dark moths and always light moths from the earliest observations. All that changed was the percentage of moths in the two categories: that's what creationists call *variation within kind*. (For details, see the master's thesis by one of my students, Chris Osborne.[3])

According to the biblical outline of history, struggle and death began when man's rebellion ruined God's perfect creation. Natural selection is just one of the processes that operates in our present *corrupted* world when the created kinds spread throughout the earth in all its ecologic and geographic variety. In fact, 24 years before Darwin's *Origin*, a scientist named Edward Blyth published the concept of natural selection in the biblical context of a corrupted creation. A book reviewer once asked, rather naively, if creationists could accept the concept of natural selection. The answer is, "Of course. *We* thought of it first."

If natural selection is such a profound idea, and Blyth published it before Darwin, then why isn't Blyth's name a household word? Perhaps because Blyth made no more of natural selection than could be scientifically observed. It was not the *scientific* applications of natural selection that attracted attention in 1859; it was its presumed *philosophic* and *religious* implications.

Evolutionists were not content to treat natural selection as simply an observable ecological process. Darwin himself was a cautious scientist, painstaking in his work, but others, especially T.H. Huxley and Herbert Spencer, insisted on making natural selection the touchstone of a new religion, a "religion without revelation," as Julian Huxley later called it. For them, as for many others, the real significance of the Darwinian revolution was *religious* and *philosophic,* not scientific, a reason to place human opinion above

God's Word. These early evolutionists were basically anti-creationists who wanted to explain design without a Designer.

In spite of what might be claimed, natural selection has been observed to produce only variation within kind: merely shifts in populations, for example, to moths with greater percentages of darker moths, to flies resistant to DDT, or to bacteria resistant to antibiotics. Modern evolutionists believe, however, that such small changes *plus vast amounts of time* could lead to huge changes, "macroevolution," change from one kind to another: *Fish to Philosopher*, as the title of Homer Smith's book puts it, or *Molecules to Man*, the subtitle of the government-funded BSCS "blue version" high school biology textbook.

Macroevolution is the kind of change through time pictured as millions of years of struggle and death producing a "*tree of life*" rooted in chance chemical combinations forming life, and life branching out through a few simple forms to the twigs representing all the complex and varied species we have today, including man.

Beliefs about macroevolution certainly go far beyond our scientific observations of natural selection. Still, I must admit that there is a potential connection between *observed* natural selection within kind and *hypothetical* evolution from one kind to another. That connection is called "extrapolation," following a trend to its logical conclusion. Scientists extrapolate from population records, for example, to predict changes in the world population. If world population growth continued at the rate observed in the 1960s, statisticians said, then the world population by A.D. 2000 would be over six billion (as observed). Similarly, if natural selection continues over very long periods of time, evolutionists say, the same process that changes moths from mostly light to mostly dark forms will gradually change fish to philosophers or molecules to man.

Now there's nothing wrong with extrapolation in principle, but there are things to watch for in practice. For example, simple extrapolation would suggest a population of a "zillion" by A.D.

3000. Of course, there will come a point when the earth is simply not big enough to support any more people. In other words, there are *limits,* or *boundary conditions,* to logical extrapolation.

Consider my jogging (or should I say "slogging") times. Starting years ago at an embarrassing 12 minutes per mile, I knocked a minute off each week: a mile in 11 minutes, then 10, 9, 8, 7, 6, 5, 4, 3, 2, 1. Wait a minute! As you well know, I reached my limit long before the one-minute mile! (Just where, I'll keep secret!) This is an embarrassing example, but it makes an important point: no scientist would consider extrapolation without also considering the logical limits or boundary conditions of that extrapolation.

Evolutionists are aware of the problem. They distinguish between *SUBspeciation* and *TRANSspeciation.* "Sub" is essentially variation within species, and "trans" is change from one species to another. Darwinian evolutionists believe that one can "extrapolate" from variation *within* species to evolution *between* species. But other evolutionists believe that such extrapolation goes beyond all logical limits, like my running a one-minute mile.[4]

What does the evidence suggest? Can evolution from "molecules to man" be extrapolated from natural selection among dark and light moths? Or are there boundary conditions and logical limits to the amount of change that can be produced by Darwin's war of nature — time, chance, struggle, and death?

The answer seems to be: *"Natural selection, yes; evolution,* **no.**" As it turns out, there are several factors that sharply limit the amount of change that can be produced by time, chance, and Darwinian natural selection.[5]

Darwin published his theory in 1859, before Abraham Lincoln became president, long before DNA's significance was discovered, and even before the germ theory of disease and the modern sciences of genetics and ecology were founded. It is perhaps not surprising, then, that over the past century and a half scientists have discovered a long list of factors that set definite *limits to the kind and amount of change natural selection can produce* — **no matter what the time involved**. You could calculate how long it would take you, pedaling a bicycle at 10 mph (16 kph), to reach the moon, but such an extrapolation would ignore serious limits to getting to the moon on a bicycle — even if you had zillions of years to do it!

Following are some of the limits that prevent extrapolation from natural selection to evolution — limits causing a growing number of 21st century scientists to say, *"Natural selection, yes; evolution, no."*

Natural Selection, Yes; Evolution, No

(1) *What does "fittest" mean?*

The definition of "fittest" guarantees that *natural selection must be accepted as a fact*. Most people assume that "fitness" refers to features of structure, function, or behavior that suit an organism for a particular role in its environment. It doesn't. Fitness is defined by scientists solely in relation to relative reproductive success. *Members of a population that leave the most offspring to the next generation are fittest by definition.*

You may have thought the dark-colored peppered moth was fittest to survive in a polluted forest because it was most camouflaged. But what if the extra melanin production interfered with, say, sex hormone production and made the dark-colored moths sterile? Obviously, the superior camouflage would *not* make such a moth fittest to survive! Evolutionists think the camouflage helped, of course, but the dark moths were really determined to be "fittest to survive" because a greater percentage of their offspring survived in polluted forests than the percentage for any other color form.

Think about zebras. Their survival depends on their ability to outrun lions. So, the fastest zebra would be fittest, right? Not necessarily. Suppose the fastest zebra was hard of hearing or had a poor sense of smell. It could have outrun the lion and the rest of the herd — if only it had sensed the lion's coming! Or suppose the fastest zebra had bones that broke easily, poor digestion, and/or caught diseases easily. What looks fit to us superficially may not turn out to be fittest in nature.

So, the only way to determine fitness is to make notes on organisms in the first generation, *wait for the struggle for survival to take place*, then see which organisms actually left the most offspring to the next generation. To see how scientists calculate fitness, let's work through Figure 12, a simple example involving one pair of genes, A and a, which produce three varieties of organisms: AA, Aa, and aa. These gene combinations (genotypes) could be used to represent a variety of traits (phenotypes), e.g., tall-medium-short, fast-medium-slow, red-pink-white, smart-average-dull, heavy-medium-light, etc.

We'll start the first generation with 100 individuals: 50 AA, 30 Aa, 20 aa. The second generation coming through the struggle for survival includes 20 AA, 60 Aa, and 20 aa. All other things being equal, it's already obvious that organisms with genotype Aa were fittest, winning the struggle for survival, since they're the only group that increased in numbers. The *numerical fitness* of each group can be easily calculated. First, divide the number in the second generation in each category by the number in the first; that gives 20/50 = 0.4 for AA; 60/30 = 2.0 for Aa; and 20/20 = 1.00 for aa.

Note the highest survival ratio is the 2.0 for the Aa fittest, or winners, in this example. Calculate the *standardized fitness* value by dividing each "survival ratio" by the highest (2.0 for Aa here). This last step always gives the *winner* a fitness value of *1.00* and ranks other groups from 0 (a loser with no survivors) to some fraction of 1.00. The aa fitness here is 1.0/2.0=0.5, meaning the aa's survived about "half as well" as the fittest Aa's. The AA's did worst at surviving, about "20 percent as well" as the fittest (20/50 = 0.4 and 0.4/2.0 = 0.2).

Several profound and often misunderstood consequences follow from the simple calculation of fitness:

CALCULATION OF FITNESS, or NET RELATIVE REPRODUCTIVE EFFICIENCY

Trait categories	A. Static Population				B. Increasing Population				C. Decreasing Population			
	AA	Aa	aa	Tot.	AA	Aa	aa	Total	AA	Aa	aa	Tot.
First generation, G_1	50	30	20	100	50	30	20	100	50	30	20	100
Second generation, G_2	20	60	20	100	40	120	40	200	10	30	10	50
G_2/G_1 ratio	20/50	60/30	20/20		40/50	120/30	40/20		10/50	30/30	10/20	
"Numerical fitness"	0.4	2.0	1.0		0.8	4.0	2.0		0.2	1.0	0.5	
H, highest ratio (survival winner)		2.0				4.0				1.0		
Ratio $G_2/G_1 \div$ H	0.4/2	2/2	1/2		0.8/4	4/4	2/4		0.2/1	1/1	0.5/1	
"Standardized fitness"	0.2	1.0	0.5		0.2	1.0	0.5		0.2	1.0	0.5	
Fittest		**1.0**				**1.0**				**1.0**		

Figure 12. The calculations above compare the fitness of three variations of a trait (AA, Aa, aa, which could represent, for example, "large-medium-small" or "red-pink-white", etc.). Dividing numbers in the second generation by the first (G_2/G_1) gives the "numerical fitness," which is standardized by dividing each by the highest ratio (H). Based on counts of survivors (and *not* on any particular adaptation, such as intelligence, speed, or camouflage), standardized fitness values range from 0 (no survivors) to 1.0 (top survivor). Note that Aa is the top survivor above (fitness = 1.0) whether the population of its species is static (A), increasing (B), or decreasing (C). In case C, Aa is the "high scorer" on a "losing team," *winning the natural selection battle within its species, but possibly becoming extinct as its species is losing the ecological war with others.*

(a) *"Survival of the survivors."* The definition of fitness is grounded ultimately in reproductive success, so it is sometimes called *differential reproduction* or *net relative reproductive efficiency.* In far less than pompous-sounding phrases, what that boils down to is **survival of the survivors**. *Now you can see why natural selection, or survival of the fittest, is a fact.* How is it determined which organisms will be "naturally selected" as fittest? Wait for the struggle for survival to play out from one generation to the next, then count who survived in greatest numbers! An organism may be ugly, slow, or stupid, but if its offspring survive in greatest numbers, it's the fittest! (That may comfort some of us, as well as the opossum!)

Notice that natural selection is **NOT** some awesomely powerful scientific theory that enables scientists to predict future changes in populations. *"Natural selection" is really just a high-sounding, misinforming term* applied to the *observation* that some organisms in a varied population survive in greater numbers than others do — *survival of the survivors. After* scientists *observe* which organisms are "fittest" (i.e., survived in greatest relative numbers), then they can begin to *speculate on why.* Was it camouflage, speed, intelligence, fecundity (having lots of offspring easily), disease resistance, some combination or none of these, or just "blind luck"? Ecclesiastes 9:11 says, "The race is not to the swift, nor the battle to the strong [in our fallen world] . . . but time and chance happeneth to them all" (ASV).

Natural selection is a fact because it's a *tautology* or *truism,* a form of *circular reasoning. It is argued that the fittest are those that survive in greatest relative numbers and those that survive in the greatest relative numbers are defined as the fittest.* That's definitely *true,* but it's really just an observation, not a profound theory, and begs the question of what makes some organisms fitter than others.

The story is told of a student walking to school who saw in the grass a mouse that remained absolutely motionless as a hawk soared overhead. When she asked her teacher why, the teacher explained that mice which ran were seen and killed by the hawk, so natural selection produced those which remained motionless. The next day, the student saw a mouse running to its burrow as a hawk soared overhead. When she asked her teacher why, the teacher explained how mice that remained motionless were easy targets for the sharp-eyed hawk that killed and ate them, so natural selection favored survival of the mice which ran. The "nice" thing about "survival of the survivors" is that it can explain anything: why mice run or stay put, why some species (e.g., horseshoe crabs) never changed in "600 million years" while others changed rapidly and quickly (e.g., an insect-eater thought to have evolved into horses, whales, and bats in less than "5 million years"). The so-called "proof" that natural selection produced evolution is too often merely the argument that survivors survived!

(b) *Natural selection versus ecological competition.* Most people just assume "natural selection" for the "fittest" means the selected variety must be increasing. Actually, natural selection has nothing to do with whether a species as a whole is increasing or decreasing in numbers or staying the same (static or stable). Look back at the calculation of fitness in Figure 12. In case A, the population was static or stable; the second generation had 100 individuals like the first one did. Now imagine the population doubled to 200, and the second generation contained 40 AA, 120 Aa, and 40 aa. What would the new fitness values be? The winner ("fittest") being "naturally selected" is still Aa, and its reproductive efficiency is $120/30 = 4.0$, which is the highest value. That means the standardized fitness of Aa, $4.0/4.0$, is 1.00, the maximum value, just as it was in the static population. The fitness values for the other two groups are also exactly the same in the expanding population as they were for the static case. The reproductive efficiency for aa is $40/20 = 2.0$, so its standardized fitness is $2.0/4.0$ (the "winning" efficiency) $= 0.5$, "one-half" the maximum, as before. The numbers for AA are $40/50 = 0.8$, and $0.8/4.0 = 0.2$, exactly 20 percent of maximum as in the static population.

What if the species population is decreasing? Who's the fittest then? Imagine the population declined by half, and the second generation was 10 AA, 30 Aa, 10 aa (50 total). Again, Aa is the best survivor or fittest, this time because it declined the least in population. Aa's numbers are 30/30 = 1.0, and 1.0/1.0 (the highest) is 1.0. The aa's again did "half" as well: 10/20 = 0.50, and 0.5/1.0 = 0.5. The AA "losers" got a fitness score of "20 percent" maximum, just as before: 10/50 = 0.2, and 0.2/1.0 = 0.2. Notice, however, the species population is decreasing dramatically. *In this case, being the "fittest" only means being the high scorer on the losing team!*

Being the fittest, then, is no guarantee of survival at all. *It may only mean you are likely to be the last of your kind to die out!* Fitness has to do with competition *within* a group; survival of the group often depends on competition among different groups, often related to changing environmental factors — loss of habitat, increase or decrease in temperature or moisture levels, changes in the saltiness of aquatic and soil environments, catastrophes like fires, floods, earthquakes, underwater landslides, etc. So, for example, it's **NOT** natural selection that determines whether the dull and sluggish opossum or the sleek and daring cheetah survives; it's ecology, interaction among different groups and the environment (and so far the opossum is outscoring the cheetah in the ecological competition!).

(c) *Intra- versus interspecific competition.* Many people have the mistaken notion that natural selection involves, for example, competition between lions and zebras. Not at all. Natural selection is NOT lion versus zebra; it's *lion versus lion* (which can catch a zebra) and *zebra versus zebra* (which can escape the lion). In other words, natural selection is NOT **INTER***specific* competition (**between** species); it's **INTRA***specific competition* (**within** species). By analogy to humankind, natural selection is competition among classmates and friends for dates on a Saturday night and jobs at McDonald's, or competition among brothers and sisters for family favors. Natural selection is the *ultimate sibling rivalry*, a struggle to the death among members of the same species. Even members of a plant species compete with one another (not consciously, of course) for water and minerals from the soil and a place in the sun. Some variants of a species are more likely to leave more offspring to the next generation than others, but *at most* the *intraspecific competition of natural selection* produces *variation within kind*, NOT change from one kind to another. *Natural selection, yes; evolution, no.*

A classic lab kit sold to demonstrate natural selection does nothing of the sort. The kit includes *two different species* of flour beetle, *Tribolium confusum* and *T. castaneum.* By changing temperature and moisture conditions and adding predators and different hiding places, students can see one beetle species survives better under this condition, the other beetle species under that. Competition between different species as conditions change is *ecological competition*, not at all natural selection among members of the same group.

Evolutionists, however, did report an example of natural selection that once occurred in a flour beetle experiment. A mutant beetle occurred in one species, and offspring of that beetle eventually wiped out other members of that species — natural selection in action. The supposedly "new and improved" beetle species then lost the ecological competition with the other beetle species under conditions that the pre-mutant beetle species formerly won. As evolutionists recognize, *winning the natural selection battle can lead to losing the ecological war* — "*mischievous results*" of natural selection one evolutionist called it.

(d) *Succession versus evolution.* Evolution is a *hypothetical* process that is supposed to change a few simple forms over time into many complex and varied forms. There is a real process of change through time in which a few life forms *are* followed by a series of more and more complex and varied forms, but the *real* process is *ecological succession*, NOT evolution. If you watched an area of bare rock over time, as farmers and scientists have, you could observe a series of changes from lichens to moss, ferns, shrubs, and trees, but the lichens didn't evolve into the moss, nor the moss into the ferns, etc. Rather, each living community changed the environment in ways that paved the way for the next community to move in. (Plants "move" by scattering spores and seeds which sprout when conditions are right.) Lichens can break down rock, producing enough soil for mosses. Mosses build more soil, and hold moisture, paving the way for shrubs. Shrubs break up the rock further, anchor the soil, and provide shade to decrease moisture loss, paving the way (in the proper climate) for trees.

As the plant communities change, so do the animals. Protozoans are followed successively by worms, insects, birds, and mammals. *Existing species* from another area move in as conditions become favorable — **ecology, not evolution**. It is *migration* of different kinds, *NOT mutation* of one kind into others, that produces ecological succession. Succession involves only *tens or hundreds of years*, NOT millions.

Death is *not* a necessary part of ecological succession, and at least some kinds in early (pioneer) communities survive through various seral stages into the final (climax) community. Lichens grow on bare rock, for example, but lichens also grow on tree bark in climax forests. Ecological succession on a global scale would have followed both creation ("multiply and fill") and the Flood (migration from Ararat).[6] As discussed later, dramatic environmental changes caused by the Flood would favor both (a) selection for different adaptations among pre- and post-Flood members of the same kind, and also (b) survival of different kinds in different proportions in the pre- and post-Flood ecologies.

Ironically, natural selection and ecological competition don't really provide adequate explanation for presumed evolutionary changes, but they do help explain changes important in the creation model.

(e) *Long term versus short term advantage*. Richard Dawkins, Great Britain's leading spokesman for evolution, refers to evolution by natural selection as the "blind watchmaker."[7] In contrast to creation by plan and purpose looking toward a goal, natural selection, Dawkins asserts, is a "blind" process that does not plan, has no purpose, and can't look ahead toward goals. Natural selection is merely opportunistic, rewarding chance combinations of traits with a slight advantage in Darwin's ceaseless "war of nature."

Dawkins is right about natural selection, but wrong about the nature of the living world. *Natural selection cannot plan ahead*; selection is only the observation that certain trait combinations will win the immediate struggle for survival, becoming, by definition, the fittest — *no matter what that does to the future of the species*. That can have a devastating impact on living things, the exact opposite of the evolutionist's hopes and dreams.

Consider territorial population control.[8] Many birds and mammals regulate their population through a series of complex instincts and "ritualistic combat" in which no death occurs and no predators are necessary. Sea lions, for example, limit their population by "allowing" breeding only on certain restricted territories on small beaches. Males who fail to stake out a territory one year must wait until later years to breed. That guarantees plenty of food for the species as it cruises the Pacific. Suppose a chance mutation knocked out the instinct for territorial recognition. Such a mutant male might establish a new breeding colony on another island and pass on his unrestricted urge to breed. Descendants of such a male would automatically win the struggle for survival in the *short term,* but the *long term effects* might include over-hunting their range and even bringing the species to extinction — or at least replacing gentle territorial control with harsher predatory control. Indeed, some evolutionists blame a large percentage of extinction on the exploitation of environmental resources automatically rewarded by natural selection, which is "blind" to long term consequences.

□ □ □ □ □ □ □ □ □ □ □ □ □ □

Natural selection tends to favor specialists, and that also produces problems long term. In a given environment, *specialists* are usually more efficient at exploiting food sources than *generalists,* and evolutionists recognize the tendency for natural selection to convert generalized ancestral populations into ever more specialized descendants. When the environment changes, *highly adapted, specialized* varieties tend to lose out to the *adaptable, generalized* forms — if there are any left. Again, *natural selection seems to promote short-term survival at the expense of long-term extinction.* As we shall see in the chapter on fossils, the long-term survivors over and over again are the generalized, adaptable forms like those God created to multiply and fill the earth, *not* the specialized forms natural selection generated to exploit short-term advantage.

Dawkins is right about the blindness and failure to plan by natural selection, but that makes him wrong about evolution and the history of life on earth.

(f) *Brake or accelerator?* Remember, evolution may not be true, but natural selection is. Natural selection *is* a process at work in our fallen world; it is a description of what happens when different varieties of the same gene-trading species compete for limited resources. As we have seen, the results of natural selection in action are often the opposite of what evolutionists expected, and the exact opposite of what the public is told.

Calling natural selection "survival of the fittest" conjures up an image of a positive, progressive process. Natural selection really operates as the "great eliminator" or "terminator," and might be better called *"unsurvival of the unfittest."* Think back on the famous peppered moth case. Natural selection did **NOT** produce a "new and improved moth"; the dark moth was already present. Pollution made the light form less camouflaged, and so (presumably) natural selection eliminated more light than dark moths. Had natural selection "gone to completion" and totally eliminated the light moth, the species might now be well on the road to extinction, since reduction in pollution has now made the light moth more camouflaged again.

Note also that natural selection only promoted increased death of less camouflaged moths; it did nothing to produce either dark or light color. Mutations are supposed to produce new traits for selection to select, but known mutations are either neutral (having no effect) or harmful, producing defects, disease, and disease organisms. Perhaps the most important role of natural selection in a fallen world (corrupted creation) is acting as a *brake,* slowing down the accumulation of harmful mutations, **eliminating** or reducing genetic decay by producing *"unsurvival of the unfittest."*

All scientists agree that *elimination of the unfit* is a major consequence of natural selection in our present world, but a process that works at best to make tomorrow no worse than today is no process for producing the evolutionist's dream of upward, onward progress. Eliminating defects to repair an old car may keep it running, but it will never turn a mini-van into a Formula 1 race car!

(g) *Fitness versus adaptation.* **Adaptations** *are features and functions that suit an organism for its roles in its environment.* Fitness is determined by counting survivors in Darwin's "war of nature;" *adaptation is determined by engineering or design analysis.* A woodpecker is admirably designed for drilling holes in wood, regardless of how well it is surviving. Professional evolutionists freely admit that *fitness and adaptation are quite different concepts determined in quite different ways,*[9] but that major difference is almost always overlooked in popular nature programs and children's literature, and is often ignored in introductory college biology textbooks. Professional evolutionists do believe that at least some of the time well-adapted organisms should show greater fitness: i.e., leave more offspring to the next generation than their competitors. Creationists already know, of course, that organisms were created with adaptations for survival so they could multiply and fill the earth.

There is no convincing evidence or argument that fitness or natural selection lead to adaptation, but there is ample evidence and logic for the *reverse: adaptation can lead to natural selection*!

If organisms already have certain adapted or adaptable traits, then, as they multiply over the earth, they will more likely survive as the "fittest" and be "naturally selected" in some environments rather than others. In his article on "Adaptation" in the *Scientific American* book *Evolution,* Lewontin[10] emphasizes this point over and over again:

> . . . evolution cannot be described as a process of adaptation because all organisms are already adapted. . . .

> . . . adaptation leads to natural selection, natural selection does not necessarily lead to greater adaptation. . . .

That is, adaptation has to come *first, before* natural selection can act. Natural selection obviously cannot explain the origin of traits or adaptations if the traits have to be there first.

Lewontin recognizes that this simple (but crucial) point is often overlooked, so he gives an example. As a region becomes drier, he says, plants can respond by developing a deeper root system or a thicker cuticle (waxy coating) on the leaves, but "*only if* their gene pool contains genetic variation for root length or cuticle thickness" (emphasis added). Here again, the genes for deep roots and thick, waxy coats must be present among the genes of a kind *before* natural selection can select them. If the genes are already there, we are talking only about variation within kind, i.e., creation, not evolution. As creationists were saying *even before* Darwin's time, natural selection does *not* explain the *origin* of species or traits, but only their *preservation* — how and where certain varieties survive as they multiply and fill the earth.

Lewontin is an evolutionist and outspoken anti-creationist, but he honestly recognizes the same limitations to natural selection that creation scientists do:

. . . natural selection operates essentially to enable the organisms to *maintain* their state of adaptation rather than to improve it (emphasis added).

Natural selection does not lead to continual improvement (evolution); it only helps to maintain features that organisms already have (creation). Lewontin also notes that extinct species seem to have been just as fit to survive as modern ones, so he adds:

. . . natural selection over the long run does *not* seem to improve a species' chances of survival, but simply enables it to "track," or *keep up with,* the constantly changing environment (emphasis added).

Natural selection works only because each kind was created with adaptations (design features) and sufficient variety to multiply and fill the earth in all its ecologic and geographic variety. Without realizing it at the time, Darwin actually discovered important evidence pointing both to God's *creation* (adaptation and variation) and to the *corruption* of creation (struggle and death).

The seven points above are all *logical limits* to *extrapolating* the *hypothetical* process of evolution (macroevolution) from the *observable* process of natural selection. It really looks like using natural selection to "reach" evolution is like using a bicycle to reach the moon; the barriers are insurmountable, no matter how much time you take. Evolutionists face two even more serious difficulties in trying to explain evolution as a result of natural selection: "compound traits" and the "origin" of new traits.

(2) *Compound traits or "irreducible complexity"*

Many believe any genius Darwin had is found in explaining how all the complex and varied structures and functions of living things could be produced *one step at a time* by the process of natural selection. Imagine you are standing at the bottom of the Empire State Building. Getting to the top looks impossible, especially if you have to do it in one huge jump. Then someone shows you the stairway. What looked like an impossibility now seems like a certainty. The climb may be long and hard, but you could make it from the bottom to the top if you took **one step at a time**. That's the way most people now look at the world of living things. Producing life without the outside help of a Creator once seemed *impossible*. Now, say the evolutionists, the production of all life forms from simple beginnings is a virtual *certainty* — **IF AND ONLY IF** each feature is produced slowly and gradually, *one step at a time.*

Darwin himself, however, recognized that adaptations in living systems often depend on many parts working together simultaneously, and Darwin called such features "difficulties with the theory." Such *compound traits,* or systems of *irreducible complexity,* are considered the most powerful argument **against** Darwinism and have fostered the burgeoning growth of the *"Intelligent Design" (ID)* movement among secular scientists today.[11] Remember, *natural selection can be used to turn the impossible into the highly probable* **IF AND ONLY IF each step** *in the development of an adaptation has survival value, allowing it to increase in numbers relative to its competitors.*

Throwing dynamite into the fire started by Michael Denton (*Evolution: A Theory in Crisis,* 1985)[12] and Phillip Johnson *(Darwin on Trial,* 1991),[13] biochemist Michael Behe brought popularity to the Intelligent Design (ID) movement among secular scientists with the publication of his book (*Darwin's Black Box,* 1996),[14] describing stunning examples of *irreducible complexity* found in the "molecular machinery" of living cells: the astonishing rotary motor of the bacterial flagellum, photoreceptor/effector systems ("eyes"), complex stimulation/inhibition interactions in blood clotting and the immune system, etc.!!! Right now, let's look at examples of compound traits on a larger scale.

Perhaps the biggest problem for evolutionists is "the marvelous fit of organisms to their environment." As I mentioned in the first chapter, many adaptations involve whole groups of traits working together, and none of the individual pieces has any survival value ("Darwinian fitness") until the whole set is functioning together. Remember the woodpecker? Let's look at another example.

Since death entered the world, there are many large, predatory fish that roam the oceans. As they feed on smaller fish and shrimp, their mouths begin to accumulate food debris and parasites. Lacking recourse to a toothbrush, how is such a fish going to clean its teeth?

For several kinds of fish, the answer is a visit to the local cleaning station. These are special areas usually marked by the presence of certain shrimp and small, brightly colored fish, such as wrasses and gobis. Often fresh from chasing and eating other small fish and shrimp, a predatory fish may swim over to take its place in line (literally!) at the nearest cleaning station. When its turn comes, it opens its mouth wide, baring the vicious-looking teeth.

You might suspect, of course, that such a sight would frighten off the little cleaner fish and shrimp. No, into the jaws of death swim the little cleaners. Now even a friendly dog will sometimes snap at you if you try to pick off a tick, and it probably irritates the big fish to have a shrimp crawling around on its tongue and little fish picking parasites off the soft tissues of the mouth. (Try to imagine shrimp crawling around on *your* tongue!) But the big fish just hovers there, allowing the cleaners to do their work. It even holds its gill chambers open so that the shrimp can crawl around on the gill filaments, picking off parasites!

At the end of all this cleaning, the second "miracle" occurs. You might think the fish would respond, "Ah, clean teeth; SNAP, free meal!" But, no. When the cleaning is done, the big fish lets the little cleaner fish and shrimp back out. Then the big fish swims off — and begins hunting again for little fish and shrimp to eat!

The fantastic relationship just described is called *cleaning symbiosis*. Perhaps you have seen cleaner fish in a major public aquarium, or seen pictures of their behavior in television footage or nature magazines. Cleaning symbiosis is a well-known example

Woodpecker

Eye

Cleaner Fish

Bombardier Beetle

Figure 13. Darwin included structures requiring many interdependent parts in a chapter titled "Difficulties with the Theory." Before it can have any survival value, every part of a bombardier beetle's "cannon" must be in place, and the same is true for the woodpecker's set of "drilling tools" and the "nerve wiring" for cleaner-fish behavior. Evolutionist Lewontin says such "perfection of structure was," and I say *is*, "the chief evidence of a Supreme Designer."

of mutualism, an intimate relationship of benefit to both types of species involved, in this case, the "cleaner and the cleanee."

Obviously, cleaning symbiosis has survival value for both types of species involved, but does survival value explain the *origin* of this special relationship? Of course not. It makes sense to talk about survival value only *after* a trait or relationship is already in existence. Question: Did the survival value of this cleaning relationship result from time, chance, and struggle, *or* from plan, purpose, and special acts of creation?

The major problem is using Darwinian fitness to explain traits with many interdependent parts when none of the separate parts has *any* survival value. There's certainly no survival value in a small fish swimming into a large fish's mouth on the hope that the big fish has somehow evolved the desire to let it back out! Sea creatures don't provide the only examples of cleaning symbiosis, either. A bird, the Egyptian plover, can walk right into the open mouth of a Nile crocodile — and walk back out again, after cleaning the croc's mouth! On an evolutionary basis, each cleaning relationship would have to be explained separately on the basis of time, chance, struggle, and death, operating on variants of each species involved. Remember, natural selection can help explain the origin of compound traits one step at a time *IF AND ONLY IF* each separate step has survival value on its own.

The situation is even more dangerous for the famous "bombardier beetle." The bombardier is an ordinary-looking beetle, but it has an ingenious chemical defense mechanism. Imagine: Here comes a mean ol' beetle-eater, a toad, creeping up behind the seemingly unsuspecting beetle. Just as he gets ready to flash out that long, sticky tongue, the beetle swings its cannon around, and "boom!" It blasts the toad in the face with hot noxious gases at the boiling point of water, and coats the toad's tongue with a foul-tasting residue. Now that doesn't actually kill the toad, but it surely kills its taste for beetles! Pictures show the toad dragging its tongue across the sand trying to get rid of the foul taste.

Successful firing of the bombardier beetle's cannon requires two chemicals (hydrogen peroxide and hydroquinones), enzymes, pressure tanks, and a whole series of nerve and muscle attachments for aim and control. Try to imagine all those parts accumulating by time, chance, and natural selection. One crucial mistake, of course, and "boom!" the would-be bombardier beetle blows *itself* up, and there's surely no evolutionary future in that! Trial and error can lead to improvement only if you survive the error!

Creationists and evolutionists agree that adaptations such as the woodpecker's skull, cleaning symbiosis, and the bombardier beetle's cannon all have survival value. The question is, how did they get that way: by time, chance, struggle, and death, or by plan, purpose, and special acts of creation? When it comes to adaptations that require several traits all depending on one another, the more logical inference from the evidence seems to be creation.

(3) *Origin of Traits*

Darwin's theory also points us back to creative acts when it comes to the origin of traits. In spite of the title of his book, *Origin of Species*, the one thing Darwin never really dealt with was the *origin* of species. That is, he never explained the origin of the truly new traits needed to produce a truly new kind of organism, something *more* than just a variation of some existing kind. There are many other logical limits to extrapolation from natural selection to evolution, but the simplest is this: natural selection cannot explain the *origin* of traits.

Take the famous example of "Darwin's finches" (Figure 14). On the Galapagos Islands, Darwin observed a variety of finches, some with small beaks for catching insects, others with large beaks for crushing seeds, and one with the ability to use spines to pry insects from their tunnels. How did Darwin explain the "origin" of these various finches? Exactly the same way a creationist would. He saw finches with variation in beak type on the South American mainland and presumed these finches might have

Figure 14. "Darwin's Finches." Darwin explained the location of finches with different beak types on the Galapagos Islands the same way a creationist would, by starting with a population of finches with variation in beak type. In fact, the creationist Edward Blyth published the concept of natural selection 24 years before Darwin did, and he used it to help explain how created kinds spread throughout different environments after sin brought struggle and death to the earth.

reached the islands on a vegetation mat or something similar. The ones with seed-crushing beaks survived where seeds were the major food source, and those with insect-catching beaks out-reproduced others where insects were the major source of food. Given finches with a variety of beak types, then, natural selection helps us to explain *how* and *where* different varieties *survived* as they multiplied and filled the earth. That, of course, is just what a creationist would say—except that a biblical creationist would add that the "struggle and death" part of migration did not begin until man's rebellion ruined the world God had created without death. (Contrast Genesis 1–2 with the Fall in Genesis 3.)

(a.) Pangenesis: Use and Disuse. Darwin called natural selection "the preservation of favored races," and he recognized that selection alone could not explain origin. When it came to the actual origin of new traits, Darwin wrote that it was "from use and disuse, from the direct and indirect actions of the environment" that new traits arose. About 40 years before Darwin, a famous French evolutionist, Jean Lamarck, argued for this kind of evolution based on the *inheritance of traits acquired by use and disuse.* Most books on the subject hint that we should laugh at Lamarck – but Darwin believed exactly the same thing.

Consider the supposed origin of the giraffe. According to both Darwin and Lamarck, the story begins back on the African prairies a long time ago. Because of prolonged drought, the prairie dried up. But there were green leaves up in the trees, and some of the animals started stretching their necks to reach them. As a result, their necks got a little longer (Figure 15). Now that could be partly true. If you really work at it hard enough and long enough, you could add a little bit to your height. People used to do that to get into the army or some special service where you have to be a certain height. The problem, however, is that the offspring of "stretched" parents start off just as small as all the others. The long neck could not be passed on to the next generation.

Figure 15. For the *origin* of new traits, Darwin (like Lamarck) resorted to "use and disuse" and the inheritance of acquired characteristics. Giraffes got longer necks, for example, because their ancestors stretched for leaves in trees, then passed on more neck "pangenes" to their offspring. This idea of "progress through effort" contributed to the early popularity of evolution, but has since been disproved.

Like others of his time, Darwin didn't know about the mechanism of heredity. He thought that each organ produced "pangenes" that would collect in the blood and flow to the reproductive organs; so, a bigger neck made more neck pangenes. Some people still believe this sort of concept. You've probably run into people who say, for instance, that people will eventually have bigger heads because we think a lot, and no toes because we wear shoes all the time. Darwin even used pangenes to "explain" why (in his opinion) wives grew to resemble their husbands as both got older.

It seems people knew as little about giraffes in Darwin's time as they did about heredity. Because their neck is so long, there's a huge distance between a giraffe's heart and its brain. It needs auxiliary pumps to get blood to the brain so it won't faint when it raises its head up — and it needs pressure reducers so that when it bends its head down to take a drink, it won't blow its brains out! A long neck without these features would be deadly.

Science has since disproved these "flimsy facts" of early evolutionary thought, but back in Darwin's time, pangenes captured people's imagination probably even more than natural selection did. To some, Darwin's original theory of evolution suggested continual progress. How do you make something happen? By use and disuse. If you want to get smarter, use your brain, and both you and your children will be smarter. If you want to be strong, use your muscles, and not only will you get stronger, but so will your children.

Well, almost unfortunately, that's not the modern theory of evolution. The use-disuse theory didn't work and had to be discarded. The modern evolutionist is called a *neo-Darwinian*. He still accepts Darwin's ideas about natural selection, but something new (neo-) has been added. The modern evolutionist believes that new traits come about by chance, by random changes in genes called "mutations," and *not* by use and disuse.

(b.) Mutations. Almost everyone has heard about mutations — from Saturday morning cartoons or horror movies, if nowhere

else. In those flicks, some atomic disaster produces people with gnarled skin, one big bulging eye, and other "new traits." In the real world, mutations are responsible for a number of genetic defects, including hcmophilia (bleeders' disease), loss of protective color in the skin and eyes (albinism), and certain kinds of cancer and brain malfunction.

We have abundant evidence that various kinds of radiations, errors in DNA replication, and certain chemicals can indeed produce mutations, and mutations in reproductive cells can be passed on to future generations. Figure 16 shows some of the changes that have been brought about in fruit-fly wings because of mutations: shorter wings, very short wings, curled wings, spread-apart wings, miniature wings, wings without cross veins. Students in my genetics classes work with these fruit flies each year, crossing different ones and working out inheritance patterns.

Then there's the flu virus. Why haven't we yet been able to solve the flu problem? Part of the problem is that this year's vaccine and your own antibodies are only good against last year's flu. (They don't usually tell you that when you get the shot, but it's already out of date.) The smallpox virus has the common decency to stay the same year in and year out, so once you're vaccinated or build up an immunity, that's it. The flu virus mutates quite easily, so each year its proteins are slightly different from last year's. They are still flu viruses, but they don't quite fit our antibodies, so we have to build up our immunity all over again. When it recombines with animal viruses (on the average of once every ten years), the problem is even worse.

Mutations are certainly real. They have profound effects on our lives. And, according to the *neo-Darwinian evolutionists, mutations are the raw material for evolution.*

Is that possible? Can mutations produce real evolutionary changes? Don't make any mistakes here. Mutations are real; they're something we observe; they do make changes in traits. The question remains: do they produce *evolutionary* changes?

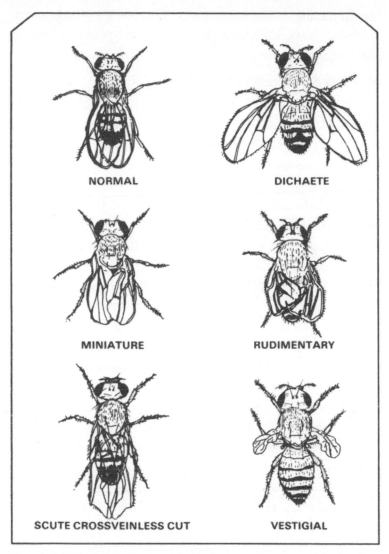

NORMAL

DICHAETE

MINIATURE

RUDIMENTARY

SCUTE CROSSVEINLESS CUT

VESTIGIAL

Figure 16. Mutations are random changes in genes (DNA), often caused by radiation. The mutations in the wings above were produced by x-raying fruit flies. According to the modern, neo-Darwinian view, mutations are the source of new traits for evolution, and selection culls out the fittest combinations (or eliminates the "unfittest") that are first produced just by chance. Mutations certainly occur, but are there limits to extrapolating from mutational changes to evolutionary changes (e.g., "fish to philosopher")?

Do they really produce *new* traits? Do they really help to explain that postulated change from molecules to man, or fish to philosopher?

MUTATIONS, YES; EVOLUTION, NO

The answer seems to be: *"Mutations,* **yes**; *evolution,* **no**." In the last analysis, mutations really don't help evolutionary theory at all. There are three major problems or limits (and many minor ones) that prevent scientific extrapolation from *observed* mutational change to *hypothetical* evolutionary change.

(1) Mathematical challenges. Problem number one is the mathematical. I won't dwell on this one, because it's written up in many books and widely acknowledged by evolutionists themselves as a serious problem for their theory.[15]

Fortunately, mutations are very rare—or are they? They occur on an average of perhaps once in every ten million duplications of a DNA molecule (10^7, a one followed by seven zeroes). That's fairly rare. On the other hand, it's not *that* rare. Our bodies contain nearly 100 trillion cells (10^{14}). So the odds are quite good that we have a couple of cells with a mutated form of almost any gene. A test tube can hold millions of bacteria, so, again, the odds are quite good that there will be mutant forms among them.

The mathematical problem for evolution comes when you want a *series* of *related* mutations. The odds of getting two mutations that are related to one another is the product of their separate probabilities: one in 10^7 x 10^7, or 10^{14}. That's a one followed by 14 zeroes, 100 trillion! Any two mutations might produce no more than a fly with a wavy edge on a bent wing. That's a long way from producing a truly new structure, and certainly a long way from changing a fly into some new kind of organism. You need more mutations for that. So, what are the odds of getting *three* mutations in a row? That's one in a billion trillion (10^{21}). Suddenly, the ocean isn't big enough to hold enough bacteria to make it likely for you to find a bacterium with three simultaneous or sequential related mutations.

What about trying for *four* related mutations? One in 10^{28}. Suddenly, the earth isn't big enough to hold enough organisms to make that very likely, and we're talking about only four mutations. It would take many more than that to change a fish into a philosopher, or even a fish into a frog. It was at this level (just four related mutations) that microbiologists gave up on the idea that mutations in asexual lines could explain why some bacteria are resistant to four different antibiotics at the same time. The odds against the mutation explanation were simply too great, so they began to look for another mechanism — and they found it.

First of all, using cultures that are routinely kept for long periods of time, they found out that bacteria were resistant to antibiotics, even *before* commercial antibiotics were "invented." Resistant bacteria were even found in the bodies of explorers frozen more than a century before medical antibiotic use. Genetic variability was "built right into" the bacteria. Did the nonresistant varieties get resistant by mutation? No. Resistant forms were already present. Furthermore, certain bacteria have little rings of DNA, called plasmids, that they trade around among themselves, and they passed on their resistance to antibiotics in that way. It wasn't mutation and asexual reproduction at all, just ordinary recombination and variation within kind.

Bacteria *can* be made antibiotic resistant by mutation, but such forms are "evolutionary cripples." The mutation typically damages a growth factor, so that the mutationally crippled bacteria can scarcely survive outside the lab or hospital. The antibiotic resistance carried by plasmids results from enzymes produced to break down the antibiotic. Such bacteria do not have their growth crippled by mutation. Their resistance is by design.

But why, you might well ask, would God create antibiotic resistance? It's possible God designed antibiotic resistance in bacteria, and antibiotic production by fungi, to balance the growth of these prolific organisms in the soil. Only after the corruption of creation did some bacteria become disease causers, making antibiotic resistance "inadvertently" a medical problem.

Contrary to popular opinion, drug resistance in bacteria does *not* demonstrate evolution. It doesn't even demonstrate the production of mutations that add information for new categories of protein to the bacterial genome. It *does* demonstrate natural selection (or a sort of artificial selection, in this case), but only selection among already existing variations within a kind. It also demonstrates that when the odds that a particular process will produce a given effect get too low, good scientists normally look for a better explanation, such as the plasmid explanation for resistance to multiple antibiotics.

At this point, evolutionists often say that "time is the hero of the plot." That's what I used to say to my students. "Sure, the odds are low, but there's all that time, nearly five billion years!" Five billion years is only about 10^{17} seconds, and the whole universe contains fewer than 10^{80} atoms. So even by the wildest "guesstimates," the universe isn't old enough or big enough to reach odds like the 1 in $10^{3,000,000}$ that Huxley, an evolutionist, estimated as the odds against the evolution of the horse. Evolutionists like Huxley do believe in miracles; they just don't believe in the Miracle Worker.

In his chapter "Beyond the Reach of Chance," Denton[16] discusses attempts to simulate evolutionary processes on computers. He concludes with these strong words:

> If complex computer programs cannot be changed by random mechanisms, then surely the same must apply to the genetic programs of living organisms. *The fact that systems in every way analogous to living organisms cannot undergo evolution by pure trial and error* [i.e., by mutation and selection] and that their functional distribution invariably conforms to an improbable discontinuum *comes, in my opinion, very close to a formal disproof of the whole Darwinian paradigm of nature.* By what strange

capacity do living organisms *defy the laws of chance* which are apparently obeyed by all analogous complex systems? (emphasis added).

Most gratifyingly, Denton seems to look beyond the merely negative insufficiency of chance to glimpse a solution to "The Puzzle of Perfection," as he calls it, in the "design hypothesis":

> It is the sheer universality of perfection, the fact that everywhere we look, we find an elegance and ingenuity of an absolutely transcending quality, which so mitigates against the idea of chance. . . . In practically every field of fundamental biological research ever-increasing levels of design and complexity are being revealed at an ever-accelerating rate. The credibility of natural selection is weakened, therefore, not only by the perfection we have already glimpsed but by the expectation of further as yet undreampt of depths of ingenuity and complexity (p. 342).

In God's handiwork, unlike man's, the closer we look, the more marvelous is the perfection we see. Unfortunately, we also have evidence that the transcendent ingenuity and design Denton sees has been marred and scarred. In that sense, mathematics isn't even the most serious challenge to using mutations as the basis for evolution.

(2) Upward or downward? Even more serious is the fact that mutations are "going the wrong way" as far as evolution is concerned. Almost every mutation we know is identified by the disease or abnormality that it causes. Creationists use *mutations* to explain the *origin of parasites and disease,* the *origin of hereditary defects,* and the *loss of traits.* In other words, time, chance, and random changes do just what we normally expect: tear things down and make matters worse. Using mutations to explain the *breakdown* of existing genetic order (creation-corruption) is quite the opposite of using mutations to explain the *build up* of genetic order (evolution).

Clearly, creation-corruption is the most direct inference from the effects of mutations that scientists actually observe.

By producing defects or blocking the normal function of certain genes, mutations have introduced numerous genetic abnormalities into the human population. The hemophilia (bleeders' disease) that afflicted the royal houses of Europe may have arisen as a mutant of a clotting-factor gene in Queen Victoria, for example; and the dreaded Tay-Sach's Disease may have arisen in Czechoslovakia in the 1920s as a mutation in the gene for producing an enzyme crucial to brain function.

Some people like to call mutations "the means of creation," but mutations don't create; they corrupt! Both logically and often observationally, as in the examples above, the ordered state must come before mutations can disorder it. Mutations are real, all right, but they point to a *corruption* of the created order by time and chance.

As a matter of fact, human beings are now subject to over 5,000 mutational disorders. Fortunately, we don't show as many defects as we carry. The reason they don't show up is that we each have two sets of genes, one set of genes from our mothers and another set from our fathers. The "bad genes" we inherit from our mothers' side are usually covered up by our fathers' genes, and vice versa. We can see what is likely to happen when an animal is born with only one set of genes. Figure 17, based on a description in a genetics textbook, represents the rare case of a turkey that was hatched from an unfertilized egg, so it had just one set of chromosomes. The poor bird couldn't hold its head up; instead, it bobbed up and down from a neurological disorder. The feathers were missing in patches, and it finally had to be transferred to a germ-free chamber because its resistance to disease was so low.

Now here's the basis for a good horror story. Picture a mirror at the end of a dark hall. You claw your way through the spider webs to reach the mirror, and then you press a button. The mirror

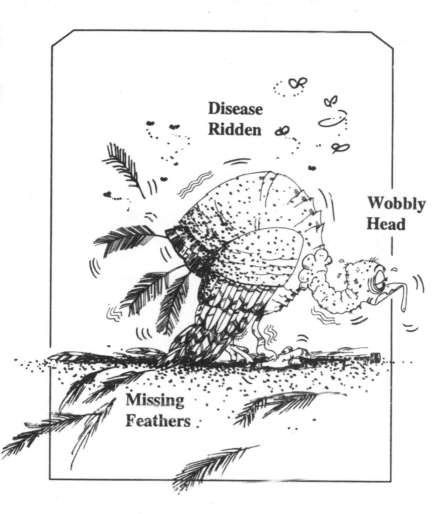

Figure 17. Mutations are mostly harmful, and, as time goes on, they impose an increasingly heavy *"genetic burden"* on a species. The turkey above, lacking a second set of genes to mask its hereditary defects, could scarcely survive. Creationists use mutations to help explain the origin of parasites and disease. Some evolutionists still believe that time, chance, and occasional favorable mutations provide the raw material for "upward-onward" progress, but the "post-neo-Darwinists" are looking for other means to explain evolution.

then splits you in two halves, so you can see what you would look like if you had only those genes you inherited from your mother's genes or only those from your father. In the next scene, you're writhing there in agony, your hair turning white as you fall over backward and die of fright! Unfortunately, that picture exaggerates only slightly what mutations have done to human beings and to the various kinds of plants and animals as well. If it weren't for having two sets of genes, few of us would be able to survive.

Evolutionists recognize, of course, the problem of trying to explain "onward and upward" evolution on the basis of mutations that are harmful at least 1,000 times more often than they are helpful. No evolutionist believes that standing in front of x-ray machines would eventually improve human beings. No evolutionist argues that destruction of the earth's ozone layer is good because it increases mutation rates and, therefore, speeds up evolution. Evolutionists know that decrease in the ozone layer will increase mutation rates, but they, like everyone else, recognize that this will lead only to increased skin cancer and to other harmful changes. Perhaps a helpful change *might* occur, but it would be *drowned in the sea of harmful changes*.

Because harmful mutations so greatly outnumber any supposed helpful ones, it's considered unwise nowadays (and illegal in many states) to marry someone too closely related to you. Why? Because you greatly increase the odds that bad genes will show up. By the way, you also increase the odds of bringing out really excellent trait combinations. But did you ever hear anybody say, "Don't marry your first cousin or you'll have a genius for a child?" They don't usually say that, because the odds of something bad happening are far, far, far, far, far greater.

That would not have been a problem, by the way, shortly after creation (no problem for Cain and his wife, for example). Until mutations had a chance to accumulate in the human population, no such risk of bad combinations existed. Mutations are often carried as "hidden genes" (recessives) that are difficult to eliminate by selection, so they tend to build up in populations. The build-up of mutations with time poses a serious problem for plants and animals, as well as for human beings, and time, evolution's "hero," only *worsens* the problem of mutational decay.

Geneticists, even evolutionary geneticists, refer to the problem as *"genetic load"* or *"genetic burden,"* terms meant to imply a burden that "weighs down" a species and lowers its genetic quality. In his article "The Mechanisms of Evolution" in the *Scientific American* book *Evolution*, Francisco Ayala[17] defines a mutation as "an error" in DNA. Then he explains that inbreeding has revealed that mutations in fruit flies have produced "extremely short wings, deformed bristles, blindness, and other serious defects." Does that sound like "the raw material for evolution?"

It's not that beneficial mutations are theoretically impossible. Bacteria that lose the ability to digest certain sugars, for example, can regain that ability by mutation. That's no help to evolution, however, since the bacterium only gets back to where it started, but at least the mutation is helpful.

A classic example used for decades to illustrate a beneficial mutation is *sickle-cell anemia*. Sickle-cell anemia is a disease of red blood cells. Why would anyone call that a beneficial mutation? Well, in certain parts of Africa, the death rate from malaria is quite high. Malaria is caused by a tiny, one-celled organism that gets inside the red blood cells and eats up the hemoglobin. Now, that particular germ doesn't like sickle-cell hemoglobin. Carriers of one sickle-cell gene produce about half normal and half sickle-cell hemoglobin, and the malaria germ leaves them alone, too. So, carriers don't get malaria. But the cost is high: 25 percent of the children of carriers can die of sickle-cell anemia, and another 25 percent are subject to malaria. If you want to call that a good mutation, you're welcome to it! It seems doubtful to me that real improvement of human beings would result from accumulating that kind of "beneficial" mutation, and certainly hemoglobin's ability to carry oxygen was not improved.

The gene for sickle-cell anemia has built up to high levels in certain African populations, not because it is "beneficial" in some abstract sense, but simply because the death rate from anemia in those areas is less than the death rate from malaria. Natural selection is a "blind" process that automatically accumulates genes for short-term survival, even if it reduces the long-term survival of the species. For that reason, evolutionists recognize that natural selection can occasionally lead to "mischievous results" detrimental to genetic quality. That's the effect I think we're seeing with sickle-cell anemia (Figure 18).

Furthermore, when the frequency of the sickle-cell gene reaches 18 percent, natural selection for it "stops." That's the point at which the death rates from sickle-cell anemia and malaria balance, demonstrating conclusively that sickle-cell anemia is not a suitable model for the continuous genetic expansion that evolutionists seek.

Suppose I told you I had found a way to make cars run uphill without using gasoline. Then, as you watched in eager anticipation, I showed you how applying the brakes would make the car run downhill more slowly. Would you believe I had discovered a means for getting cars to run uphill without fuel? Similarly, natural selection can and does slow the rate of genetic decay produced by accumulating mutations (as it does with sickle-cell hemoglobin), but that hardly proves that mutation-selection produces upward and onward progress!

A better example of favorable mutation might be found in a change from teosinte into corn, but the mutation was favorable to people, not to corn, which has been described as a "biological monstrosity" that could not survive on its own without man's special care. There are many other examples of mutations "beneficial" to people: seedless grapes, short-legged sheep, hairless dogs, but these would all be harmful to the organism in its own environment and, hence, harmful in evolutionary perspective.

While taking a graduate course in evolution on his way to a master-of-science degree in biology, one of my graduates asked

SICKLE-CELL TRAIT

NORMAL BLOOD   **SICKLE-CELL ANEMIA**

cell

protein

DNA

G G A C T T C T T

G G A C A T C T T

* **MUTATION**

Figure 18. "Sickle-cell anemia" is often given as an example of a favorable mutation, because people carrying sickle-cell hemoglobin in their red blood cells (Ss) are resistant to malaria. But the price for this protection is high: 25 percent of the children of carriers may die of the anemia (ss), and another 25 percent (SS) are subject to malaria. The gene will automatically be selected where the death rate from malaria is high, but evolutionists themselves admit that short-term advantages — all that natural selection can ever favor — can produce "mischievous results" detrimental to long-term survival. What do you think? Is sickle-cell anemia a "mischievous result," or a good example of evolutionary progress? (Drawing from Parker, Reynolds, and Reynolds, *Heredity*, 2nd edition [Chicago, IL: Educational Methods, Inc., 1977]).

his professor a simple question during a lecture on mutations as the raw material for evolution: "Would you please give us some examples of beneficial mutations?" After an uncomfortably long pause, the professor finally replied, "I can't think of any right now, but there must be hundreds of them." He did *not* come back to the next class with a list — but, to his credit, he didn't try to use sickle-cell anemia to illustrate helpful mutations.

Once again, let me say that *it's not that good mutations are theoretically impossible; rather, the price is too high.* To explain evolution by the gradual selection of beneficial mutations, one must also put up with the millions of harmful mutations that would have to occur along the way. Even though he has been one of the "old guard" defenders of classic neo-Darwinian evolution, Ayala faces the problem squarely in his article in the *Scientific American* book *Evolution.* He is talking about variation within species (not kind, but species, the smallest possible unit). He says that variation within species is much greater than Darwin postulated. He speaks of such variation as "enormous" and "staggering." Yet when he gets to the actual figures, the variation is less than I, as a creationist, would have expected. (Ayala did say his figures *underestimated* the real variation.)

For creationists, all this variation poses no problem at all. If living things were created to multiply and fill the earth, then great variation within kind is simply good design. There would be no price to pay for created variability, since it would result from creation, *not* from time, chance, struggle, and death (natural selection). (Mutations have introduced further variability since creation was corrupted, but it's the kind of variability a bull introduces into a china shop!)

What problem did Ayala, as an evolutionist, see with all this staggering variability? Just this: For each beneficial mutation a species accumulated, the price would be a thousand or more harmful mutations. When genetic burden gets too great, offspring are so likely to have serious hereditary defects that the ability of the species to survive is threatened. Take the Florida panther, for example, which is considered an endangered species. What endangers it? Highway traffic? No. Hunting? No. Habitat destruction? No. It's endangered by too much "evolution," i.e., the accumulation of mutations that have riddled the reproductive and circulatory systems with so much "evolutionary progress" (read that "genetic burden") that the small, inbred population of panthers was unable to produce a cub that could survive and reproduce.

I told my students that Florida officials should import panthers from out West to cross with the Florida panther to dilute the effects of these harmful mutations. To my surprise, that's what happened! The Florida panther is now making a comeback — except that as it becomes a healthier panther, it is less a "Florida" panther (which was never a true species anyway). Unfortunately, there are other cases where "endangered" sickly subspecies with multiple mutational defects are "protected" from good health by preventing their interbreeding with others of their kind.

Time only makes this evolutionary problem worse. Thanks to our accumulated genetic burden, serious hereditary defects are present in perhaps 5 percent of all human births, and that percentage greatly increases among the children of closely related parents. All of us have some genetic shortcomings, and it's really only by common consent that most of us agree to call each other "normal."

Natural selection cannot save us from this awful situation either. Selection can and does eliminate or reduce the worst mutations — but only when these mutants come to visible (phenotypic) expression. Most mutations "hide" as recessives, "invisible" to selection, and continue to build up in secret at multiple loci, somewhat like a "genetic cancer" slowly but steadily eating away at genetic quality.

If early evolutionists had known what we know now about mutations, it's most unlikely that mutations would ever have been proposed as the pathway to evolutionary progress.

(3) Mutations point back to creation. Mathematics and genetic load are huge problems for evolution, but the biggest reason mutations cannot lead to evolution is an extremely simple one. It's so simple, I'm almost afraid to say it. But really, *mutations presuppose creation.* After all, *mutations are only changes in genes that already exist.*

Most mutations are caused by radiation or replication errors. What do you have to have before you can have a mutation? Obviously, the gene has to be there first, before the radiation can hit it or before it can make a copying mistake. In one sense, it's as simple as that: the gene has to be there *before* it can mutate. All you get as a result of mutation is just a varied form of an already-existing gene, i.e., variation within kind (Figure 19).

Uncritical acceptance of evolution has so stunted scientific thinking that people give mutations god-like qualities. They act as if a cosmic ray striking a cell can cause a "mutation" that somehow assembles over 1,500 DNA bases into a brand new gene, regulators and all, that suddenly begins producing a brand new protein responsible for a brand new trait, raising the lucky mutated organism to the next higher rung on the evolutionary ladder! NOTHING remotely like that has ever, or could ever, happen!

Mutations are NOT genetic "script writers"; they are merely "typographic errors" in a genetic script that has already been written. Typically, a mutation changes only one letter in a genetic sentence averaging 1,500 letters long.

To make evolution happen — *or even to make evolution a theory fit for scientific discussion* — evolutionists desperately need some kind of "genetic script writer" to *increase the quantity and quality of genetic* **INFORMATION**. Mutations have no ability to compose genetic sentences, no ability to produce genetic information, and, hence, no ability to make evolution happen at all.

That simple, absolutely foundational fact completely stumped Richard Dawkins, the world's leading spokesman for evolution as

Abrupt Appearance: Stasis

Figure 19. The most logical inference from our scientific observations of mutation, selection, and genetic recombination would seem to be *variation within created kinds*. There's no "genetic burden" to bear if variety is produced by creation instead of time, chance, and mutation. But could there be enough variation in each created kind to produce all the diversity we see today? Creationists now have some promising answers to that question. (Drawing from Bliss, *Origins: Two Models,* 2nd edition [Green Forest, AR: Master Books, 1978]).

of this writing. In a video production featuring several evolutionist and creationist leaders and skeptics,[18] Dawkins argued eloquently that millions of years of mutation and natural selection would serve as a "blind watchmaker,"[19] producing all appearance of design among living things without any help from some supernatural Designer. Then in a quiet, non-threatening voice, not knowing what the answer would be, the narrator asked Dawkins to give an example of a mutation that *adds information*.

The usually effusive Dawkins gestured, opened his mouth, but stopped before he spoke. With his eyes shifting back and forth as if searching for some answer, he started to speak several times, but always checked himself. Finally, after a long embarrassing silence, the program resumed with Dawkins speaking on a different subject — leaving unanswered the ultimate question, the origin of genetic information.

Yet, molecules-to-man evolution is all about phenomenal expansion of genetic information. *It would take thousands of information-adding mutations to change "simple cells" into invertebrates, vertebrates, and mankind.* If there were any scientific merit at all to mutation-selection as a mechanism for evolution, Dawkins' reply should have been enthusiastic and overwhelming, "My three favorite examples of mutations adding information are. . . . Excellent examples among plants are . . . among insects are . . . among bacteria are. . . ." His answer, instead, was silence, and with no mechanism to add genetic information, the "evolutionary tree" can't grow.

The problem with evolution is not some shortcoming in Dawkins, however. The problem is with the fundamental nature of information itself. The information in a book, for example, cannot be reduced to, nor derived from, the properties of the ink and paper used to write it. Similarly, the information in the genetic code cannot be reduced to, nor derived from, the properties of matter nor the mistakes of mutations; its message and meaning originated instead in the mind of its Maker.

□□□□□□□□□□□□□□

As cogently presented by two of the world's leading information theorists,[20] *information comes only from pre-existing information.*[21] Information systems have the "exherent," created kind of design, which can be logically inferred from our scientific observations as explained earlier (Figure 1). Although mutations may corrupt it and selection may sort variations into different environments, it was not a "blind watchmaker" that composed the genetic script for each kind of organism, but a Creator with a plan and purpose and eyes wide open.

If the evidence and logic is so convincingly clear, why is evolution still so popular? Laying aside personal biases and spiritual concerns, there is a serious semantic problem that could cause honest confusion. After all, evolution is about the continual production of new and different genes, and mutations are continually producing new and different genes — or are they?

Genes of the *same kind,* like those for straight and curly hair or those for yellow and green seeds, are called *alleles.* There are over 300 alleles of the hemoglobin gene. That's a lot of variation, but all those alleles produce hemoglobin, a protein for carrying oxygen in red blood cells (none better than the normal allele). By concept and definition, alleles are just variants of a given gene, producing variation in a given trait. *Mutations produce only alleles,* which means they can produce only variation *within kind* (creation), *not* change from one kind to others (evolution).

Genes of the same kind can be defined objectively as segments of DNA that *occupy corresponding positions* (*loci;* sing. *locus*) *on homologous chromosomes.* Homologous chromosomes are pairs that look alike, but come from two different parents, so their genetic content is similar but not identical. They pair up and then separate in the kind of cell division (meiosis) required for sexual reproduction. Genes that pair up in meiotic cell division, therefore, can be identified *as genes of the same kind.* Genes of the same kind are also turned on and off by the same gene regulators. Notice, it is not subjective human opinion that is telling us which genes are the same kind; it is objective, observable cellular processes.

Mutations, random changes in the genetic code, do produce "new genes" not present at creation, but the so-called "new genes" are still found at the same locus, still pair the same way in meiosis, and are still turned on and off by the same regulators, so they are really only *genes of the same kind* as the original, and represent only *variation within kind* (usually harmful variation in the case of mutations).

Notice the terms "new genes" or "different genes" can have two radically different meanings. As geneticists normally do, we have been calling genes of the same kind *alleles.* The genes for tongue rolling and non-rolling are *"different genes"* in one sense, but only variations of the *same kind* of gene — affecting the same trait, found in corresponding positions (loci) on homologous chromosomes, pairing up in meiosis, and turned on and off by the same regulators. They are NOT different genes in the sense that genes for tongue rolling, and genes for making sickle cell hemoglobin are! Similarly, the sickle cell gene is a "new gene" in the sense that it was not present at creation, but it is only a new (and harmful!) *version of a pre-existing* gene, one that occupies the same chromosomal position, pairs the same way, and is turned on and off by the same regulators as the gene for making normal hemoglobin. In fact, the gene for sickle cell hemoglobin differs in base sequence at only one position out of several hundred in the normal gene for making hemoglobin, again just *variation within kind* or *allelic variation.*

We need a new and different term to describe genes that are *truly new and different* — genes with **information** affecting a *different category of trait* — not just information on varieties of shirts, for example, but information on motorcycles! To refer to genes that do NOT occupy corresponding loci on homologs, that do NOT pair in meiosis, and that DO contain information on distinctive categories of traits, we will use the word ***genon.***

Genes for tongue rolling and non-rolling are different alleles, for example, but genes for tongue rolling and genes for making hemoglobin are different genons, with genes for normal and sickle cell hemoglobin as alleles of the hemoglobin genon.

The complete set of DNA specifying a kind is called its *genome*. The human genome includes at least 30,000 different genons, each of which could have been created in four different allelic varieties (two in each parent). Genetic defects and diseases occurring since the corruption of creation have introduced *many new alleles*, but *no new genons*. All the genes in one generation available to be passed on to the next are called the gene pool. Members of the **same kind** *may also be defined* as organisms that share the *same gene pool*.

The number of genes for different kinds of traits (genons) can be called the **depth *of the gene pool.*** Using earlier examples, we could say the human gene pool is 30,000 genons deep, the *E. coli* bacterial gene pool about 5,000, while the gene pool of a small virus may be only a dozen genons deep. The **width** of the gene pool refers to the amount of its *"horizontal"* allelic variation. Among dogs, for example, the width of a greyhound's gene pool is very narrow; crossing pure bred greyhounds just gives you more greyhounds, all very similar in speed, color, intelligence, hair length, nose length, etc. Crossing two "mongrels," however, can give you big dogs and small dogs, dark and light and splotchy colored dogs, dogs with long and short hair, yappy and quiet dogs, mean and affectionate dogs, etc., etc.! The *width* of the mongrel's gene pool (its allelic variability) is quite large compared to the greyhound's, but the *depth* of the gene pool (the number of genons) is the same for both dogs.

"**Kind**" is defined in terms of **depth** of the gene pool, the total number of different **genons** in a genome and a list of the traits they influence. **Variation within kind** is defined in terms of the **width** of the gene pool, the number of **alleles** at each gene site (locus or genon).

Variation, Yes; Evolution, No

I have been saying, perhaps too often, that the weight of evidence points to "variation within the created kinds." Do I really mean that all the tremendous variety we see today was built right into the created kinds? Could there be enough variation in two created human beings, for example, to produce all the variation among human beings we see today?

Answer: "Yes, indeed; no problem!" I get some help here from an unexpected source, evolutionist Francisco Ayala.[22] He says that human beings are "heterozygous" for 6.7 percent of their genes on the average. That means that 6 or 7 times in 100, the pair of genes for a given trait differ, like the genes for free or attached ear lobes, or for rolling or not rolling the tongue. Now this may not seem like much, but Ayala calculates a single human couple with just "6.7 percent variety" could produce 10^{2017} children (mathematically, not physically!) before they would run out of variation and have to produce an identical twin. That's a 1 followed by 2,017 zeroes! The number of atoms in the known universe is a mere 10^{80}, nothing at all compared with the variety that is present in the genes of just two human beings!

Take human skin color, for example. First of all, it may surprise you to learn that all of us (except albinos) have exactly the *same* skin-coloring agent. It's a protein called melanin. We all have the same basic skin color, just different amounts of it. (Not a very big difference, is it?) How long would it take to get all the variation in the amount of skin color we see among people today? A million years? No. A thousand years? No. Answer: *just one generation!*

Let's see how that works. The amount of skin color we have depends on at least two pairs of genes. Let's call these genes *A* and *B*. People with the darkest skin color have genes *AABB* as their genotype (set of genes for a trait); those with very light skins have *aabb*. People with two "capital-letter" genes would be "medium-skinned," and those with one or three such genes would be a shade lighter or a shade darker.

Suppose we start with two medium-skinned parents, *AaBb*. Figure 20 is a genetic square that shows the gene combinations in the children they could have. Less than half (only 6 of the 16 combinations) would be medium-skinned like their parents. Four each would be a shade darker or lighter. One in 16 of the children of medium-skinned parents *(AaBb)* would have the darkest possible skin color *(AABB)*, while the chances are also 1 in 16 that a brother or sister will have the very lightest skin color *(aabb)*. (For details, see Parker, Reynolds, and Reynolds.[23])

The Bible doesn't tell us what skin color our first parents had, but, from a design point of view, the "middle" makes a great beginning. Starting with medium-skinned parents *(AaBb)*, it would take only one generation to produce all the variation we see in human skin color today. In fact, this is the normal situation in India today. Some Indians are as dark as the darkest Africans, and some — perhaps a brother or sister in the same family — as light as the lightest Europeans. I once knew a family from India that included members with every major skin color you could see anywhere in the world. The TV news in early 2006 showed fraternal twins born to parents of medium skin tone; one twin was quite dark and one was quite light.

Now let's see what happens when human beings are separated into isolated groups by barriers such as geography, culture, or language (such as at the Tower of Babel in Gen. 11). If those with very dark skins *(AABB)* migrate into the same areas and/or marry only those with very dark skins, then they only have capital *A* and *B* genes to pass on and all their children will have very dark skins. Similarly, parents with very light skins *(aabb)* can have only very light-skinned children, since they have only *a* and *b* genes to pass on.

Even certain medium-skinned parents *(AAbb* or *aaBB)* can get "locked-in" to having only medium-skinned children, like the Orientals, Polynesians, and my ancestors, the Native Americans. Each *AAbb* parent, for example, will pass on one *A* and one *b*,

Maximum Variation
AaBb x AaBb

	AB	Ab	aB	ab
AB	AA BB	AA Bb	Aa BB	Aa Bb
Ab	AA Bb	AA bb	Aa Bb	Aa bb
aB	Aa BB	Aa Bb	aa BB	aa Bb
ab	Aa Bb	Aa bb	aa Bb	aa bb

Only Dark AABB   Only Medium aaBB or AAbb   Only Light aabb

Figure 20. All human beings have *the same* basic skin-color agent (melanin), just different amounts of it. From parents created with medium skin color as diagrammed, all the variation we see today could be produced in just *one generation*. In the same way, plants and animals created with a mixture of genes could have filled all of the earth's ecologic and geographic variety. As people break up into groups, however, some groups would develop limited variability — only dark, only medium, or only light as indicated.

so the children of *Ab* egg and sperm cell union will all be *AAbb*, like their parents.

Where people with different skin colors get together again (as they do in the West Indies, for example), you find the full range of variation again — nothing less, but nothing more either, than what we had at the beginning. Clearly, all this is *variation within kind.*

There are at least four skin color genes in the human gene pool: *A, a, B, b.* That total human gene pool for skin color can be found in just one person with medium skin color *(AaBb)*, or it can be "spread around" among many people with visibly different skin colors. In fact, the gene frequencies (percents of each gene) in one *AaBb* medium-skinned person are exactly the same as the gene frequencies in the 16 children that show five different amounts of skin color. All that *individual variation* occurs in a *group that remains constant: creation and variation within the created kind!*

The tendency for gene percentages to remain the same, generation after generation, is expressed mathematically as the *Hardy-Weinberg law.* For evolutionists, this fundamental law of population genetics represents *resistance* to change, and might be called *genetic inertia.* Creationists could call it the *law of conservation of genetic variability* instead, and see it as a way to define mathematically both the constancy of the group and the individual differences that characterize "variation within kind."

Geneticists call the shuffling of pre-existing genes *recombination.* Perhaps you've played a game with the common deck of 52 cards that includes four groups (hearts, diamonds, clubs, and spades), each with 13 different numbers or "faces" (2–10, plus J, Q, K, A). In one game, called "bridge," each of four players gets a "hand" of 13 cards. You can play bridge for 50 years (and some people do!) without ever getting the same group of 13 cards! The "hands" you are dealt are constantly changing, and each is unique — but the deck of cards remains always the same.

Although the comparison is not perfect, a deck of bridge cards illustrates the concept of *variation within created kind.* The bridge hands dealt are *unique, different, and constantly changing,* like the *individual* members of a population, but the deck of 52 cards remains *constant, never changing, always the same,* like the *created kind.* **Ever-changing individuals** in a **never-changing group**, or **individual variation** plus **group constancy**; that's **variation** within **created kinds**.

What happened as the descendants of medium-skinned parents produced a variety of descendants? Evolution? Not at all. Except for albinism (the mutational loss of skin color), the human gene pool is no bigger and no different now than the gene pool present at creation. As people multiplied, the genetic variability *built right into* the first created human beings came to visible expression. The darkest Nigerian and the lightest Norwegian, the tallest Watusi and the shortest Pygmy, the highest soprano and the lowest bass could have been present right from the beginning in two quite average-looking people. Great variation in size, color, form, function, etc., would also be present in the created ancestors of all the other kinds (plants and animals) as well.

Evolutionists *assume* that all life started from one or a few chemically evolved life forms with an extremely small gene pool. For evolutionists, enlargement of the gene pool by selection (struggle and death) among random mutations is a slow, tedious process that burdens each type with a "genetic load" of harmful mutations and evolutionary leftovers. Creationists *assume* each created kind began with a large gene pool, designed to multiply and fill the earth with all its tremendous ecologic and geographic variety, so no struggle and death or long time need be involved at all.

Neither creationist nor evolutionist was there at the beginning to see how it was done, but at least the creationist mechanism works, and it's consistent with what we observe. The evolutionist assumption *doesn't* work, and it's *not* consistent with what we presently know of genetics and reproduction. As a scientist, I prefer ideas that *do* work and *do* help to explain what we can observe, and that's creation!

According to the creation concept, each kind starts with a large gene pool present in created, probably "average-looking," parents. As descendants of these created kinds become isolated, each average-looking *(generalized)* type would tend to break up into a variety of more *specialized* descendants adapted to different environments. Thus, the created ancestors of dogs, for example, have produced such varieties in nature as wolves, coyotes, and jackals. Human beings, of course, have great diversity, too. As the Bible says, God made of "one blood" (or one gene pool) all the "tribes and tongues and nations" of the earth (Figure 21). When asked about race on my census form, I checked "Other" and wrote in "Human"; there's only one race, the human race, and we're all parts of it (Acts 17:26).[24]

Varieties within a created kind have the same genes (genons), but different percentages of various alleles. Differences from average allele percentages can come to expression quickly in small populations (a process called *genetic drift*). Take the Pennsylvania Amish, for example. Because they are descendants of only about 200 settlers, the founders, who tended to marry among themselves, they have a greater percentage than their ancestors of genes for short fingers, short stature, a sixth finger, and a certain blood disease.

All the different varieties of human beings can, of course, marry one another and have children. Many varieties of plants and animals also retain the ability to reproduce and trade genes, despite differences in appearance as great as those between St. Bernards and Chihuahuas. Varieties of one kind may also lose the ability to interbreed with others of their kind. For example, fruit flies multiplying through Central and South America have split up into many subgroups (Figure 21). Since these subgroups no longer interbreed, each can be called a separate species.

Figure 21. Descendants of created kinds tend to break up into different varieties. Even varieties that no longer interbreed (B) can be recognized as the same kind because they possess only alternate forms (alleles) of the same genes. The existence of distinct types, both living and fossil, said Harvard's Stephen Gould, "fit splendidly with creationist tenets of a pre-Darwinian era." Although Gould rejected creation, the facts seem to me to fit creation in our present "post-neo-Darwinian era" just as well.

SPECIATION, YES; EVOLUTION, NO

Whoops! Two or more species from one kind! Isn't that evolution?

Some evolutionists certainly think so. After I participated in a creation-evolution debate at Texas A & M, a biology professor got up and told everyone about the flies on certain islands that used to interbreed but no longer do. They've become separate species, and that, he said, to a fair amount of applause, proves evolution is a fact — period!

Well, what about it? Barriers to reproduction do seem to arise among varieties that once interbred. Does that prove evolution? Or does that make it reasonable to extrapolate from such processes to *real* evolutionary changes from one kind to others? As I explained to the university-debate audience (also to applause), the answer is simply no, of course not. It doesn't even come close.

Any real evolution (macroevolution) requires an *expansion* of the gene pool, the *addition* of new genes (genons) with new information for new traits as life is supposed to move from simple beginnings to ever more varied and complex forms ("molecules to man" or "fish to philosopher"). Suppose there are islands where varieties of flies that used to trade genes no longer interbreed. Is this evidence of evolution? No, exactly the opposite. Each variety resulting from *reproductive isolation* has a *smaller* gene pool than the original and a *restricted* ability to explore new environments with new trait combinations or to meet changes in its own environment. The long-term result? Extinction would be much more likely than evolution.

Of course, if someone insists on defining evolution as "a change in gene frequency," then the fly example "proves evolution" — but it also "proves creation," since varying the amounts of already-existing genes is what creation is all about (Figure 22).

If evolutionists really spoke and wrote only about observable variation within kind, there would be no creation-evolution controversy. As you know, textbooks, teachers, and television "docudramas" insist on extrapolating from simple variation within kind to the wildest sorts of evolutionary changes. Of course, as long as they insist on such extrapolation, creationists will point out the *limits* to such change and explore creation, instead, as the more logical inference from our scientific observations. All we have ever observed is what evolutionists themselves call "subspeciation" (variation within kind), never "transspeciation" (change from one kind to others) (Figure 22).

Evolutionists are often asked what they mean by "species," and creationists are often asked what they mean by "kind." Creationists would like to define "kind" in terms of interbreeding, since the Bible describes different living things as "multiplying after kind," and evolutionists also use the interbreeding criterion. However, scientists recognize certain bower birds as distinct species *even though* they interbreed, and they can't use the interbreeding criterion *at all* with asexual forms. So, both creationists and evolutionists are divided into "lumpers" and "splitters." "Splitters," for example, classify cats into 28 species; "lumpers" (creationist *or* evolutionist) classify them into only one!

Perhaps each created kind is a unique combination of *non-unique* traits. Look at people, for instance. Each of us has certain traits that we may admire (or abhor): brown hair, tall stature, or even a magnificent nose like mine. Whatever the trait, someone else has exactly the same trait, but nobody has the same *combination* of traits that you do or I do. Each of us is a *unique combination* of *non-unique traits.* In a sense, that's why it's hard to classify people. If you break them up according to hair type, you'll come out with groups that won't fit with the eye type, and so on. Furthermore, we recognize *each person as distinct.*

We see a similar pattern among other living things. Each created kind is a unique combination of traits that are individually shared with members of other groups. The platypus (Figure 9), for example, was at first considered a hoax by evolutionists, since its "weird" set of traits made it difficult even to guess what it was

Change and Variation

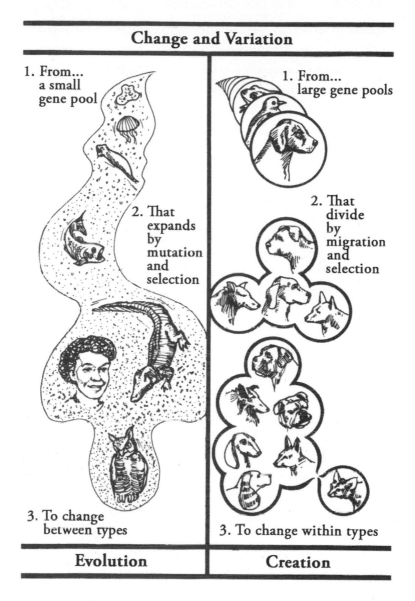

1. From... a small gene pool

2. That expands by mutation and selection

3. To change between types

Evolution

1. From... large gene pools

2. That divide by migration and selection

3. To change within types

Creation

Figure 22. Change? Yes — but which kind of change? What is the more logical inference, or the more reasonable extrapolation, from our observations: unlimited change from one kind to others (evolution), or limited variation within kinds (creation)? Given the new knowledge of genetics and ecology, even Darwin, I believe, would be willing to "think about it."

evolving from or into. Creationists point out that *each* of its traits (including complex ones like its electric location mechanism, leathery egg, and milk glands) is complete, fully functional, and well-integrated into a distinctive and marvelous kind of life.

Perhaps God used a design in living things similar to the one He used in the non-living world. Only about a hundred different elements or atoms are combined in different ways to make a tremendous variety of non-living molecules or compounds. Maybe creationists will one day identify a relatively few genes and gene sets that, in unique combinations, were used to make all the different types of life we see. It would take a tremendous amount of research to validate this "mosaic or modular" concept of a created kind, but the results would be a truly objective taxonomy that would be welcomed by all scientists, both creationists and evolutionists. We might even be able to write a "genetic formula" for each created kind, as we can write a chemical formula (a unique combination of non-unique atoms) for each kind of compound.

Why should we be able to classify plants and animals into created kinds or species at all? The late Stephen Gould,[25] famed evolutionist and acrimonious anti-creationist, wrote that biologists have been quite successful in dividing up the living world into distinct and discrete species. "But," said Gould, "how could the existence of distinct species be justified by a theory [evolution] that proclaimed ceaseless change as the most fundamental fact of nature?" For an evolutionist, why should there be species at all? If all life forms have been produced by gradual expansion through selected mutations from a small beginning gene pool, organisms really should just grade into one another without distinct boundaries. Darwin also recognized the problem. He finally ended by denying the reality of species. As Gould pointed out, Darwin was quite good at *classifying* the species whose ultimate reality he denied. And, said Gould, Darwin could take no comfort in fossils, since he was also successful in classifying them into distinct species. He used the same criteria we use to classify plants and animals today.

In one of the most brilliantly and perceptively developed themes in his book *Evolution: A Theory in Crisis*, Denton[26] shows how leaders in the science of classification, after a century of trying vainly to accommodate evolution, are returning to, and fleshing out, the creationist typological concepts of the pre-Darwinian era. Indeed, the study of biological classification was founded by Karl von Linné (Carolus Linnaeus) on the basis of his conscious and explicit biblical belief that living things were created to multiply after kind, and that these created kinds could be rationally grouped in a *hierarchical pattern* reflecting themes and variations in the Creator's mind. If evolution were true, says Denton, classification of living things ought to reflect a *sequential pattern*, like the classification of wind speeds, with arbitrary divisions along a continuum (e.g., the classification of hurricanes into categories 1, 2, 3, 4, and 5 along a wind speed gradient). In sharp contrast, living things fit into distinctly bounded hierarchical categories, with each member "equi-representative" of the group, and "equidistant" from members of other defined groups.

"Actually," concluded Gould, "the existence of distinct species *was* quite consistent with *creationist* tenets of a pre-Darwinian era" (emphasis added). I would simply like to add that the evidence *is* also quite consistent with the creationist tenets of the present *post-neo-Darwinian* era. In Darwin's time, as well as the present, "creation" seems to be the more logical inference from our observations.

The collapse of neo-Darwinism has sparked interest in creation among secular intellectuals, leading to the influential movement now called *"Intelligent Design"* or *ID*. ID spokesmen present evidence for intelligent design without tying it to the Bible or any other overtly religious position. ID gained worldwide notoriety with *Darwin on Trial* in which a prestigious law professor from the University of California at Berkeley, Phillip Johnson,[27] demonstrated that Darwinian evolution was based on so many errors in logic and violations of the rules of evidence that it represented little more than a thinly veiled apologetic for philosophic naturalism. Books and visuals by Jonathan Wells show that popular *Icons of Evolution*[28] still used in textbooks, museum displays, and television programs were discredited scientifically years ago.

ID took the scientific offensive with *Darwin's Black Box*[29] in which biochemist Michael Behe pointed to "irreducible complexity" in DNA and numerous subcellular "molecular machines" and interactive physiological systems as powerful evidence both (1) falsifying the Darwinian concept of step-by-step evolution that requires survival rewards at each step, and (2) supporting the concept that multiple parts, each functionless until organized as a whole, require plan, purpose, and intelligent design. Other ID publications and productions press the point for secular audiences.[30]

It's no wonder that in recent times evolutionists have left the defense of evolution largely to lawyers, judges, politicians, educators, the media, and the clergy, NOT *to scientists. Even secular and agnostic scientists are becoming creationists!*

The evidence is forcing secular scientists to admit the severe inadequacy of mutation-selection, *but* these same processes are being picked up and used by creationists. What would Darwin say about that? A man as thoughtful and devoted to detail and observation as Darwin was would surely be willing to "think about it."

MUTATION-SELECTION IN BIBLICAL PERSPECTIVE

Hold it! Mutation-selection in *biblical* perspective? Isn't that some sort of contradiction in terms? Not at all. Like thousands of other scientists (including many evolutionists), I think the scientific evidence is quite clear: Evolution demands an increase in the quantity and quality of genetic information, and mutation-selection, *no matter how long you wait,* cannot provide it. *But, both mutation and selection are* very real, observable processes going on around us every day. *Evolution,* **no,** *but mutation-selection,* **yes**!

They don't produce evolutionary changes, but mutation and selection do indeed produce changes. Mutations are no real help in explaining the origin of *species,* but they are great for explaining the origin of disease, disease organisms, and birth defects. Natural selection is no real help in explaining the *origin* of really new species, but it's great for explaining *how* and *where* different specialized subtypes of the various created kinds "multiplied and filled the earth" after death corrupted the creation and, again, after the Flood.

I've already told you that I'm an evolutionist turned creationist, so this may surprise you: I don't believe we live in the world God created! Or, at least, we don't live in the world *as* God created it. I've also told you I'm now the "worst kind" of creationist, a "biblical creationist." One reason is my answer to the same problem that puzzled Darwin: How could there be so much pain, suffering, disease, death, and disaster in a world created by an all-powerful, all-loving God?

According to the Bible, God did *not* create the world full of pain and death. Instead, it was the self-centered, arrogant wickedness of human beings that ruined the world of perfect peace and harmony that God had created. In the words of Romans 8:19–21, because of man's evil, the creation was "subjected to futility . . . and a bondage to corruption." Remember, there are *four "Cs" in the biblical outline. The first, creation, was followed by the second, corruption.*

The Bible seems clearly to be "telling it like it is." Our world is full of far too much evidence of design, beauty, plan, and purpose to be a product of the blind processes of time, chance, struggle, and death. Our world is also full of too much pain, suffering, imperfection, and decay to be the work of a kindly "Mother Nature." "Nature lovers" may wish to preserve the whale and the wolf, but few are willing to push for saving the tapeworm or the AIDS virus! The rose has thorns! "Mother Nature" can be, and often is, a "wicked old witch." Our world really looks like a "corrupted creation." If you already have genes working together in coordinated sets (creation), then random changes like mutations can produce disease, death, and other defects in design (corruption).

What about viruses? Viruses have the DNA-protein (triplet base-R) coding relationship that suggests they were deliberately created. Viruses also have "docking proteins" that must attach to corresponding receptor proteins on a cell's membrane before they can enter that cell. You never got a virus infection that you didn't invite into your cells! That's why a virus will affect one organ system and not others, and why, for example, dogs get some viral diseases that don't affect humans, and vice versa. Some people may even be resistant to the AIDS virus because they don't have the receptor protein it needs to get into their cells.

It seems to me that in God's originally perfect creation, the interlocking of docking and receptor proteins was designed to allow viruses to insert their DNA (or RNA) into only those cells in which gene transfer would be beneficial. In properly programmed receptor cells, some viruses can splice their DNA into the cell's genome, and the added (pre-existent, pre-programmed!) genetic information multiplies along with the cell. In genetic engineering labs today, scientists use viruses as carriers and splicers of genetic information. Perhaps God, the ultimate Genetic Engineer, designed viruses as gene carriers, especially for bacteria, which are incredibly streamlined for genetic efficiency and rapid response to environmental stimuli.

Then with the corruption of creation came mutations affecting both viral docking and cellular receptor proteins. Now mutated viruses inject genetic information into the wrong cells, where it causes havoc and disease. Time, chance, struggle, and death reward the immediate victors in Darwin's war of nature, but they ruin a relationship God had originally created for the benefit of life on earth.

Evolutionists often taunt proponents of intelligent design (ID), as I once would have, by saying such things as "Great job your intelligent Designer did with the AIDS virus! He/she/it must really be proud of the malarial parasite, too, and bubonic plague bacteria were a real masterpiece of intelligent design."

I do think the 4 Cs of biblical history (creation, corruption, catastrophe, Christ) provide far richer and deeper scientific explanations for real world observations than intelligent design, especially when it comes to billions of dead things buried in rock layers (fossils) and to imperfections (defects, disease, death, and disaster) in our present fallen world.

ID scientists who want to avoid any reference to the Bible can give at least a partial answer to the problem of imperfection. After all, essentially all of the examples of imperfection used to taunt intelligent design — viruses, mutations, diseases, birth defects, so-called "vestigial" (functionless) organs, etc. — are examples of *breakdowns* in previously well-designed systems. Mutations, for example, only damage genes that previously had a beneficial function, and such damage may cause birth defects, viral and bacterial disease, and even loss of organ function. But the design came first.

A car breaking down on the highway certainly does not prove that no intelligent design was involved in making the car originally. Imperfections in systems previously designed are a challenge, not to ID scientists, but to evolutionists. To support their theory, evolutionists don't need examples of designed systems breaking down; they need examples of incomplete parts coming together to produce new and improved structures and functions. The world is still waiting for the first example of that kind of evolutionary progress.

Meantime, DNA defects are also responsible for a host of hereditary diseases, some fatal and many debilitating: sickle-cell anemia, galactosemia, PKU, Tay-Sachs disease, hemophilia A, and a few thousand others, and gene defects are responsible for some cancers and perhaps for some aspects of the aging process.

Time, the usual hero of the evolutionary plot, only makes matters *worse. The more time that goes by, the greater the genetic burden or genetic corruption.* Natural selection can't save us from this genetic decay, since most mutations are recessive and can sneak through a population hidden in carriers, only rarely showing up as the double recessive which can be "attacked" by natural selection. Even leading evolutionists admit that, as time goes by, accumulating genetic decay threatens the very survival of plant, animal, and human populations.

In the last chapter of their classic textbook *Evolving: The Theory and Processes of Organic Evolution*,[31] leading evolutionists Ayala and Valentine asked the question, "What does the future hold?" When I was an evolutionist, I would have expected that chapter to be full of bright prospects: higher IQs, greater mathematical and musical genius, faster runners and higher jumpers, nutritious and delicious foods in abundance, the conquest of disease. Instead, Ayala seemed despondently concerned with basic survival: How can we save ourselves from mutations? He saw decay in genetic quality in plant, animal, and human species everywhere. He even wondered if the government might have to step in and license human reproduction, allowing couples to have children only after they pass extensive genetic tests.

What can natural selection, the evolutionist's substitute for God, do to save us from this mutational corruption? Not enough. By eliminating the worst mutations as they come to visible expression, natural selection can *slow* the process of genetic decay, but that's something like giving aspirin to a cancer patient to slow the rate of dying. Since natural selection can select only among combinations of genes that already exist or their mutational alleles, selection can no more lift us out of the quagmire of genetic decay than flapping our arms would lift us off the ground.

Darwin was certainly right about one thing: there is a struggle for survival! That comes as no surprise, of course, to a Bible student. We read about it almost right away, in the third chapter of the first book, Genesis. The first two chapters describe the perfect peace of paradise as God created it. The third chapter describes how human self-centeredness and arrogance corrupted God's creation, bringing thorns and thistles, pain, struggle, and death. Our hope is also right there in Genesis: the first promise of the salvation and restoration to new and abundant life that we have in Jesus Christ (Gen. 3:15).

Understanding the evolutionary process of mutation-selection forced me to give up the popular views called *theistic evolution* and *progressive creation*. Like most people, I grew up learning only evolution. When I became a Christian, it seemed only natural to put evolution and the Bible together. "Evolution is just God's means of creation," I told myself triumphantly. Besides that, I don't like to fight. So when I heard creationists and evolutionists arguing, I was only too happy to step in as the great peacemaker: "Calm down. You're both right. The Bible tells us *that* God created. Evolution tells us *how* He did it."

That's certainly an extremely popular view, and it's a temptingly easy solution, but I think many people who opt for theistic evolution or progressive creation have the same mistaken, highly *romanticized concept of the evolutionary process* I once had. We tend to think of evolution as just step-by-step, upward-onward progress, and that sounds like something God might do. By contrast, remember how Charles Darwin described the evolutionary process in the closing paragraphs of his *Origin of Species:*

> . . . thus, from the war of nature, famine and death,
> the production of higher animals directly follows.

The *"war of nature, famine and death."* Evolution is a gruesome cycle of millions of years of struggle and death. Unless carriers of part of a species' gene pool die, there can be no evolutionary change. Even the evolution of altruism or cooperation can proceed only over the dead bodies of all those who don't cooperate.

That's what evolutionists still believe today. Describing human origins, the late Carl Sagan,[32] whose TV series *Cosmos* continues to preach evolution worldwide, put it this way:

> Only through an immense number of deaths of slightly maladapted organisms are you and I — brains and all — here today.

Again, death and accident, death and accident, over countless generations. That's what the evolutionary process is all about. Could that be the way God created the world that He called "all very good" (Gen. 1: 31)?

The more I thought about it, the more I wondered, "How could evolution be God's means of creation?" God even tells us that He was "grieved to His heart" at the "violence and corruption" that filled the earth after people turned away from Him (Gen. 6:5–11). If God was grieved by violence and corruption, how could He use it as His means of creation, or endorse it as part of a "good creation" before man ruined it? Jacques Monod, famous atheist and biochemist, once said that he was surprised that any Christian would believe that God would use such a *cruel, wasteful,* and *inefficient* process as evolution for His means of creation.

We need to do a much better job of *teaching evolution*! I really think that if more people understood the evidence and how evolution is supposed to work, far fewer people would believe it. Certainly *there should be far, far fewer Christians willing to compromise the biblical message of new life in Christ with evolution's millions of years of struggle and death.*

Why would Christ come to conquer death and to raise us to newness of life if God's plan for step-by-step improvement were based on time, chance, struggle, and death? Evolution is not just at odds with a verse or two in the Bible, or with someone's interpretation of the word "day." *Evolution is the opposite of the whole gospel message* — the good news that death is the loser, and rich and abundant life the winner, through Jesus Christ, the Author of life as Creator, and the Redeemer of life as our Savior![33]

I haven't given up "believing in" mutation-selection! When I'm explaining how the generalized created kinds multiplied and filled the earth with variously specialized sub-types after death entered, and again after the Flood, I use natural selection (and genetic drift, gene migration, and reproductive isolation) as freely and easily as any evolutionist. When I'm explaining the origin of disease, disease agents, and aging, I freely and easily appeal to the effects of mutations. *Mutations and selection* have major roles to play in the history of our planet, *not in its origin, but between its corruption and its restoration in Christ.*

In fact, in an attempt to be as "nice" as possible, I used to say I accepted "microevolution," a term often given to mutation-selection working together to change the percentages of genes in a population, but then a friend told me that could be confusing. Saying I accept microevolution, a "little evolution," might make some think that if only I believed in enough time, a little evolution ("microevolution") would lead to a lot of evolution ("macro-evolution"). Nothing could be further from the truth. Even leading evolutionists now recognize that "micro" and "macro" evolution are "de-coupled," and that great variation within kind ("micro") by itself could never, even in infinite time, lead to macroevolution. More time would just let microevolution produce more little changes, but never a "macro" change — like shooting more arrows for more time would hit more targets, but never hit the moon.

After I explained some of these things to a hostile radio interviewer one time, he snapped, "You mean evolution explains the bad changes and creation explains the good changes." With a smile he did not find appealing, I replied: "Yes! You've got it!"

Let me add one more thing. After a lecture in which I was describing the depressing decline in genetic quality resulting from the continuous build-up of harmful mutations, someone asked plaintively, "Isn't there some good news in all these gene combinations?" There is. With God, as with us created in His image, "variety is the spice of life." God seems to have endowed the first of each created kind with dazzling genetic variability, and the Hardy-Weinberg law, the fundamental law of population genetics, acts to conserve that created variability. God created just two people, for example, with all the genes needed to produce children dark and light, tall and short, bass and soprano, etc.!

That means each child is an absolutely unique, never-to-be-repeated combination of traits. There's a children's song, "God made me special; I'm the only one of my kind." And that is true!! *Each person is a treasure, with a place in God's plan that no one else can take.*

That's not all. To the extent that these things depend on gene combinations, we may not yet have seen the greatest mathematical or musical genius, the fastest runner or highest jumper, the most skilled artist or craftsman. God's plan at creation is still unfolding before our very eyes. That's not evolution (adding something that was not there before); that's **"entelechy"** — the unfolding of creativity written ahead of time in the fabulous genetic code of DNA! Maybe it's time we treated each other as the miraculous marvels we are! THINK ABOUT IT!

Endnotes

1. Thomas Kelly, producer, *Puzzle of the Ancient Wing,* Canadian Broadcasting Corporation, "Man Alive" television series, 1981.

2. Will Durant, "Historian Will Durant: We Are in the Last Stage of Pagan Period," *El Cajon (CA) Daily Californian,* April, 8, 1980 (by Rogers Worthington of the *Chicago Tribune*).

3. Chris D. Osborne, *A Reevaluation of the English Peppered Moth's Use as an Example of Evolution in Progress,* Master's thesis, Institute for Creation Research, Santee, CA. 1985.

4. Theodosius Dobzhansky, F. Ayala, L. Stebbins, and J. Valentine, *Evolution* (San Francisco, CA: W.H. Freeman and Co., 1977).

5. Lane Lester and Ray Bohlin, *The Natural Limits to Biological Change* (Grand Rapids, MI: Zondervan, 1984).

6. Gary Parker, *Exploring the World Around You* (Green Forest, AR: Master Books, 2002).

7. Richard Dawkins, *The Blind Watchmaker* (New York: W.W. Norton, 1986).

8. Parker, *Exploring the World Around You.*

9. Dobzhansky, Ayala, Stebbins, and Valentine, *Evolution.*

10. Richard C. Lewontin, "Adaptation," *Scientific American* (and *Scientific American* book *Evolution)* (September 1978).

11. Jonathan Wells, *Icons of Evolution* (Washington, DC: Regnery Pub., 2000).

12. Michael Denton, *Evolution: A Theory in Crisis* (London: Burnett Books, 1985).

13. Phillip Johnson, *Darwin on Trial* (Washington, DC: Regnery Gateway, 1991).

14. Michael Behe, *Darwin's Black Box* (New York: The Free Press, 1996).

15. Paul S. Moorehead and Martin M. Kaplan, *Mathematical Challenges to the Neo-Darwinian Interpretation of Evolution,* Wistar Symposium No. 5 (Philadelphia, PA: Wistar Institute Press, 1967).

16. Denton, *Evolution: A Theory in Crisis.*

17. Francisco Ayala, "The Mechanisms of Evolution," *Scientific American* (and *Scientific American* book *Evolution)* (September 1978).

18. Gillian Brown, *From a Frog to a Prince*, video, Keziah Productions.

19. Dawkins, *The Blind Watchmaker.*

20. Werner Gitt, *In the Beginning Was Information* (Green Forest, AR: Master Books, 2006).

21. Lee Spetner, *Not By Chance* (New York: Judaica Press, 1997).

22. Ayala, "The Mechanisms of Evolution."

23. Gary Parker, W. Ann Reynolds, and Rex Reynolds, *Heredity,* rev. ed., Programmed Biology Series (Chicago, IL: Educational Methods, Inc., 1977).

24. Ken Ham, Carl Wieland, and Don Batten, *One Blood: The Biblical Answer to Racism* (Green Forest, AR: Master Books, 1999).

    Gary E. Parker and Mary M. Parker, *Skeletons in Your Closet, Discovering Your Real Family Tree* (Green Forest, AR: Master Books, 1998).

25. Stephen Jay Gould, "A Quahog Is a Quahog," *Natural History* (August/ September 1979); also published in *New Scientist* as "Species Are Not Specious" (August 2, 1979).

26. Denton, *Evolution: A Theory in Crisis*, chapters 5–9.

27. Phillip Johnson, *Darwin on Trial* (Washington, DC: Regnery Gateway, 1991). See also Norman MacBeth, *Darwin Retried* (Boston, MA: Gambit, 1971).

28. Wells, *Icons of Evolution.*

29. Behe, *Darwin's Black Box.*

30. Illustra Media, *Unlocking the Mystery of Life*, DVD/VHS, 2002.

31. Francisco Ayala and James W. Valentine, *Evolving: The Theory and Processes of Organic Evolution* (Menlo Park, CA: Benjamin-Cummins Publishing Company, 1979).

32. Carl Sagan, "A Gift for Vividness," as quoted in *Time* (October 20, 1980): p. 68.

33. Ken Ham, *The Lie: Evolution* (Green Forest, AR: Master Books, 1987).

Chapter 3

The Fossil Evidence

INTRODUCTION

After I spoke on creation to a packed auditorium of students and professors at a Tennessee University, one of the professors accused me of misrepresenting evolution when I called it a progressive change from a few simple life forms to many complex and varied ones. He explained that there is nothing inherent in the process of mutation-selection that promotes either complexity or progress. Mutations occur at random in no particular direction, and selection merely rewards and propagates the most reproductively successful exploiters of environmental resources in each generation.

I had to admit that he was right about the presumed evolutionary mechanism of mutation-selection (TCSD). Then I asked if he, as an evolutionist, believed that there was a time in the earth's past when the most complex forms of life were bacteria. He said, "Yes, of course." Then I asked if he believed there was a later time when life on earth included bacteria but also a wide variety of invertebrates (clams, snails, worms, etc.), but no vertebrates. Even though he now knew where I was going, as an evolutionist he still had to say, "Yes." He had to agree that later still the earth included a wide variety of vertebrates (fish, dinosaurs, people) in addition to invertebrates and bacteria. So, I concluded for him, earth's history involved a progression from a few simple life forms to many complex ones. But, as he himself had stated in challenging me, there is nothing about mutation-selection (time, chance, struggle, and death) which explains that kind of progression. Mutation-selection (TCSD), yes; evolution, no.

Much of the public accepted that evolution had occurred in the past because they were taught to see mutation-selection at work in the present. Nobody (except creationists) told them that professional scientists in the second half of the 20th century seriously challenged or even abandoned mutation-selection as a mechanism for molecules-to-man evolution. Discoveries in computer-assisted math, cell ultrastructure, DNA, and molecular biology during the 1950s, 60s, and 70s forced a "revolution in evolution" when the world's leading experts on evolution met in Chicago in 1980. As summarized professionally by Lewin in *Science*[1] (and popularly by Adler and Carey in *Newsweek*[2]),

> The central question of the Chicago conference was whether the mechanisms underlying microevolution [mutation-selection] could be extrapolated to explain the phenomena of macroevolution.

That's the central question considered in the last chapter: Can changes from molecules-to-man *(macroevolution)* be explained by (extrapolated from) the process of mutation-selection *(microevolution)*? You know my answer; how did the world's leading evolutionists answer that question?

> At the risk of doing violence to the positions of some of the people at the meetings, *the answer can be given as a clear,* **No** (emphasis added).

Just plain **NO.** Experts from around the world looking at supposed evidences for evolution in their own scientific disciplines reached the same conclusion for the same reasons creationists had already cited. You just can't get from microevolution (mutation-selection) to macroevolution (molecules-to-man), *no matter what the time involved*, just like you can't get to the moon by riding a bicycle. There are just too many logical and scientific limits to such an extrapolation.

You would think that this major revolution in evolution would have stimulated vibrant national dialogue, numerous talk show appearances, and changes in the world of education. But textbooks, television programs, and museum displays chose to ignore these advances in science, just as they have chosen to ignore advances in molecular machinery, DNA coding, and information theory that have heaped more challenges onto evolutionary theory since 1980.

Indeed, textbooks, television programs, and museum displays in the early 21st century continue to present the arguments for evolution used in the late 19th and early 20th centuries! Now you can see why the professor at the Tennessee University was so frustrated; I was criticizing evolutionist arguments that professional evolutionists had already discarded. Perhaps you can also see why I was frustrated; I still had to debunk those falsified evolutionist ideas because they were still being palmed off on the public by the new *"edutainment"* industry producing textbooks, television programs, museum displays, and other "docudramas" in which *marketing a message* is much more important than mere scientific facts and the pursuit of truth.

Why don't more scientists speak out against such an abuse of science? One answer: *fossils.*

Many scientists admit they have no evidence of, nor use for, evolution in their own specialized branches of science, but there's a *"widespread feeling"* among scientists and the general public that fossils somehow "prove evolution" anyway. "Maybe mutation-selection doesn't explain *how* evolution occurred," a knowledge-able evolutionist might say, "but fossils prove that evolution *did* occur. The evidence for *millions of years of struggle and death* is right under our feet as fossils — billions of dead things, buried in rock layers, laid down by water, all over the earth!"

The showcase for evolution is, of course, *the Grand Canyon.* As a professor enthusiastically pushing evolution, I used to think "If only these Christian students would take a trip to the Grand Canyon, they would see the evidence for evolution laid out right before their very eyes. If they could just look at those rock layers a mile deep, full of fossils showing the stages of evolution, maybe they'd just throw their Bibles over the edge, and try to get in touch with a 'god' more in sync with modern science."

Now I've ruined everything! If only I hadn't mentioned fossils, maybe I could have convinced you that the evidence we've looked at (biochemistry, embryology, homology, ecology, genetics, adaptation, classification, variation) really supports plan, purpose, and special acts of creation, not time, chance, struggle, and death, but if we're going to honestly "think about it," we've got to include fossils.

Fossils used to scare me. After my heart and mind were opened to consider the 4C biblical outline for origins in contrast to evolution, I gradually convinced myself (over a three-year period!) that the evidence in *biology* overwhelmingly favored the biblical view, but friends knew how to stop me cold: "Look, Parker, if you only knew anything about fossils (paleontology), then you'd give up this creationist nonsense and come on back into the scientific age with the rest of us!" I even began to wonder whether some parts of the Bible and evolution could *still* be made to fit together — "progressive creation" maybe?

About that time, God did something wonderful for me. I won a grant from the National Science Foundation for 15 months of full-time work on my doctoral degree. To my major in biology, I added a minor in geology, emphasizing the study of fossils and origins. I had done my master's degree work as a practicing atheist and evolutionist. Now, I was sure I was a Christian, and

I leaned toward creation, but if the fossils didn't work out, I just wouldn't talk about creation any more.

Well, I fell in love with fossils. My family and I (that's two rock hounds and four pebble pups!) have collected oodles of fossils from numerous sites in America, Canada, and Australia, and a few spots in Europe, South America, and Asia, and I regularly lead university students in field-study courses to the Grand Canyon and to well-known fossil sites.

Fossils are the remains or traces of once-living things preserved largely in sedimentary deposits. They represent the closest we can come to *historical* evidence in this matter of origins, so they are of prime importance in comparing biblical and evolutionary pictures of history. Actually, fossils can help us with two types of questions: First, *what kinds* of plants and animals once populated the earth? Second, *how fast* were fossils, and the rock layers that contain them, formed?

I. WHAT KINDS?

When the modern version of the creation-evolution dialogue got started in the middle of the 1800s, creationists and evolutionists had radically different ideas of the kinds of life they expected to find as fossils.

The evolutionist, of course, expected to find fossils that showed stages through which one kind of animal or plant changed into a different kind. According to evolution, the boundaries between kinds should blur as we look further and further back into their fossil history. It should get more and more difficult, for example, to tell cats from dogs and then mammals from reptiles, land animals from water animals, and finally life from non-life. They expected also that the criteria we use to classify plants and animals today would be less and less useful as older and older fossils showed the in-between characteristics of presumed common ancestors for different groups.

If the different kinds of life we see today are the descendants of created kinds, as the creationist says, then all we ought to find as fossils are just *variations of these kinds,* with decline and even extinction evident as a result of corruption and the catastrophe of Noah's flood. The same kind of criteria we use to classify plants and animals today ought to work just as well with fossils, and each kind should represent a mosaic of complete traits.

Certainly, the evolutionist and the creationist had radically different concepts of what would be found, as the systematic study of fossils began in earnest in the middle of the 1800s. Let's take a look now at the evidence. Which concept does it support — evolution, or the biblical concepts of creation, corruption, catastrophe, and Christ?

INVERTEBRATES: ANIMALS WITHOUT BACKBONES

Take a look at Figure 23. If you live near the seashore or like to visit marine aquaria, I'm sure most of the animals there are quite familiar to you. There are some jellyfish floating in the background. On the bottom, you can find sea urchins and sea lilies, members of the starfish group; a couple of snails; sponges; lampshells; and members of the earthworm group. That large fellow stretched out along the right side is a nautiloid, a squid-like animal that is a member of the most complex group of invertebrate animals we know anything about (the cephalopod mollusks). The nautiloid belongs to the group of animals that has an eye somewhat like ours, as I mentioned in the first chapter.

What does this illustration show? A picture of present-day sea life off the Florida coast or around some tropical island? No, not at all. It pictures *not* sea life today, but the "first" or simplest community of plants and animals to leave abundant fossil remains. This illustration shows life in the so-called "Age of Trilobites" (what I'll later call the "Zone of Trilobites"), the Cambrian geologic system.

Trilobites, by the way, are fascinating creatures. Many trilobites, such as the one pictured in the inset in Figure 23, had extremely complex eyes. When I take students snorkeling and scuba diving, I have to warn them that organisms and objects

Figure 23. The "first" or simplest community to leave abundant fossils, the lower "Trilobite Seas" (Cambrian system), contains almost all the major groups of sea life, including the most complex invertebrates, the nautiloids, and the highly complex trilobites (inset above). Darwin called the fossil evidence "perhaps the most obvious and serious objection to the theory" of evolution.

underwater appear closer and larger than they really are (so that big, nearby shark is really smaller and farther away!). Some trilobites didn't have that problem. They had double-lens systems that made the correction for underwater vision, sort of "hand-crafted prescription face masks," masterpieces of design.

Trilobites belong to the same complex group that insects do (the arthropods). Unfortunately, no trilobites are known to be alive today. Trilobites are very famous as fossils, however, and may have a lot to tell us about how life began. As my paleontology professor, an evolutionist, said: "Never let anyone tell you a trilobite is a simple animal."

Suppose we could scuba dive in the ocean back when the trilobites were alive. If we compared life in the trilobite seas with what we see in the oceans today, what would we say? "Look at all the new forms of life, the increased variety, and greater complexity!" No, that's not what we would say at all. Rather, we might say, "What happened? Where did everything go? What happened to all the trilobites? Where are all the lampshells? There used to be several thousand species of lampshells (brachiopods); now only a handful are left!" We might also wonder what happened to the great nautiloids, so much bigger and more varied in the Cambrian seas than those today. Today, the only shelled squid we have is the modest pearly nautilus.

Decline and even extinction, *not* evolution, is the rule when we compare fossil sea life with the sort of marine invertebrates we find living today. In fact, all major groups, except perhaps the groups including clams and snails, are represented by *greater variety* and *more complex* forms as *fossils* than today.

It's hard to imagine how absolutely crushing this evidence is to evolution. Suppose, for example, that you had a burning desire to find out where snails came from. You search the fossil evidence all over the world, all the way back to the "beginning," the "first" abundant fossils in Cambrian deposits, and, sure enough, snails come from snails. Where did the most complex of all the invertebrates, members of the squid and octopus group, the cephalopods, come from? Again, you search through all the fossil evidence, all the way back to the very "beginning," and, sure enough, "squids" come from "squids." In fact, the first "squids" (cephalopods), the nautiloids, are more impressive than most modern forms. Of course, trilobites seem only to come from trilobites. There's no evidence they evolved from, or into, anything else.

In other words, you find snails and squids and trilobites as fossils; you don't find "snids" and "squails" and "squailobites," or some other in-between form or common ancestor. The "missing links" between these groups are *still* missing.

In fact, few scientists, if any, are still looking for fossil links between the major invertebrate groups. The reason is simple. All the groups appear as separate, distinct, diversified lines in the deepest fossil-rich deposits. Evolutionists are well aware of these facts, and several have admitted that this "explosion" of life in Cambrian ("lower trilobite") rock seems to favor the concept of creation.

The sudden appearance of a multitude of complex and varied life forms at the very bottom of the fossil-rich portion of the geologic column is now routinely called the *Cambrian explosion*. A far greater variety of basic body plans is present among Cambrian fossils than among life forms along Australia's Great Barrier Reef, perhaps the richest life zone today! Evolutionists had expected life to begin with a few simple life forms thrown together by time, chance, and chemistry, and they had expected the variety and complexity of life to build gradually as natural selection culled the best from random mutational changes. Although it's still taught, the Cambrian evidence renders this classic view flatly false!

To a creationist, Cambrian fossils are simply the descendants of the created (and corrupted) kinds first buried in the catastrophe of Noah's flood. When I was a graduate student trying to decide between creation and evolution, the Cambrian fossil evidence made it very hard to believe in evolution, very easy to accept what the Bible says about creation, corruption, catastrophe, and Christ.

Evolutionists have come up with just about every explanation for the Cambrian explosion *except* the biblical model. Francis Crick, the Nobel laureate who argued chemical evolution was impossible on earth and must have occurred on another planet, followed up by suggesting that the "seeds of life" arrived on earth in some sort of rocket ship that accidentally or deliberately hit the earth, giving life an explosive extra-terrestrial "jump start."

Many evolutionists still cling to their traditional belief that life did start slowly and gradually on earth, but that the *evidence rotted away* since the early forms lacked the hard parts that make the best fossils. The Cambrian explosion, then, is simply an explosion of hard parts occurring simultaneously in many different animal groups. Besides being *an appeal to faith* rather than *an inference from science,* the "hard part hypothesis" requires multiple mathematical miracles for the repeated origin of gene sets for hard parts by time-and-chance in different lines. The view also contradicts the most reasonable of all evolutionary assumptions, that complex features, like hard parts, have descended by variation from a common ancestor in which the feature originated by just one "miracle," not many miracles after the lines diverged.

The hard-part hypothesis also contradicts the fossil evidence. Although rare, soft parts *do preserve,* and, although rare, Precambrian fossils *are found.* What does the Precambrian soft-part evidence tell us about life before the Cambrian deposits were laid down?

Evolutionists used to say that they would have found the ancestors of Cambrian life there if only the evidence hadn't rotted or been destroyed by heat in the rocks. That "excuse" no longer works. Although most Precambrian rock is the igneous and metamorphic type unsuitable for fossil preservation, we have now discovered great stretches of Precambrian sedimentary rocks that could and should have preserved soft parts and the common ancestors of the diverse and complex Cambrian life — if any such evolutionary ancestors existed.

□□□□□□□□□□□□□□□

Actually, Precambrian fossils strongly support the creation concept. My wife, Mary, and I have found soft-bodied jellyfish and members of the earthworm group (annelids) in the famous Ediacara beds of South Australia. What lessons do we learn from the "oldest" animal fossils? Once a jellyfish, always a jellyfish; once an "earthworm" (annelid), always an "earthworm." Most people think of segmented worms as fish bait, but to a biologist, they are marvelously complex. The "lowly" earthworm, for example, has five "hearts," a two-hemisphere brain, and a multi-organ digestive system. It looks like Precambrian animal fossils are telling us the same thing about the origin of life that Cambrian fossils are: Living things look as if they were created well designed to multiply after their kinds and to fill the earth with stupendous and soul-satisfying variety!

Creation is also supported by our ability to use the same criteria to classify both living plants and animals and those found as fossils. Even among extinct types, we don't find "in-between forms," or forms that are any harder to classify (when the fossil evidence is complete enough) than plants and animals living today.

Most people just assume that fossils and evolution go hand in hand. Some people even seem to think that "believing in" fossils is almost the same as "believing in" evolution. We've been so thoroughly indoctrinated with "educational" materials and entertainment touting evolution, that it's hard even to think that fossils argue so strongly *against* evolution *and for* the biblical outline of history.

Could I be right about that? Is there anyone else who thinks that the fossils argue *against* evolution? Yes, indeed . . . Charles Darwin, for one. That's right, Charles Darwin, the father of the modern concept of evolution. Darwin thought that the fossil evidence was "perhaps the most obvious and serious objection which can be urged against the theory [of evolution]." Why? Because he knew some of the same things that we know about fossils.

Darwin's chapter on the fossil evidence was titled "On the Imperfection of the Geologic Record." In that chapter, he dealt with "the sudden appearance" of groups of fossils in the lowest known fossil-bearing strata (the Cambrian). When it came to intermediate links (those types of fossils supposed to show how one kind of life evolved into others), Darwin wrote the following:

> . . . intermediate links? Geology assuredly does *not* reveal any such finely graduated organic change, and this is perhaps the *most obvious and serious objection* which can be urged against the theory [of evolution] (emphasis added).

So Darwin was faced with a conflict. Theory (evolution) and facts (fossils) didn't agree. Which was he going to throw out, the facts or the theory? Darwin chose to throw out the facts. *Normally,* of course, a scientist doesn't do that, but Darwin had reason, or at least hope, for doing so. He blamed the conflict between fact and theory on "the imperfection of the geologic record." In his time, the science of paleontology (fossil study) was just getting under way. He hoped that as new fossil evidence was unearthed around the world, the "missing links" would be found to support his theory.

It's now well over a century since Darwin made that statement, and we've unearthed thousands of tons of fossils from all over the world. What does all this massive amount of evidence show? Have we found the "missing links" required to support the theory of evolution, or have we merely unearthed further evidence of variation within the created kinds?

David Raup reviewed the evidence for us when he was curator of the famous Field Museum of Natural History in Chicago. That museum houses 20 percent of all fossil species known, so Raup was in a position to speak with considerable knowledge about the fossil evidence. The title of his article in the *Field Museum Bulletin* is "Conflicts Between Darwin and Paleontology,"[3] and the thrust is repeated and expanded in a second article, "Geology and Creationism."[4]

Raup starts by saying that "most people assume that fossils provide a very important part of the general argument made in favor of Darwinian interpretations of the history of life. Unfortunately, this is not strictly true." He then quotes the same passage from Darwin that I did, and points out that Darwin was "embarrassed" by the fossil evidence. He goes on to say that we now have a rich body of fossil knowledge, so that we can no longer blame the conflict between evolutionary theory and the fossil facts on the "imperfection of the geologic record." He mentions also, as I did, that Darwin expected those gaps in his theory, those missing links, to be unearthed by future discoveries. Then Raup summarizes those discoveries:

> Well, we are now about 120 years after Darwin, and knowledge of the fossil record has been greatly expanded. ... Ironically, we have *even fewer examples* of evolutionary transition than we had in Darwin's time. By this I mean that some of the classic cases of Darwinian change in the fossil record, such as the evolution of the horse in North America, have had to be *discarded* or *modified* as a result of more detailed information (emphasis added).

What a statement! Darwin said that the fossil evidence was perhaps the most obvious and serious objection against his theory. Raup is saying that 120 years of research have made the case for Darwinian evolution *even worse.* Raup says we have "even fewer examples" now, since new evidence has forced evolutionists to change their minds about examples, like the horse, that were once used. (For details, see the master's thesis by Walter Barnhart[5] or my discussion of fossil horses in *Fossils: Key to the Present*[6] and/or *The Fossil Book,*[7] and see Figure 27, page 175.)

Raup's words still eloquently summarize the fossil evidence. Except for a couple of flawed exceptions we'll discuss later, those of us who do creation-evolution debates and/or speak for university audiences still encounter the same old candidates for "missing links" used in the late 1800s and early 1900s — *if* our evolutionist opponents even try to bring up fossil evidence at all.

Raup goes on to say that "we still have a record which *does* show change, but one that can hardly be looked upon as the most reasonable consequence of natural selection." In comparing fossil forms with modern forms, we do see change all right, but it's *not* the kind of change associated with evolution by natural selection. It's simply *variation within the created kinds,* plus decline and even extinction, reflecting corruption and catastrophe.

Raup is still an evolutionist, but he's beginning to argue for "survival of the luckiest," instead of "survival of the fittest." Condemning with faint praise, he says, "Natural selection as a process is okay. We are also pretty sure that it goes on in nature, although good examples are surprisingly rare." Genetic studies suggest that mutation-selection *could not* lead to evolutionary change; the fossil evidence seems to confirm that it *did not.*

Raup then tries to argue that "optimal engineering design" is the best evidence of evolution — exactly the same kind of evidence that geneticist Lewontin conceded as the best evidence of *creation!* One of the reasons evolution continues to survive is that paleontologists believe geneticists have the real evidence, and geneticists believe that paleontologists have the evidence, and so on around the various specialties within biology, each one passing the buck for evidence to the next one. Since professionals in different disciplines rarely talk with one another about such matters, the *myth* of overwhelming support for evolution continues.

After he bemoaned the repeated failures of evolution to come to grips with the fossil evidence, paleontologist Niles Eldredge[8] lamented that the only alternative is "special creation." As we have seen, the fossils of invertebrates, the most abundant by far of all fossils, *do* offer strong support for the concept of creation, specifically the biblical concepts of creation, corruption, catastrophe, Christ. But let's look now at fossil evidence from other groups.

FOSSIL PLANTS

Did you ever wonder what kind of plants the dinosaurs tromped around on? The answer may surprise you. Some of these unfamiliar animals wandered around among some very familiar plants: oak, willow, magnolia, sassafras, palms, and other such common flowering plants.

In the geologic sequence, the flowering plants first appear suddenly and in great diversity in Cretaceous ("upper dinosaur") rock. Darwin was aware of the situation and called the origin of these plants "an abominable mystery." As my professor of paleobotany summarized it, nothing has happened in the last century or so to solve that mystery. As far as the fossil evidence is concerned, we simply find different varieties of the same types of plants we have today, plus decline and/or extinction in many cases.

There is a tendency to give every different fossil fragment a different scientific genus-species name. Five different genus names were given to fossil specimens that later turned out to be parts of just *one* type of tree, the *Lepidodendron.* Many of the flowering plants are so easily recognizable that they are classified using the same scientific names we use today.

Other fossil plants are as easily classified as the flowering plants. The ferns and fern allies appear suddenly and simultaneously in Silurian/Devonian rock in far greater diversity than we have today (Figure 24), yet none of these fossil plants has any features of anatomy, morphology, or reproduction that are hard to understand in terms of what we observe among living plants. The difference is this: There used to be many more kinds of ferns and fern allies on the earth than there are today. And some of these that are small and inconspicuous today, like the "ground pine" *(Lycopodium)* and "horsetail" *(Equisetum),* had fossils with similar parts that grew to be huge trees (e.g., *Lepidodendron* and *Calamites,* respectively). The structural design and classification of plants seem to point to creation; the decline in size and variety to the corruption and catastrophe that followed.

Figure 24. Fossil plants are easily classified using the same criteria we use today and, perhaps because of extinction following the Flood, we find even greater variation among fossil plants than we find now. As Professor Corner of Cambridge put it, ". . . to the unprejudiced, the fossil record of plants is in favor of special creation."

Even the algae are recognizable from their first appearance in the fossil sequence as greens, blue-greens, reds, browns, and yellow-browns, the same groups we have today. The "oldest" fossils found so far are some Precambrian cyanobacteria or blue-green algae that form rocky structures called *stromatolites*. (I've had the privilege of examining and photographing these on both the west and south coasts of Australia.) Are these "simple" forms of life like evolutionists had hoped to find? Exactly the opposite! When it comes to energy biochemistry, those "simple" organisms are more complex than we are. They can take sea water and turn it into living cells, using just sunlight for energy — a *fantastically* intricate feat of biochemical engineering called photosynthesis. (Don't you wish we could run on just water, air, and sunlight!?)

Blue-greens are also found living the same way just offshore from their "old" Precambrian fossils. What's the lesson from these "oldest" plant fossils? Evolution — change from simple beginnings to more complex and varied kinds? Not at all. The lesson from the "oldest" plant fossils seems to be the same as that from the "oldest" animal fossils: Living things were created complex and well designed to multiply after kind.

New fossil discoveries are usually reported as if they support evolution, when the opposite is often true. The discovery of the first flowering plant fossil in Jurassic rock below the "Cretaceous explosion" of flowering plants was at first hailed as a breakthrough in solving Darwin's "abominable mystery," the origin of flowering plants. After the hype wore off, however, evolutionists recognized the mystery was only moved down a layer, and creationists noted the evidence still pointed to creation: the first flowering plants still well-designed to multiply after kind, with the occasional flower found, as it is today, among a profusion of cycads and conifers.

While evolution's trumpets blared, discovery of the wollemi pine growing in Australia was touted as the plant equivalent of finding a live dinosaur, since fossils had suggested it died out with the dinosaurs. But here it was, alive and well and looking just like it had always looked, stronger evidence for creation than evolution it would seem.[9]

Like *Gingko biloba* and the dawn redwood, the wollemi "dinosaur pine" is another example of a "living fossil," a rare, unchanged survivor of a once widely distributed and successful group. The lesson is not evolution but creation (well-designed, after kind) followed by corruption and catastrophe, including worldwide habitat destruction and climate change following the Genesis flood.

My paleobotany professor (an evolutionist) started his class by saying he supposed we were there to learn about the evolution of plants. Then he told us that we weren't going to learn much. What we *would* learn, he said, is that our modern plant groups go way back in their fossil history. Sure enough, all we studied was "petrified plant anatomy," features already familiar to me from the study of living plants. We encountered some difficulties in classification, of course, but only the same kinds which we encounter among the *living* plants. Summarizing the evidence from fossil plant studies, E.J.H. Corner, Professor of Botany at Cambridge University, once put it this way (even though he believed in their evolution): ". . . to the unprejudiced, the fossil record of plants is in favor of special creation."[10]

VERTEBRATES: ANIMALS WITH BACKBONES

When we come to the vertebrates, the animals with backbones, the situation changes dramatically. We run smack into the most powerful evidence of *evolution.* At least that's what I used to tell my students when I taught university biology as an evolutionist.

Sometimes I would run into a student who would ask me, "If evolution is true, where are the missing links?" "Missing links?" I'd say. "Glad you asked. It just so happens we have a perfect example: *Archaeopteryx,* the link that shows how reptiles evolved into birds!"

Archaeopteryx has been *the* showcase for evolution. Found in 1860, the Berlin specimen is pictured in nearly all biology textbooks. That specimen, along with a reconstruction in the same position, is shown in Figure 25.

At first, you may wonder what the fuss is all about. It has feathers, wings, and a beak, so it's a bird. But look closer. It has teeth in the bill, claws on the wings, no keel on the breast bone, an unfused backbone, and a long, bony tail. These are all characteristics we normally associate with reptiles. What's more, the existence of a creature like *Archaeopteryx* was predicted by evolutionists before any such specimen was found! What's a creationist going to say to a "perfect example of evolution" like *Archaeopteryx?* There's no way I can get you to consider creation without facing up to *Archaeopteryx.*

Well, first of all, the reptile-like features are not really as reptile-like as you might suppose. The familiar ostrich, for example, has claws on its wings that are even *more* "reptile-like" than those of *Archaeopteryx.* Several birds, such as the hoatzin, don't have much of a keel. The penguin has unfused backbones and a bony tail. No living birds have socketed teeth, but some fossil birds do. Besides, some reptiles have teeth and some don't, so presence or absence of teeth is not particularly important in distinguishing the two groups.

More importantly, take a look at the individual features of *Archaeopteryx.* Is there any clue as to how legs evolved into wings? No, none at all. When we find wings as fossils, we find *completely developed, fully functional wings.* That's true of *Archaeopteryx,* and it's also true of the flying insects, flying reptiles (pterodactyls), and the flying mammals (bats).

Is there any clue in *Archaeopteryx* as to *how* reptilian scales evolved into feathers? No, none at all. When we find feathers as fossils, we find *fully developed and functional feathers.* Feathers are quite complex structures, with little hooks and eyelets for zippering and unzippering them. *Archaeopteryx* not only had complete and complex feathers, but feathers of several different types, including the asymmetric feather characteristic of strong fliers.

Reconstruction

Fossil Specimen

Figure 25. At last — evidence of evolution! . . . or is it? The famous *Archaeopteryx* combines features most often found in reptiles (teeth, claws, unfused vertebrae, and a long bony tail) with features distinctive of birds (wings, feathers, and a furcula or wishbone). Does *Archaeopteryx* provide clues as to how scales evolved into feathers, or legs into wings? Is *Archaeopteryx* more likely an evolutionary link, or a mosaic of complete traits (a distinctive created kind)? Read both sides and think about it.

What about lack of a keel? Actually, muscles for the power stroke in flight attach to the wishbone or furcula, and *Archaeopteryx* had "an extremely robust furcula." A growing number of evolutionists, perhaps a consensus, now believe that *Archaeopteryx* was a strong flier and the first bird, and not a missing link between reptiles and birds (see Carey[11]).

Despite the demise of *Archaeopteryx*, evolutionists retain a deep-seated belief that someday a missing link between dinosaurs and birds will be found. As I write this, the evolutionist's faith is focused on fossils from China, where large numbers of dinosaurs, dinosaur eggs, and some birds are found.

Several mistaken claims have already been made and falsified, including the major blunder published in *National Geographic* under the title "Feathers for *T. rex.*"[12]

With all the artistic (NOT scientific) skill for which *National Geographic* is famous, the public was treated to the picture of a baby "*T. rex*-bird" covered with down feathers like a newly hatched chick. Detailed art-work showed a close-up of the presumed "dinosaur feather." In three months, over 100,000 young people saw the "proof" for dinosaur-bird evolution on display at *National Geographic*'s headquarters in Washington, D.C.

It was all **FAKE**. The supposed fossil was fake. The art work and article in *National Geographic* described a **fake**. What influenced so many students touring the *National Geographic* exhibit in Washington was the display of a **fake**.

Scientists with expert knowledge of birds, such as Storrs Olson at the prestigious Smithsonian Institute, also in Washington, D.C., recognized the scientific problems with *National Geographic*'s story almost immediately. In an open letter published in the *Smithsonian* magazine (dated November 1, 1999), Storrs Olson[13] sternly rebuked *National Geographic* for (emphasis added) ". . . UNSUBSTANTIATED, SENSATIONALISTIC, TABLOID JOURNALISM. . . ." — putting the *Geographic* article in the same class as those about alien abductions and pigs that fly. His letter included details of many other examples of "scientific malpractice" in the *National Geographic* article.

The fake was not particularly clever or subtle. Bolstering the myth that evolution is making scientific progress, a fawning and uncritical media often publicize flashy stories of exaggerated claims, only to publish an obscure retraction or "different interpretation" a few weeks later.

The "feathers for *T. rex*" turned out to be fossils of bird parts cemented together with fossils of dinosaur parts. At least this time the evolutionist's error was so huge and obvious that it did get national media attention. The article detailing the fake in *USA Today*,[14] for example, was headlined:

The Missing Link That Wasn't

The *National Geographic* debacle should encourage scientific skepticism for several reasons. First, evolutionists are human beings, and all human beings make mistakes. Second, even if it's given a scientific sounding name (like "Archaeoraptor"), a discovery announced in the news is not really scientific until other scientists have checked it out thoroughly. It only took a few weeks for scientists to disprove both *Geographic*'s claims about its "dinosaur-bird" and the news report that a NASA team had found fossils in Martian rock, but it took over 40 years to prove that "Piltdown Man" ("Eoanthropus dawsoni") was a hoax, and *Archaeopteryx* has remained in textbooks long after it was scientifically discredited as a reptile-bird link.

When you hear another fossil from China is claimed as a dino-bird link (and I'm sure you will), check out the "rest of the story" on a major creationist website such as answersingenesis.org or icr.org. Furthermore, the fossils from China currently promoted in the press are in the *wrong place* to include the ancestors of birds, because fossil birds have already been found in lower layers. By the evolutionist's own definition, a fossil qualifies as a missing link or transitional form in an *evolutionary series* IF AND ONLY

IF it is found in *both* a morphologic series *and* a stratigraphic series, i.e., it must show gradation in structural features such as a "sceather" stage between scales and feathers (*morphologic series*), and these gradations must occur from lower to higher in a series of rock strata *(stratigraphic series).*[15]

Although the Chinese fossils currently hyped are too high in the stratigraphic series, some evolutionists say the same form could one day be found in a lower layer. That's true, but it's an *act of faith, not a fact of science!*

The whole search for missing links demonstrates that evolution is really a very strong *faith-based belief system* or world view, not a strictly scientific theory. An empirical scientist would survey fossil discoveries looking for patterns of order; *an evolutionist begins with belief in Darwin's belief, and then goes looking for the evidence to support that belief,* evidence that Darwin said was missing. When I was an evolutionist, I hoped that I might one day become an "evolution hero" by finding a missing link. Fossil support for the evolutionist's "tree of life" would require finding *thousands upon thousands of missing links,* and only a handful have even been proposed. (Problems are exposed in the evolutionist's beliefs about the railroad worm, ammonites, fish-amphibian transitions, horses, and whales in books by Gish[16], Parker,[17] and Bliss, Parker, and Gish,[18] and at icr.org and answersingenesis.org, and the platypus has already been discussed). *No scientist building up a theory from the fossil evidence would ever come up with the concept of evolution guided by mutation-selection.*

Despite phenomenal fossil failure, faith in evolution remains unbounded. Evolutionists who admit that science has falsified *the neo-Darwinian interpretation*[19] of evolution don't usually turn to creation; they just propose different kinds of evolution.

A few evolutionists make it unnecessary to hunt for dino-bird links, for example, by simply saying that "birds *are* dinosaurs." A sign at the Cincinnati Zoo (1997) put it this way: "Dinosaurs went extinct millions of years go — or did they? No — birds are

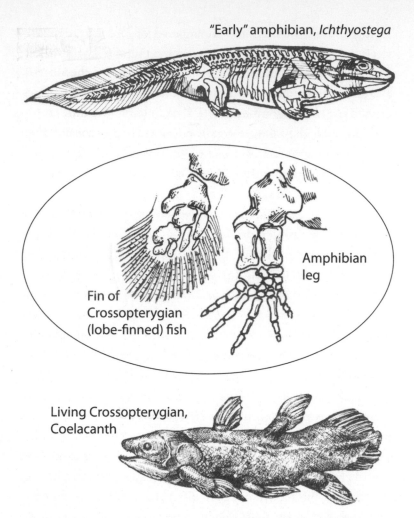

"Early" amphibian, *Ichthyostega*

Amphibian leg

Fin of Crossopterygian (lobe-finned) fish

Living Crossopterygian, Coelacanth

Figure 26. When they were known only from fossil remains, bones in the fins of the coelacanth were imagined to have joints at the wrist and elbow and to have a shoulder attachment strong enough for walking on land. Then the coelacanth was found alive and well, a fisherman's favorite deep in the Indian Ocean, having fins without wrists or elbows, designed for swimming not walking. Once again evolutionists were forced to abandon a presumed "missing link" used for decades to "prove evolution." The new evidence supported instead the creationist prediction that differences between fossil fish and amphibians would be like those between living members of these groups.

essentially modern short-tailed feathered dinosaurs." A nature encyclopedia[20] included this interesting tidbit: "The smallest dinosaur is the bee hummingbird. . . ." According to the view of this small minority, you could order "Kentucky-fried dinosaur," or point to a hummingbird and say "What a cute little dinosaur."

A more serious *post-neo-Darwinian* theory did spark considerable scientific discussion. During the late 1970s and early 1980s, a group of evolutionists led by Harvard's Stephen Gould tried to resurrect the idea that evolution happened in big jumps — "The Return of Hopeful Monsters" Gould called it.[21] The hopeful-monster idea (variously expressed as *punctuated equilibrium*, saltatory evolution, or quantum speciation) was proposed to explain why the links required by gradual evolution have never been found.[22] "Big jumpers" argued that mutations in embryonic regulator genes could effect major changes in multiple systems simultaneously, but known examples produced only hopeless monstrosities (like four-winged flies that couldn't fly), never hopeful monsters! Nor could "big jumpers" answer this crucial question about the first appearance of any hopeful-monster: *with what would it mate?*

At least the creationist and the post-neo-Darwinian punctuationalist *agree that the missing links are missing.* What is the scientific difference between saying that the missing links can never be found (the "new" evolution) and saying that they never existed at all (creation)?

Sometimes it's kind of fun to be a creationist. The "rear-guard" neo-Darwinian evolutionists like to point out the apparent absurdity of hopeful-monster evolution and claim that *evolution could not happen fast.* The punctuational evolutionists point to genetic limits and the fossil evidence to show that *evolution did not happen slowly.* The creationist simply agrees with both sides: Evolution couldn't happen fast, and it didn't happen slowly — because evolution can't and didn't happen at all! In terms of the kind of variation that *can* and *did* occur, the creation concept seems to be the far more logical inference from our observations.

At least the hopeful monster concept avoids the problem of missing links. But notice: this alternate concept of *evolution* is based on the fossils we *don't find* and on genetic mechanisms that have *never been observed*. The case for *creation* is based on thousands of tons of fossils that we *have found* and on genetic mechanisms (variation within kind) that we *do observe* and see occurring every day. As a scientist, I prefer a model that's based on what we *do* see and *can* explain (creation), rather than one that's based on what we *don't* see and *cannot* explain (evolution).

Human Beings

What about ourselves? What can we infer from the fossil evidence regarding the origin of human beings? Evolutionists now give us two choices. Either human beings are the result of time, chance, struggle, and death, or else we began as "a hopeful monster whose star was a bit more benevolent than most."[23] According to creationists, the evidence suggests, instead, that we are here by the plan, purpose, and special creative acts of God.

I was part of a television program on creation-evolution produced by the *secular* Canadian Broadcasting Corporation (CBC).[24] The program opened with a medieval princess wandering in a castle garden, apparently looking for something. Then the camera panned over to a rock ledge around a pond. There it was, big bulging eyes and all: a frog. Right before our incredulous eyes, the princess leaned over and kissed the frog. Stars sparkled across the TV screen, then a handsome prince appeared. As the prince and princess embraced, the narrator stepped into the scene with this introduction: If you believe a frog turns into a prince instantly, that's a fairy tale; if you believe a frog turns into a prince in 300 million years, that's evolution.

When I believed and taught evolution, I would not have put it that way, of course. As I look back, I realize *that* story reflects what I really was teaching. According to evolution, if you simply wait long enough, time, chance, struggle, and death (mutation and selection) will gradually turn some amphibians, like that

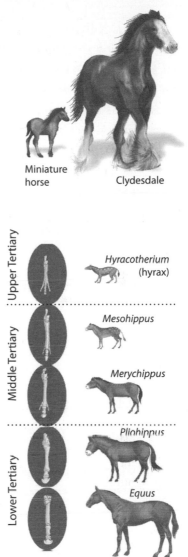

Figure 27. Horse fossils were once thought to illustrate the two parts of an *evolutionary series*: (1) *morphological series*, graded structures from many to one hoof per foot, short to long face, small to large size, and browsing to grazing teeth; (2) *stratigraphic series* from lower to higher in the geologic column diagram.

However, (a) the animal at the bottom is a hyrax (the biblical coney) which seems to have "multiplied after kind"; (b) the size range is less than the variation within kind from miniatures to Clydesdales; (c) fossils once thought to be different stages of evolution are found buried together; and (d) South American fossils reverse the sequence, having large grassland grazers with one hoof on the bottom and small forest browsers with multiple hooves on top. The series, therefore, may be ecological, not evolutionary.

frog, into reptiles, mammals, apes, and finally man, like that prince. Clearly the *burden of proof lies with the evolutionist* to find a series of fossils suggesting the change from frog to prince, or at least ape to man.

The first fossils proposed as links between apes and mankind were the "cave men" called Neanderthals. The Neanderthal was originally portrayed as a "beetle-browed, barrel-chested, bow-legged brute" (a suitable ancestor for a mugger, if nothing else!). The creationists in those days responded, "Hey, wait a minute. Neanderthals are just plain people, some of whom suffered bone diseases." The first Neanderthals discovered came from harsh inland environments in Europe, where they could easily have suffered skeletal abnormalities, especially from lack of seafood with iodine in the diet and from shortage during the long winters of sun-induced vitamin D necessary for calcium absorption.

Neanderthals from the Palestine area do not show the more stooped and massive features. The brain volume of Neanderthals is slightly *larger* than the average brain volume of people today, and brain casts show the Broca's area involved in the complex speech that so distinctively sets mankind apart from apes. Neanderthal peoples had a well-developed culture, art, and religion. Nowadays, many evolutionists agree completely with creationists: Neanderthals were just plain people, no more different from people living today than one living group is different from another. What were the "cave men"? Just people who lived in caves. (And at today's housing prices, that may once again be a good idea!)

There was a secular museum in Germany where the curator dressed the wax model of a Neanderthal Man in a business suit and tie. His reason? He said it was time to quit deceiving the public. Neanderthals were just plain people. Indeed, scientists now classify Neanderthals as *Homo sapiens,* the same scientific name given to you and me.

Tragically, Neanderthals have not been the only people once considered subhuman "missing links." In an article reprinted in

Natural History as part of an issue on the history of evolutionary thought, there's a short but very sad article by Henry Fairfield Osborn.[25] Osborn says that a hypothetical unbiased zoologist from Mars would classify people into several distinct genera and many species. Thus, said Osborn, Negroes would be classified as a separate species, not yet evolved to full human stature. "The standard of intelligence of the average adult Negro," wrote Osborn as a so-called fact of evolution, "is similar to that of the 11-year-old youth of the species *Homo sapiens* [which, for Osborn, meant Caucasians only]." Osborn was a leading evolutionist of the 1920s, and it is easy to see how his kind of evolutionary thinking (rejected by modern evolutionists) helped to pave the way for Hitler's Nazi racism in the 1930s and 1940s. Hitler's racism fed further on the false sciences of eugenics and "craniometry."[26]

The Australian Aborigines were also once treated as subhuman evolutionary links, and were classified as Australian animals by Germany's leading evolutionist, Ernst Haeckel. The natives of Tasmania were deliberately slaughtered by settlers who justified themselves by saying it was okay to kill wild dogs as farm pests, so why not other non-humans? As her dying wish, the last surviving Tasmanian, Truganini, asked that she be buried with her "people," not embalmed as a museum specimen. She died, was embalmed, and preserved as an evolutionary link. Warning: Few Christians stood against this horror, perhaps because many churches had already accepted evolution into their thinking. Christians standing on the Bible would have known there's only one race, the human race, and we're all parts of it (Acts 17:26).

In 1912, speculation about man's ancestry shifted to Piltdown Man, dignified by the scientific name *Eoanthropus dawsoni.* Almost everyone knows that Piltdown Man turned out to be a deliberate hoax, but Piltdown Man wasn't shown to be a hoax until the 1950s. For over 40 years, the subtle message of the textbooks was clear: You can believe in creation if you want to, but the facts are all on the side of evolution. *The facts,* in this case, turned out to be a bit of ape jaw and human skull stained to make them look older.

One mystery is who perpetrated the Piltdown hoax, but the real mystery is *why did anyone believe it?* It was *not* a particularly clever hoax. When people looked at the teeth with the right hypothesis in mind, "the evidences of artificial abrasion [filing] immediately sprang to the eye. Indeed, so obvious did they seem that it may well be asked — how was it that they had escaped notice before?"[27] The age-stain was better done, but the imported mammalian fossils and hand-crafted tools were again obvious frauds. People *wanted* to believe in evolution, so they were able to see what they *wanted to believe* (a "people problem" that can only be solved by honestly looking at alternate sides of an issue).

Sometimes people ask me how virtually all the evolutionists in the world could be so wrong about such an important issue as human origins. Answer: it wouldn't be the first time. Science is a human endeavor, and human beings make mistakes. Evolution goes far beyond the limits of science, and is even more easily influenced by human bias. I can understand that both intellectually and personally since I once accepted the evolutionary bias and its view of the evidence.

The "human factor" in the study of human origins is apparent in the multiple and varied interpretations of Java and Peking Man *("Homo erectus")* recounted in a very readable, yet thoroughly documented, book by Marvin Lubenow, *Bones of Contention.*[28]

Joining Neanderthals, Blacks, Aborigines, and Piltdown Man as proposed witnesses for human evolution at the famous Scopes trial[29] in 1925 was Nebraska Man. Nebraska Man was dignified by the scientific name *Hesperopithecus haroldcookii,* but he was never known by anything but a tooth. By imagination, the tooth was put in a skull, the skull was put on a skeleton, and the skeleton was given flesh, hair, and a family! Figure 28 includes a picture of Nebraska Man redrawn from a London newspaper published during the year of the Scopes trial.

Two years later, Nebraska Man was back to being just a tooth. The tooth was found in the real skull, attached to the real skeleton. It turned out not to be the tooth of man's ape-like ancestor, but the tooth of a pig!

The Australian National Museum in Sydney apparently found a solution to the problem of evolutionary links still missing between apes and man. In June of 1993, we were greeted by a display describing five kinds of apes: lemurs, orangs, gorillas, chimps, and man. No need to look for links between apes and mankind if human beings are *still* apes! One display described nursing behavior in various apes, including people. Another showed that man and chimps are the only apes that murder their own kind. A third pictured love-making among people and other apes. The text mentioned that some apes were monogamous, others polygamous or promiscuous, and that some men were like gorillas, others like chimps, etc. It was a truly inspiring and edifying display! Most evolutionists, of course, would be just as disgusted by the displays as would anyone else with a respect for science (or for common sense).

Modern speculation on mankind's ancestry centers on a group of fossils called *Australopithecus*. In the public mind, these fossils are associated especially with the work in Africa of the Leakey family and of Donald Johanson and his famous specimen, "Lucy" (Figure 29).

The name *Australopithecus* means "southern ape," and it seems that apes are just what they are. Johanson likes to point out that where he finds his australopithecine bones, he finds many of the regular African animals (rhinos, boas, hippos, monkeys, etc.), but never apes. Could it be that apes are exactly what he has been finding all along? Lucy's features are clearly ape-like — except that some claim Lucy and other australopithecines walked upright.

How crucial to the definition of man is relatively upright posture? Vincent Sarich, at the University of California in Berkeley, and Adrienne Zihlman say that if you want something

A. *Neanderthals* turned out to be just plain people, some of whom suffered from bone diseases. In proper attire, they would attract no particular attention today.

A

B. *Piltdown Man (Eoanthropus dawsoni)* was a deliberate (but not very clever) hoax palmed off as "proof of evolution" to students for more than two generations. It turned out to be a bit of ape jaw and human skull artificially aged.

B

C. *Nebraska Man (Hesperopithecus)* was reconstructed, family and all, from a tooth — a tooth that later was found to belong to a pig!

C

Figure 28. A few of the many discarded candidates for man's ancestor.

that walks upright, consider the living pygmy chimpanzee or bonobo, *Pan paniscus.* This rain-forest chimpanzee is only slightly shorter than the average chimpanzee, but it spends a fair amount of time walking upright. (I've watched them in the San Diego Zoo.) Since all the other features of the australopithecines are so apelike, perhaps Johanson and the Leakeys have discovered the ancestor of the living pygmy chimpanzee!

Did the australopithecines indeed walk upright? In the *American Biology Teacher,* eminent anatomist Charles Oxnard[30] said:

> In one sense you may think there is no problem. For most anthropologists are agreed that the gracile australo-pithecines . . . are on the main human lineage. . . . This is the view that is presented in almost all textbooks; I expect that it has been your teaching in the classroom; and it is widely broadcast in such publications as the "Time-Life Series" and the beautiful [television] story of "The Ascent of Man." However, anatomical features in some of these fossils provide a warning against a too-ready acceptance of this story. . . .

As part of his warning, Oxnard reminds his readers of gross errors once made in the cases of Piltdown Man and Nebraska Man.

In a PBS TV program on Lucy,[31] Donald Johanson finally contradicted his earlier assertions and admitted that Lucy's pelvis never really fit with the idea that she walked upright — because the bones of the pelvis fit together too perfectly (something paleontologists usually desire!). So, he shows a scientist sawing up a replica of Lucy's pelvis and gluing the pieces back together — and then claims the sawed-and-glued pelvis shows Lucy did walk upright after all. I saw the TV program first while speaking on creation in New Zealand. A newsman there commented that Johanson's standard of evidence might be acceptable in America, but it was not acceptable in New Zealand!

A. bosei
(Reconstructed)

A. africanus
(Artist's conception)

A. afarensis
("Lucy")

Figure 29. Australopithecines, including Johanson's "Lucy" and the Leakey finds in Africa, are the current candidates for man's ancestors. Anatomist Charles Oxnard says the fossils "provide a warning against too ready acceptance of this view." He reaches two conclusions. One is scientific: "If the australopithecines walked upright, it was not in the human manner." The second is educational: "Be critical." We must encourage our science students to examine evidence more critically, he says — and that means allowing students to explore evidences for and against both evolution and creation.

Louis Leakey started the modern interest in australopithecines (and captured the attention of *National Geographic)* way back in 1959 with his "ape man," *Zinjanthropus. Zinjanthropus* has since been reclassified as *Austalopithecus bosei* or *A. robustus,* and it is now considered grossly apelike, an extinct ape really not related to man at all.

In fact, it was not the skeletal features that attracted attention to the Leakey finds in the first place. It was tools. As I said at the beginning of this book, every scientist can recognize evidence of creation. Tools imply a toolmaker. Since the tools were found with *Australopithecus,* Louis Leakey assumed that that creature had made the tools. Thirteen years later, Richard Leakey found beneath the bones his father had unearthed "bones virtually indistinguishable from those of modern man." Perhaps those tools were used *on* the owner of the gorilla-like skull, making it more like man's meal than man's ancestor. At the time, Richard Leakey said his discovery shattered standard beliefs in evolution.

Actually, fossil discoveries have been *shattering* standard beliefs in human evolution with monotonous regularity. Each in its day was hailed as "scientific proof" that human beings evolved from ape-like animals, yet all the candidates once proposed as our evolutionary ancestors have been knocked off the list. The cover story in *Time* magazine for March 14, 1994, *assumes* that evolution is an absolute fact,[32] but it summarizes what is really the evaporating case for human evolution with these dramatic words:

> Yet despite more than a century of digging, the fossil record remains *maddeningly sparse.* With so few clues, even *a single bone* that doesn't fit into the picture *can upset everything.* Virtually every major discovery has put *deep cracks* in the conventional wisdom and forced scientists to *concoct new theories,* amid furious debate [emphasis added].

It's sad that human evolution is still taught as "fact" to school children, college students, and the general public, when "virtually every major discovery" has discredited the so-called evidence and disproved the theory. Even sadder, scientists who know the evidence are "forced to concoct new theories," but they are only concocting new theories of *how* human evolution occurred, unwilling to ask *whether* evolution occurred and to work on the truly new, non-evolutionary theories that the evidence demands. To the creationist, the evidence simply confirms that *people have always been people, and apes have always been apes, as far back as the evidence goes* (Figure 30).

Indeed, secular scientists have discovered molecular evidence that all human beings have descended from one woman and one man, just as the Bible says. The powerhouse organelle in living cells, the mitochondrion, contains its own loop of DNA, and mitochondrial DNA is passed from parents to children only through the mothers' egg cells. Comparative studies of mitochondrial DNA suggest all human beings had just one mother, whom the media dubbed "Mitochondrial Eve." In the Bible, Eve is called "the mother of all living" people. Studies of the Y chromosome, which is passed only from fathers to sons, suggests all people had just one father, whom we might call "Y chromosome Adam."

The first evolutionary estimates for the times of origin, however, showed a 100,000 year difference between the first man and first woman. (Talk about waiting around on a Saturday night for the telephone to ring!) Compromising assumptions were made to put the first man and woman at the same time and place — which God did by creating Adam and Eve on the same day and placing the first couple together in the Garden of Eden (which means Garden of Delight).

The Bible describes Adam and Eve as created mature, ready and able to talk with each other and with God, and to assume stewardship responsibilities for care of the earth. Until the late 1900s, skeptics were inclined to scoff at the idea that Adam, made from dust, could be walking and talking the day of his creation, but now mankind, made in the image of the Creator, has done

Figure 30. Footprints are more distinctive of man than most bone fragments are. If the Laetoli footprints above are accepted as human, as discoverer Mary Leakey and other scientists concluded after detailed study, then evolutionists would have to say that people existed "before" mankind's supposed ancestors. Creationists say that these footprints, and many other evidences, simply suggest that people have always been people, beginning with the first created human beings.

something nearly as creative. Think about computers. The chips are made primarily of silicon, just "dust of the ground." When you plug in the computer and hook up the printer and voice synthesizer, what happens? At first, the computer just grunts, but after several weeks, it can utter words, and after a few years full sentences. Of course not! The computer can speak and write, complete with grammar, syntax, and spell-checker, right from the moment it's created and activated. If mankind, a reflection of the Creator, can program such devices for instant complex functions, how much easier would it be for God to create mature human beings?

Sometimes I like to think we could enter the data regarding human origins into a computer free of human biases and social pressures. I think the computer's conclusion about human origins would be something like this: "You got here the same way I did. Someone made you with a purpose. By the way, whoever made you did a lot better job than you did making me!"

SUMMARY: FOSSIL KINDS

As far as the fossil evidence is concerned, different kinds of animals and plants have always been different kinds of animals and plants, and people have always been people. It seems to me that "creation" is clearly the logical inference from our scientific knowledge of fossil kinds.

If the fossil evidence is as clear and simple as I'm suggesting it is, then even evolutionists would accept my description of the facts (even if they violently disagreed with my biblical inferences), and they do. At a rare conference of scientists from different specialties, leading evolutionists from around the world meeting in Chicago at least agreed on the same assessment of the fossil evidence reached (and predicted) by creationists long ago. As the summary in *Newsweek* put it (emphasis added):

> *Evidence from fossils now points overwhelmingly away from the classical Darwinism which most Americans learned in high school.*[33]

In building up to that monumental conclusion (which should be posted as a plaque in all the nation's science classrooms), the writer starts with man (emphasis added):

> The missing link between man and the apes . . . is merely the most glamorous of a whole hierarchy of *phantom creatures*. In the fossil record, *missing links are the rule. . . . The more scientists have searched for the transitional forms between species, the more they have been frustrated.*

The concept of evolution touted in textbooks, then, is based on phantoms and figments of the imagination, *not* on fossils and the facts of science. In a landmark paper that helped pave the way for the Chicago conference, Gould and Eldredge[34] put it this way: "Phyletic gradualism [gradual evolution] was an *a priori* assertion from the start [something believed ahead of time]; it was never 'seen' in the rocks." *Evolution was never seen in the rocks!* Evolution is *not* a logical inference from scientific observations, because the observations were contrary to the theory right from the start, even as Darwin said.

If it wasn't based on evidence or logic, then, where did the concept of evolution come from? Gould and Eldredge supply the answer: "It [gradual evolution] expressed the cultural and political biases of 19th century liberalism." That's what has been passed off in our school systems for 100 years as the "fact of evolution" — *"the cultural and political biases of 19th century liberalism."*

When it comes to the fossil evidence, what are the facts? Believe it or not, when it comes to fossils, *evolutionists and creationists now agree on what the facts are.* The overwhelming pattern that emerges from fossils we have found is summarized in the word *stasis*. *Stasis* and *static* come from the same root word, a word that means "stay the same." Gould and Eldredge are simply saying that most kinds of fossilized life forms appear in the fossil sequence abruptly and distinctly as discrete kinds, show relatively minor variation within kind, then often abruptly disappear.

Steven Stanley,[35] fossil expert from Johns Hopkins University, provided several examples of stasis. Elephants appear as a distinct group abruptly in the fossil sequence, diversify immediately into three subtypes, which then persist unchanged (except those which became extinct) without noticeably changing into anything else. Similarly, the modern horses *(Equus)* appear abruptly, Stanley said, "and their origin is not documented by known fossil evidence." Stanley also noted that the excellent fossil history of bowfin fishes shows only trivial changes, and no basic shift of adaptation, making them very much like their descendants.

The victory of stasis over gradualism did not come easily at the Chicago conference. As Lewin[36] mentioned in his professional summary for *Science,* "The proceedings were at times unruly and even acrimonious," but, on the positive side, "many people suggested that the meeting was a turning point in the history of evolutionary thought."

Perhaps the most dramatic response came from leading evolutionary geneticist Francisco Ayala. After admitting that neo-Darwinists "would not have predicted stasis from population genetics [extrapolation from mutation and selection]," he concluded, "but I am now convinced from what the paleontologists say that *small changes do not accumulate"* (emphasis added). No one finds it easy to change years of thinking, but a willingness to adapt theory to fact is the mark of a true scientist, and Ayala deserves a lot of credit for his statement.

When the dust finally settled, Gabriel Dover of Cambridge University summarized the Chicago conference by calling species stasis "the single most important feature of macroevolution." Note, again, that at least the creationists and evolutionists agree on what the fossil facts represent, namely, stasis: *sudden appearance of complete forms, minor variation, and sudden disappearance.*

Perhaps you also detected a note of irony in Dover's comment. If stasis means anything, it means staying the same; if evolution means anything, it means change. It seems to me, then, that evolutionists are actually saying (without quite meaning to, of course) that *the most fundamental fact of their theory of change is that everything stays the same!*

Creationists prefer a much more direct approach to the evidence. Each basic kind of plant and animal life appears in the fossil sequence *complete, fully formed,* and *functional;* each classifies according to the criteria we use to distinguish groups today, with "boundary problems" generally no greater nor different for extinct forms than for those living today; and each kind shows broad but quite finite ecologic and geographic variation within its kind. The most direct and logical inference (to a heart and mind open to the possibility) appears to be, it seems to me, *creation, and variation within the basic created kinds.* Differences such as extinction and decline in size and variety seem to point to *corruption* and *catastrophe* in the created order, not at all to "upward, onward" evolution.

When Darwin published *Origin* back in 1859, no one knew what discoveries would be made or what patterns would emerge in the new science of paleontology. On the basis of their theory and observations of heredity and reproduction, creationists predicted that only distinct kinds would be found, variation only within kind, and persistence of the criteria for classification. Evolutionists predicted a series of links would be found to show how complex types today evolved slowly and gradually from common ancestral stocks that finally blurred into simple, indistinct, and difficult-to-classify early forms.

The real test of a scientific theory is its ability to predict in advance of observation. When it comes to fossils, *creation has passed the scientific test with flying colors.* The original Darwinian theory of evolution and the neo-Darwinist and punctuationalist views have been disproved twice, both by genetics and by the fossil evidence.

In his final chapter, as he reviews his reasons for calling his book *Evolution: A Theory in Crisis,* Denton[37] makes the following strong, sometimes harsh, statements:

We now know, as a result of discoveries made over the past thirty years, that not only is there a distinct break between the animate [living] and inanimate [non-living] worlds, but that it is one of the most dramatic in all nature, absolutely *unbridged by any series of transitional forms* ["missing links"], and like so many other major gaps of nature, *the transitional forms are not only empirically absent but are also conceptually impossible* [p. 347, emphasis added].

Similarly, the sorts of scenarios conjured up by evolutionary biologists to bridge the great divisions of nature, *those strange realms of "pro-avis" or the "proto-cell" which are so utterly unrealistic to the skeptic,* are often viewed by the believers [in evolution] as further powerful confirmatory evidence of the truth of the paradigm. Evolutionary thought today provides many other instances where the priority of the paradigm [i.e., the assumption that "evolution is fact"] takes precedence over common sense [p. 352, emphasis added].

For the skeptic or indeed to anyone prepared to step out of the circle of Darwinian belief, it is not hard to find inversions of common sense in modern evolutionary thought which are strikingly reminiscent of the mental gymnastics of the phlogiston chemists or the medieval astronomers [p. 351].

In a very real sense, therefore, advocacy of the doctrine of continuity [i.e., evolutionism] has always necessitated a retreat from pure empiricism [i.e., logic and observation], and contrary to what is widely assumed by evolutionary biologists today, *it has always been the anti-evolutionists* [i.e., creationists], *not the evolutionists, in the scientific community who have stuck rigidly to the facts and adhered to a more strictly empirical approach. . . . It was Darwin the evolutionist who was retreating from the facts* [p. 353–354 emphasis added].

On the positive side, Denton also notes that "there has always existed a significant minority of first-rate biologists who have never been able to bring themselves to accept the validity of Darwinian claims" (p. 327). At a conference in Sydney, Australia (April 1987), where we appeared on the platform together, Denton was willing to cautiously extrapolate that "significant minority" to "perhaps a majority" of first-rate biologists. He stressed also that those biologists willing to explore the design hypothesis do so for scientific reasons, apart from particular religious presuppositions (p. 341).

Creation-evolution was featured on CBS Television's "Sunday Morning" (November 23, 1980) in a superb cover story put together by Richard Threlkeld[38] (who ranks up there with CBC's Tom Kelly as a fair, honest, thoughtful, and thought-provoking TV journalist). The 20-minute piece starts with my students and me "in the act of discovery," hunting fossils in the desert east of San Diego. It continues with several evolutionists, other creationists, parents, students, and teachers in action and includes a computer graphic series depicting evolution.

Threlkeld makes the inevitable trip to the site of the famous Scopes "monkey trial," but he does not allow his thinking to be buried there. "The debate goes on," he observes, "and why not?" After all, nobody was there to see how life came into being, he says; at bottom both views are assumptions. But he doesn't stop thinking there, either. Instead, he treats the two ultimate assumptions, creation and evolution, as ideas which *can* be compared for their scientific merits and which *must* be compared before we can truly appreciate our origin as human beings.

II. HOW FAST?

All the courses I took concerning fossils were taught by professors who firmly believed in evolution. Yet, when it came to the kinds of life we studied, it seemed the actual evidence made it overwhelmingly difficult to believe in evolution and very easy to believe what the Bible says about creation, corruption, catastrophe, and Christ.

Even if you could accept my conclusion, or, at least, consider it reasonable, I'm sure you'd have another question. *How fast* do fossils form, and *how fast* do rock layers get stacked up like we see in the Grand Canyon? Believe me, those questions bothered me, too! I knew that some believed, for example, that even though God especially created the first of each kind, he "spaced out" His creative activity over a vast period of time, a sort of "progressive creation."

Can science help us decide how fast fossils form, and how fast those sedimentary rock layers pile up? That's what I wanted to know when I signed up for courses like stratigraphy that deal in part with rates of sediment-layer formation.

Surprisingly enough, just about everybody — creationist, evolutionist, and everyone in between — agrees that individual fossil specimens themselves begin to form very, very rapidly! If a plant or animal just dies and falls to the ground or into the water, it's quickly broken up and decomposed by scavengers, wind and water currents, even sunlight. Fallen logs, road kills, and dead aquarium fish don't just become fossils, nor did the millions of bison slaughtered in America's move west.

Most fossils are formed when a plant or animal is quickly and deeply buried, out of reach of scavengers and currents, usually in mud, lime, or sand sediment rich in cementing minerals that harden and preserve at least parts of the dead creatures. Evolutionists and creationists agree: the ideal conditions for forming most fossils and fossil-bearing rock layers are *flood conditions.* The debate is just whether it was many "little floods" over a long time, or mostly the one big flood of Noah's time. In fact, until Darwin's theory came along, most educated laymen and scientists — including the founding fathers of geology — assumed that fossils were the remains of plants and animals buried in Noah's flood.

Although professionals understand how fast fossils begin to form under flood conditions, the general public often does not. I was on a radio talk show one time when a caller said he believed the earth had to be fantastically old because he'd seen (as I have) huge logs turned to stone in Arizona's Petrified Forest. Surely, he said, it would take millions of years to turn a log six feet (2m) across and 100 feet (30m) long into solid stone! So I asked him to think about it. If a tree fell over in a forest or into a lake or stream and just laid there for millions of years, wouldn't it just rot away? Bugs, termites, fungus, and chemical action would soon turn it back into dust. *If* that tree got suddenly and deeply buried in mineral-rich sediment, *then* minerals could crystallize throughout the pore space in the log and turn it to stone before it had time to decay. To my encouragement, he replied, "You know, I believe you're right about that!"

A museum in central Tasmania has a "fossil hat" on display. A miner had dropped his felt hat, and the limey water had turned it into a "hard hat" (which the curator was kind enough to let me feel and photograph). That same process, mineral in-fill, can turn wood, bones, and shells into fossils in a short period of time. Indeed, fossils can be made in the laboratory!

Remember the Precambrian Australian jellyfish? Jellyfish often wash ashore, but in a matter of hours they have turned into nondescript "blobs" (although watch out — the stinging cells continue to work for quite a while!). To preserve the markings and detail of the Ediacara jellyfish, the organisms seem to have landed on a wet sand that acted as a natural cement. The sand turned to sandstone before the jellyfish had time to rot, preserving the jellyfish's markings, somewhat as you can preserve your handprint if you push it into concrete during that brief time when it's neither too wet nor too dry. Indeed, the evolutionist who discovered the Ediacara jellyfish said the fossils must have formed in *less than 24 hours*. He didn't mean one jellyfish in 24 hours; he meant millions of jellyfish and other forms throughout the entire Ediacara formation, which stretches about 300 miles (500 km) from South Australia into the Northern Territory, had fossilized in less than 24 hours! In short, **floods form fossils fast!** (See Figure 31.)

Like most Americans, I was mis-taught in grade school that it takes millions of years and tremendous heat and pressure to turn sediments (like sand, lime, or clay) into rock (like sandstone, limestone, or shale). We all know better. Concrete is just artificial rock. Cement companies crush rock, separate the cementing minerals and large stones, and then sell it to you. You add water to produce the chemical reaction (curing, not drying), and rock forms again — easily, naturally, and quickly, right before your very eyes. Indeed, you can make rock as a geology lab exercise, without using volcanic heat and pressure or waiting millions of years for the results. Time, heat, and pressure can and do alter the *properties* of rock (including "Flood rock"), but the initial *forma-tion* of most rocks, like the setting of concrete, is quite rapid.

Knowledgeable people readily agree that both fossils and rock layers can and do form very rapidly. But there's a catch. Fossils and rock layers are *not* just found "one at a time." Rocks chock full of fossils are buried in layers stacked on top of one another, in places about two *miles* (*three km*) *thick!* Not only that, but there's a tendency for fossils to be found together in certain groups, and a tendency for these groups to be found one after the other in a certain sequence called the *"geologic column."*

According to evolution, the geologic column (Figure 32) lays out the story of evolution chronologically, from bottom to top, right before our eyes. Maybe science hasn't explained how evolution works yet, but the "fact of evolution" is plain to see in the "record in the rocks." Life started with a few simple life forms (originally produced by time, chance, and chemistry), and we can chart its progress, the net increase in variety and complex-ity produced by Darwinian struggle and death, as we move up through the rock layers. Only an ignorant, fundamentalist fanatic

Figure 31. Because massive flooding seems to be the most logical inference from our observations of fossil deposits, a number of evolutionary geologists are now calling themselves "neo-catastrophists." Catastrophist geology, originally a creationist idea associated with Noah's flood, has stimulated a great deal of research, and it helps us to understand how fossils form (above) and why such huge numbers are spread over such broad areas (below).

with his nose in the Bible could fail to see evidence so clear and convincing as the "rock-hard" geologic column!

Or at least that's the way textbooks, television, museums, and magazines usually tell the story, and that's the evolutionary story I used to teach, too. Well, there really are lots of fossils out there, and they really are stacked in thick layers of sedimentary rock —

> billions of dead things,
> buried in rock layers,
> laid down by water,
> all over the earth.

What do these thick layers of fossil-rock mean to a scientist who believes the Bible?

Actually, most scientists and scholars before Darwin took billions of fossils buried in rock layers laid down by water all over the earth as extremely powerful evidence *confirming* the Bible, a record in stone of the worldwide flood in Noah's time described in Genesis — and also in the traditions, oral and written, of hundreds of cultures (the descendants of Noah) from around the world.

In the Genesis account (Gen. 6–9), the corruption of God's perfect creation by man's wickedness filled the earth with so much grief, violence, and death that God destroyed the world in a global *catastrophe*, the Flood, and gave it a fresh start with Noah and those with him on the ark: creation, corruption, catastrophe, Christ (deliverance). Noah was in the ark for a year and ten days. During the first 150 days (5 months), the waters continued to rise until finally they covered "all the high hills, that were under the whole heaven" (Gen. 7:19).

For scientists called flood geologists or catastrophists, the "major layers" or *systems* in the *geologic column* are *eco-sedimentary zones*, the remains of various ecological groups living in the pre-Flood world. The first creatures buried in greatest abundance in the rising Flood waters would be the heavy-shelled, bottom-dwelling sea creatures, and these would be followed successively by near

(12) Quaternary
(11) Tertiary
(10) Cretaceous
(9) Jurassic
(8) Triassic
(7) Permian
(6) Pennsylvanian
(5) Mississippian
(4) Devonian
(3) Silurian
(2) Ordovician
(1) Cambrian

Figure 32. Two interpretations of fossil groups (geologic systems) and their sequence (the "geologic column" diagram).

Above: According to the catastrophist model, groups of fossils are the remains of plants and animals once living in different ecological zones at the same time, and they were buried in rapid succession. (Drawings from Bliss, Parker, and Gish, *Fossils: Key to the Present* [Green Forest, AR: Master Books, 1980]).

Right: According to the uniformitarian model, systems and the geologic column represent stages in the slow and gradual evolution of life over eons of time.

shore forms and swimmers, then lowland plants and animals, and finally upland forms, with sea creatures found in all the systems of the geologic column as the waters finally covered everything. When the mountains rose and the valleys sank down (Ps. 104:8) at the end of the Flood, the continents were covered with layers of fossils formed as stages in the burial of eco-sedimentary zones during the catastrophe of Noah's flood (Figure 32).

Evolutionists and creationists agree that fossils reflect death and disaster on a colossal scale. Creationists see this as a *bad thing*, a consequence of the corruption of creation by man's turning from God. Evolutionists see it as a *good thing*, a record of millions of years of struggle and death, the buried remains of casualties in Darwin's "war of nature" that produced a net increase in the "quantity and quality" of life on earth (Figure 32).

It's hard to imagine two views more strikingly different! (In *The Fossil Book*,[39] I have a chart comparing the two views on 15 points, p. 25.) Surely scientific study of rocks and fossils should help us decide which of these two views (if either) is better supported by the evidence. Were fossil-bearing rock layers formed *rapidly and globally* (creation/Flood geology), or *slowly and locally* (classic evolution)? Once again, science has not been kind to the evolutionist's position, but has unearthed strong support for the creationist/Flood geologist instead.

Early evolutionists were dogmatically *uniformitarian*. Often summarized as "the present is the key to the past," the doctrine of uniformitarianism was introduced into geology and into Darwin's thinking by Charles Lyell. Lyell wanted scientists to forbid themselves to see any evidence of a process going on in the past *at a rate* or *on a scale* different from what we see today: *slow, gradual, and/or local* (e.g., an intense but local volcanic eruption). His idea sounds scientific (and anti-biblical), but nowhere on earth today do we have fossils forming on the scale that we see in geologic deposits. The Karroo Beds in Africa, for example, contain the remains of perhaps 800 billion vertebrates! A million fish can be killed in red tides in the Gulf of Mexico today, but they simply decay away and do not become fossils. Similarly, swamp peat is nowhere slowly turning into vast beds of anthracite coal.

Some geologic formations are spread out over vast areas of a whole continent. For example, there's the Morrison Formation, famous for its dinosaur remains, that covers much of the mountainous West, and there's the St. Peter's Sandstone, a glass sand that stretches from Canada to Texas and from the Rockies to the Appalachians. Sediment does build up slowly at the mouths of rivers, such as the Mississippi delta, but slow sediment build-up could not possibly produce such widespread deposits, such broadly consistent sedimentary and paleontological features, as we see in the Morrison and St. Peter's formations. In this case, knowledge of the present tells us that something happened on a much larger scale in the past than we see happening anywhere today. That's not appealing to faith or fancy — that's appealing to fact! For purely scientific reasons, evolutionists and creationists may both conclude these are flood deposits, even if the scale of the flood is something far beyond anything observed in historical times.[40]

Then there's the matter of "misplaced fossils." Evolutionists believe, for example, that the land plants did not appear until over 100 million years after the Cambrian trilobites died out. Yet, over 60 genera of woody-plant spores, pollen, and wood itself have been recovered from lowest "trilobite rock" (Cambrian) throughout the world. The evidence is so well known that it's even in standard college biology textbooks. The secular botany textbook by Weier, Stocking, and Barbour[41] that my students once used puts it this way: "Despite tempting fragments of evidence, such as cutinized [waxy] spores and bits of xylem [wood] dating back to the Cambrian period . . ." most evolutionists still believe that land plants did not evolve until much later. Notice, that the evolutionist argues "despite . . . evidence."

The creationist does not argue *in spite* of the evidence." Rather, *"because* of the evidence," the creationist says, "we think that land plants and Cambrian trilobites lived at the *same time* in *different places*. Normally, these sea animals and land plants would not be preserved together for ecological reasons. A few plant specimens, escaping decay, could occasionally be entombed with trilobites in ocean sediment, and that's what we see."

Misplaced fossils are common enough that evolutionists have a vocabulary to deal with them. A specimen found "too low" in the geologic column (before it was *supposed* to have evolved) is called a "stratigraphic leak," and a specimen found "too high" is called a "re-worked specimen." Often, of course, there is actual physical evidence for mixing of strata from two different sources, but sometimes, such evidence is lacking. With such a handy vocabulary available, it's quite likely that the number of misplaced fossils found — without evidence of disturbance — is far greater than the number actually recorded (which is considerable anyway).

Sometimes whole geologic systems are misplaced. While I was a graduate student in stratigraphy class, still trying to decide between the Bible and evolution, we went on a field trip to find the missing 25 million years of the Silurian. We went to a quarry in southern Indiana that was famous for building-quality limestone. The massive gray limestone was quite thick and exposed over many hundreds of yards. In the lower part of the formation, we found corals belonging to system No. 2, the Ordovician. But as we worked our way up the quarry wall, suddenly we began to find Devonian corals, those belonging to system No. 4. Where were the missing corals of system No. 3, the Silurian?

For an evolutionist, that's a crucial question. Evolutionists believe that Ordovician corals *evolved into* Silurian corals, which *evolved into* Devonian corals. Skipping the Silurian would break the evolutionary chain, and for an evolutionist would be impossible!

What was there between the Ordovician and Devonian corals in that limestone quarry in Indiana? Only millimeters separated them, and there was no change in color, no change in texture, not even a bedding plane. There was *no physical evidence at all* for those hypothetical 25 million years of evolutionary time. As the professor emphasized, such a situation is a serious problem for evolution. We simply can't imagine land just lying there for 25 million years, he said, neither eroding nor depositing, then picking up exactly where it left off!

Evolutionists have coined a term to deal with the problem: *paraconformity.* A contact line between two rock strata is called a "conformity" if the physical evidence indicates smooth, continuous deposition with no time break. "Disconformity" is used where the physical evidence indicates erosion has removed part of the rock sequence. Disconformities are often represented by wavy lines in geologic diagrams, and they often appear in the field as *real* "wavy lines" in which erosion channels and stream beds can be seen cutting into the eroded rock layer. In the case of a *paraconformity,* there is no evidence of erosion, nor any other physical evidence of a break in time, only fossils "out of place." The name even means that it *looks like* a conformity. In fact, the only way to recognize a paraconformity is by *prior commitment* to evolutionary theory. There is no physical evidence! If you believe in evolution, then you must believe there was some gap in the sequence, or else the evolutionary chain would be broken.

Creationists don't need the term *paraconformity.* Creationists can simply accept the physical evidence as it's found: smooth, continuous deposition with no time break. Suppose the Ordovician and Devonian geologic systems represent different ecological zones of creatures living at the same time. Then a change in some ecological factor, such as saltiness or temperature, could cause one group of corals to replace the other ecologically, smoothly, and continuously. Or sediment from one ecological zone could be deposited immediately on top of sediment from another zone as currents changed direction, again producing smooth continuous deposition with no time break. I included an explanation like that in my answer to an exam question about paraconformities.

I got an "A" on the essay (and on the test), and the professor was intrigued with the possibility — but said he couldn't accept it because of the time span involved.

Many people think that if Christians could only accept great age, they'd have no problem with science. Actually, they would have no problem with *evolution,* but lots of problems with *science!* Gould[42] lamented that geologists are constantly reporting ecological interpretations of fossil deposits, but he said they should quit doing that, because the time scale is all wrong for evolution. Perhaps the ecological interpretations — based on actual physical evidence — are *correct,* and it's the evolutionary time scale — based on faith in evolution — that's *wrong!* Belief in great age and slow change make it very difficult to understand many physical features of our earth.

Consider *polystratic* fossils. As the name implies, polystrates are fossils that extend through many rock layers or strata. I first heard of polystratic fossils as a geology student. The professor, an evolutionist, was talking about zoning rocks on the basis of the microscopic fossils they contain. The usual assumption, of course, is that one microfossil evolved into another, which evolved into another, and so on. The rock unit he zoned was presumed to involve about 20 million years of evolutionary time. Then the professor told us he followed the rock unit down the creek bed, and found a shellfish, with a shell shaped like an ice cream cone, perched on its tip through the whole 20 million years! How could that be, he wondered. It couldn't perch on its tip for 20 million years waiting for sediment to accumulate, and it couldn't stab itself down through rock hardened over that time.

Polystrates are indeed a mystery for an evolutionist! But they would be no mystery at all, if the whole rock unit were deposited rapidly. Some things, like trees washed out in vegetation mats after a tropical storm, may float upright for a while, and they could be entombed in that upright position if burial occurred quickly enough (Figure 33).

Polystrates are especially common in coal formations. For years and years, students have been taught that coal represents the remains of swamp plants slowly accumulated as peat and then even more slowly changed into coal. There are many reasons that this swamp idea simply cannot be true: the type of plants involved, texture of deposits, and state of preservation are all wrong; the action of flowing water, not stagnation, is evident.[43]

On a small scale, you can see the process that may have started the formation of coal deposits when a typhoon rips up mats of vegetation and floats them out to sea, but some coal seams run from Pennsylvania out across Ohio, Indiana, and Illinois into Iowa and down to Oklahoma! What kind of storm could be involved in the formation of that kind of coal seam? Answer: Catastrophic flooding on a scale like that described in the Bible for Noah's flood!

A new concept of coal formation has been developed by creationist geologists, led by Dr. Steven Austin. In his dissertation for the Ph.D. in coal geology from Penn State, Dr. Austin[44] suggested that coal was formed from plant debris deposited under mats of vegetation floating in sea water. His model explained many features of coal that the swamp model could not explain. Even more importantly, his theory — a real scientific breakthrough — is the first ever to *predict* the location and quality of coal.

Dramatic confirmation of the processes postulated by Dr. Austin was provided by the 1980 eruption of Mount St. Helens. The volcano sent mud and debris hurtling down into Spirit Lake, sloshing a wave nearly 900 feet (275 m) up its initially tree-studded slopes. The wave sheared off a million trees, enough lumber to make all the houses in a large city! The trees were sheared off their roots and stripped of their leaves, branches, and bark. The "forest" of denuded logs floated out over the huge lake. As they became water-logged, many sank vertically down into and through several layers of mud, forming polystrates on the lake bottom. Many features of the lake-bottom deposits are reminiscent of coal deposits. A fantastic video describing both the eruption of

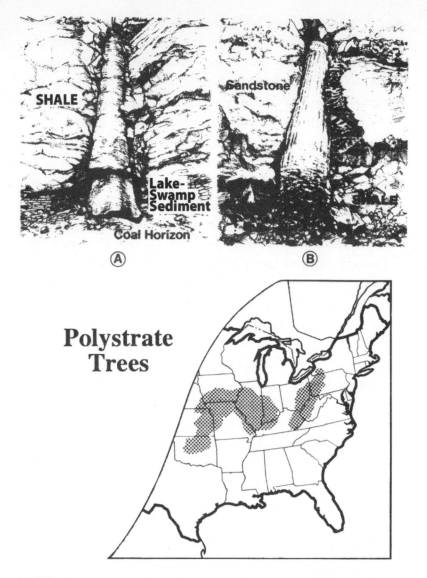

SHALE

Sandstone

Lake-
Swamp
Sediment

SHALE

Coal Horizon

Ⓐ

Ⓑ

Polystrate
Trees

Figure 33. Polystrates (above) are fossils extending through "thousands or even millions of years" of hypothetical evolutionary time. Polystrates are especially common in coal. Because coal deposits extend over such broad areas (right), a growing number of geologists (evolutionists and creationists) think that coal must have been deposited rapidly under floating mats of plants ripped up in large-scale flood catastrophes.

Mount St. Helens and his original research has been prepared by Dr. Austin,[45] and he and Dr. John Morris have the volcano's story in book form.[46]

Thanks to the eruption of Mount St. Helens, scientists have had a chance to observe, measure, and study catastrophic processes close up.[47] The energy of the initial eruption was equivalent to that released by over 20,000 atomic bombs! It blew off the top 1,300 feet (ca. 400 m) of the mountain; produced a hot-blast cloud of 400°C moving at over 100 miles per hour (160 km/hr); generated mud flows tens of feet (several meters) thick, moving at 30 miles per hour (50 km/hr); and produced a wave that, as mentioned before, sheared off a million trees. My wife and I had the opportunity to fly up Mount St. Helens, down into the crater, and out over the denuded mountainside and logjam in Spirit Lake — still awesome ten years after the first eruption. Yet, Mount St. Helens was a "tiny" volcano that never even produced a lava flow!

What supplies the power for volcanic eruptions anyway? Water. Yes, *water* — *superheated* water found in the underground liquid rock called magma. If some crack develops to release pressure, the superheated water flashes into steam, *generating colossal power* — power to blow islands apart, power that dwarfs mankind's nuclear arsenal. About two-thirds of what comes out of the average volcano is water vapor, what geologists call "juvenile water." How much water could be released by volcanic processes? Most evolutionists believe all the earth's oceans were filled by outgassing of volcanic water!

According to the Bible, the water for Noah's flood was first released when the "fountains of the great deep burst forth" (Gen. 7:11). Imagine volcanoes many times more powerful than Mount St. Helens, going off all over the world *at the same time*. That may help you begin to imagine catastrophe on a biblical scale! It's catastrophe on that biblical scale that science *needs* to explain many of the physical features of our earth.

Because of the deluge of objective evidence, a new group of evolutionary geologists has arisen. They call themselves *"neo-catastrophists."* Derek Ager,[48] past president of the British Geologic Association, said, "I have already declared myself an unrepentant 'neo-catastrophist.'" He goes on to say that the geologic evidence reminds him of the life of a soldier, full of "long periods of boredom and short periods of terror." It seems to me that the "long periods of boredom" are the contact lines between the strata (the *absence* of deposits where, *presumably,* all the evolution has occurred). The "short periods of terror" formed the fossil-bearing deposits themselves. It is rapid, large-scale processes that form the fossil-bearing deposits we actually observe.

Although Stephen Gould was an anti-creationist, he said, *"Catastrophists* were as committed to science as any gradualist; in fact, *they adopted the more 'objective' view that one should believe what one sees* and not interpolate missing bits of gradual record into a literal tale of rapid change" (emphasis added).[49]

Catastrophism helps us to understand the patterns of extinction we see when we compare living forms with their fossil relatives. Evolutionists have even proposed a global catastrophe, an asteroid impact, to explain dinosaur extinction. A catastrophe would wipe out creatures regardless of their environmental fitness. Only those that happen to be in the right place at the right time when the catastrophe hit would survive. David Raup,[50] well-known evolutionist, talked about this as "survival of the luckiest" in contrast to "survival of the fittest" (natural selection).

"Survival of the luckiest" would explain why present forms appear to be no more fit to survive than their fossil relatives. At best, only a few of each kind would survive, and these would possess less of the original created gene pool. Population genetics textbooks even refer to these consequences of a "genetic bottleneck" as the "Noah's ark effect." That would help to explain why most groups existed in greater variety in times past than they do now — the *opposite* of evolutionary expectations, a reflection instead of the biblical sequence: creation, corruption, catastrophe.

Giant forms seem to have been particularly hard hit by extinction. As fossils, we find giant dragonflies with wingspans over 2 feet (60 cm); giant fusilinids among the one-celled creatures (1/2 inch or 12 mm is giant for them); the giant reptiles, including some of the dinosaurs; even a giant beaver that reached 6 feet (2 m) in body length. (Imagine looking up into the face of a giant beaver. When he says, "I want that tree," you respond, "Take it. It's yours!") Perhaps the giant beavers were for cutting down the giant trees. As I mentioned earlier, plants such as the club mosses or ground pines (lycopods), which grow only a few inches (centimeters) tall today, are represented as fossils (with the same kind of stem and "leaf" anatomy and reproductive structures) by trees reaching 120 feet (35 m) in height (the lepidodendrons).

The decline in size and variety in so many groups may be related to a dramatic change in global climate. All scientists recognize both that the earth once had a mild climate pole to pole and that it experienced a recent "Ice Age." Although it's past maximum, we're still in the Ice Age. At its maximum, ice at higher latitudes and altitudes covered about 30 percent of the earth's surface; it still covers about 10 percent. What happened? The Genesis flood may hold the key.

Our present atmosphere is only 0.03 percent CO_2, and plants are designed for much higher levels. Carbon dioxide is a "greenhouse gas" that acts like the glass in a greenhouse to bottle up the sun's heat and spread it around.[51] At the time of the Flood, huge numbers of plants, animals, and microbes were buried and fossilized, so CO_2 from their decomposition was not returned to the atmosphere. Much CO_2 would have been consumed also in the formation of limestone, a calcium carbonate ($CaCO_3$). The result would be like throwing off the earth's blanket on a cold night. Land loses heat much more quickly than water does. So, in the first few centuries after the Flood, the earth would have *warm oceans* and, at the higher latitudes and altitudes, *cold continents* — exactly the contrasting conditions required to produce an "Ice Age."

Development of ice sheets requires *warm oceans* to produce lots of evaporated moisture; it requires areas of *cold continents* so that evaporated moisture can fall as snow and ice. The North Slope of Alaska and much of northeastern Siberia were *not* covered by glacial ice, because these areas were *too cold*, lacking the copious precipitation to make abundant snowfall. That's why evolutionary theories all fail to explain the Ice Age. Old habits are hard to break, and for the past two centuries evolutionists have been trying to explain everything in earth history as the result of slooow and gradual processes. If the earth gets slooowly colder and colder, you just get a cold earth without ice sheets, like the North Slope and northeast Siberia. The paradoxical juxtaposition of warm oceans and cold continents requires a sudden global catastrophe — exactly like the Genesis flood! Once again, evolutionists cheat themselves out of a straightforward scientific explanation based on logic and observation, all because of their unscientific commitment to uniformitarian belief, a belief that continues to fail one scientific test after another.

In warmer latitudes, the clash of warm, moist air with cold, dry air masses would generate storms, including "super hurricanes," called *hypercanes*, perhaps ten times stronger than Hurricane Katrina. Such storms may have generated the "fossil hash" deposits in Florida, where a mixture of huge land and sea Ice Age fossils are entombed side-by-side in vast shell deposits. Two other books of mine include more information on storm deposits (*The Fossil Book*[52]) and on ecological differences between the pre- and post-Flood worlds (*Exploring the World Around You*[53]).

Details on the Ice Age, on post-Flood migrations, and on the famous *frozen mammoths* are found in excellent books by meteorologist Michael Oard.[54] Oard presents evidence and scientific logic to suggest ice sheets built up to the Ice Age maximum by about 500 years after the Flood, or about 4,000 years ago.

According to paleontologists at the state museum in Florida, that's about the time the pre-Columbian peoples in Florida killed off the last of the large Ice Age mammals, many larger than the average dinosaur. The ice melted back over the next 200 years, as the difference between oceanic and continental temperatures lessened, and the scale and intensity of storms declined, but the earth never got back to its more idyllic pre-Flood climate and its ecological density and diversity.

Major environmental changes triggered by Noah's flood and the Ice Age that followed may help us understand some rare but special creatures. Scuba diving along Australia's Barrier Reef, I was startled and thrilled to find living crinoids ("sea lilies" or "feather stars"), sort of "upside-down starfish on stems." These graceful creatures (looking like plants, except that they can walk on their "roots"!) were once so abundant that the Mississippian System (Lower Carboniferous) is sometimes called the "Age (Zone) of Crinoids." I had found their fabulous fossils in Indiana, Iowa, and Nebraska, but evolutionary teaching had assured me this great group was an evolutionary dead end, unfit to survive except in a few out-of-the-way places! How stunningly untrue! Here were dozens, in a variety of brilliant colors, alive and doing very well in the richest (and most competitive) life zone on earth!

Forms like these feather stars that were once abundant but now nearly extinct are called *living fossils*. Lampshells (brachiopods) are called "living fossils" because only a few genera survive of a group once so abundant they are sometimes called "fossil weeds." The "oldest" continuously surviving animal (the one with the longest stratigraphic range) is the lampshell called *Lingula*, which, in an evolutionary sense, might be considered the world's most successful animal, remaining completely unchanged while trilobites, dinosaurs, saber-tooth tigers, and other great creatures came and went around it! Graptolites, once thought to be extinct for half a billion years, were found alive and unchanged off western Australia.

The pearly *nautilus* is called a living fossil because most members of its group, the squid-like cephalopod mollusks, have been eliminated by extinction. Why would evolution "do in" the nautiloids, the most complex (i.e., "most highly evolved") of all invertebrates, especially since the "first" nautiloids continue complete and complex — and unchanged, from the "beginning" of fossil abundance (lowest Cambrian rock)?

While it was known only from a few fossil bones presumed to be millions of years old, the coelacanth *(Latimeria)* was hailed as a "missing link," an animal caught in the act of evolving from fish to amphibian. Then they found coelacanths alive and well ("living fossils") off Madagascar — 100 percent fish in a totally deep-sea fish environment. Others of these big fish have been found off Indonesia. As regularly happens, *additional evidence disproved*, rather than supported, *evolutionary belief.* Joachin Scheven,[55] one of Europe's leading creation scientists, has a museum with spectacular displays of these and many other "living fossils."

Evolutionists have always been perplexed by "living fossils." These creatures are clearly well-fit to survive; they were complete and complex from their first appearance, and they have remained unchanged throughout vast stretches of *presumed* evolutionary time.

Unquestioning belief in vast amounts of time conflicts with so much paleontological evidence that it may be time for scientists to question belief in evolutionary time. Actually, there is a great deal of direct evidence that key fossils, and the rock layers in which they are found, are "only" *thousands* of years old, *not millions.*

Summarizing a year of media buzz, *Discover* magazine for April 2006 recounted the discovery of (emphases added) "*soft, fresh-looking tissue* inside a *T. rex* femur," a fossil presumed to be 80 million years old that contained "*lifelike tissue*" that was "*stretchy like a wet scab* on human skin," with "*supple bone cells*" and "translucent *blood vessels.*"[56] The article scoffs at creationists who propose the evidence suggests the dinosaur femur was not millions of years old, but the paleobiologist, Mary Schweitzer, who did the analysis said, "If you take a blood sample and you stick it on a shelf, you have nothing recognizable in about a week. So why would there be anything left in dinosaurs?"

Paleontologist Jack Horner, science consultant for the *Jurassic Park* films and Schweitzer's mentor said, "There may be a lot of things out there that we've missed because of our assumption of how preservation works." Indeed, the article talked about how thinking among paleontologists has been stunted by "faith among scientists" (i.e., evolutionists) and "dogma" and even by competition for funding and by peer review (read that "peer pressure" or "censorship") in journal publications. One reviewer told Schweitzer he didn't care what the data said, he knew (by his faith in millions of years of struggle and death?) that what she was finding wasn't possible. When Schweitzer wrote back and said, "Well, what data would convince you?" the reviewer said, "None." That makes a good case for opening up the discussion of origins to more than just "evolution only." It's no wonder the article was titled "Schweitzer's Dangerous Discovery."

In reality, all the media hype was "old news." Blood cells had been discovered years earlier in the famous South Dakota *T. rex* called "Sue." According to the article (but otherwise forgotten by the media), the National Science Foundation funded a grant to study these earlier *T. rex* blood cells, and "timed the announcement to coincide with the theatrical release of *Jurassic Park*." Actually, many "ancient fossils" have been recovered with organic substances remarkably intact.

Under federal permit, a team of five "creation explorers" brought back from the permafrost on the North Slope of Alaska about 200 pounds (90 kg) of "fresh-looking" dinosaur bones containing organic material (and we have a few on display at our Creation Adventures Museum in Arcadia, Florida).[57] Evolutionists believe the ice has been there only thousands of years, so the ice could not be used to explain the preservation of dinosaur bones assumed to be at least "65 million" years old. These bones, and many other fossils that include some little-altered original material, can be analyzed for DNA and protein.

During the 1990s, analysis of DNA and protein in fossils fueled fables in the media of "dinosaur cloning" and dreams among evolutionists that molecular studies might provide evidence for branching descent that the anatomical evidence had failed to provide, but scientists finally convinced evolutionists and the media that DNA decomposes in thousands of years, not millions, and protein decomposes even faster, even under ideal conditions. In a move worthy of praise, *Discover* magazine admitted that its previous articles touting DNA and protein analysis of fossils must be in error. Without explaining how, they suggested contamination as the source of DNA and protein in fossils. There is another possibility. Perhaps the DNA and protein really do belong to the fossils as originally reported by careful researchers, but the fossils are only thousands, not millions, of years old.

Even more exciting are new studies on carbon-14 reported by Dr. John Baumgardner. While a scientist at Los Alamos National Laboratories, Dr. Baumgardner was featured in *U.S. News and World Report*[58] as the world's leading expert on supercomputer simulations of plate tectonics.[59] His carbon-14 studies were done as part of a group of physicists and geologists investigating *Radioisotopes and the Age of the Earth*, the RATE team. Because carbon-14 has such a short half-life (5,730 years), evolutionists would not usually look for it in fossils thought to be more than just thousands of years old. Baumgardner did look for it — and found it — in the carbon of "ancient" coal taken from layers with "evolutionary ages" of about 300, 100, and 50 "million years" (roughly late trilobite, dinosaur, and giant mammal "ages"). The same professional radiocarbon dating labs used by evolutionists found carbon-14 at about four times the minimum detectable amount, and they found similar amounts in fossils taken from the three major levels in the geologic column (Paleozoic, Mesozoic, and Cenozoic). The data suggest, therefore, that not only are the fossils *only thousands of years old*, but also that they are *all roughly the same age, formed at the same time!* WOW!

To add thrill to excitement, Baumgardner also found carbon-14 in deep earth diamonds from seven African mines! The seven RATE team scientists found other results just as dramatic in studies of radioactive decay involving uranium, polonium, rubidium-strontium isochrons, helium diffusion, etc. The results of their eight-year research project have been published in two technical volumes for specialists in the appropriate scientific fields,[60] but they have also been made available to scientifically interested laymen in book and DVD form as *Thousands . . . Not Billions*.[61] If only the academic mind could be opened a crack (and its heart freed from fear of ridicule), there would be in these references a feast for the soul (and God at the door).

It's certainly no wonder that Darwin called fossils "the most obvious and serious objection which can be urged against the theory [of evolution]." A century and a half of fossil discovery has confirmed Darwin's worst fears. The kinds of life found as fossils suggest living things were created *well-designed* to multiply *after kind*. Rates of formation of fossils and of the rock layers in the geologic column suggest they formed *rapidly* and *recently* on a *catastrophic scale*.

THE GRAND CANYON

There's no doubt about it: the best place to see, test, and put together all these ideas about stacks of fossil-bearing rock is the Grand Canyon.[62] The Grand Canyon is an awesome gash in the earth, running for over 250 miles (400 km) along the Colorado River in the northwest corner of Arizona. The Canyon is about a mile (1.6 km) deep, and averages about 10 miles (16 km) from north to south rims. The walls of the narrow, zig-zag inner gorge expose tilted and faulted Precambrian rock, while the walls of the outer and upper gorge are streaked with thick, colorful, horizontal bands of fossil-bearing rock, representing roughly the "bottom half" of the geologic column.

I once believed and taught, like so many others, that the rock layers in the Grand Canyon represented stages in evolution laid down over vast eons of time. After leading over 40 week-long backpacking trips through the canyon, studying the rock layers and fossils close-up, I'm ready to stake the place out with Bible verses! What I once assumed was a record of a *lot of time,* now looks like evidence of a *lot of water* instead!

Actually, the canyon seems to provide an excellent contrast between rocks laid down slowly and gradually on a local scale and those laid down rapidly and catastrophically on a colossal scale. Evolutionists have argued that fossil-bearing rocks were largely laid down in local floods and/or by rivers dumping sediments into lakes or seas. Those processes do build up sediment layers; the Mississippi River, the classic example, is continuing to build up its delta right before our eyes.

When the Mississippi is flowing full and fast (often after spring rains and snow melt), gravel is carried relatively far. Later, often during the drier summer season, the river slows, so that sand is dumped where gravel was, then silt on the sand. Such slow and gradual processes produce "lumpy" sediment layers that thicken and thin over short distances and *contain virtually no fossils.*

Actually, the Precambrian sedimentary rocks in the inner gorge probably *do* represent sediment laid down somewhat slowly and gradually. Like Mississippi delta deposits, these units thicken and thin, disappear and reappear, over short distances, and they contain very few fossils. They don't have the *layer-cake* appearance — deep and wide horizontal bands of fossil-rich rocks — characteristic of *broad and rapid* flood deposits. Instead, they have the *swirl-cake* appearance — lumps of fossil-poor rock — like the sediment layers being produced at the mouth of the Mississippi River right now. To biblical creationists/Flood geologists, the Precambrian rocks at the Grand Canyon look like pre-Flood rocks formed by processes occurring like those today during the many centuries before the Flood.

Then the Flood came! There are still countless research projects to be done and questions to be answered, but let me share with you a simple model for the basic formation of the Grand Canyon, that ties together most of the ideas we've been discussing. Please treat these ideas as a stimulus to thinking, not, by any means, as the last word on the Grand Canyon.

Although most people relate the Flood to "40 days and 40 nights of rain," the Bible (Gen. 7) says that the Flood *began* when "the fountains of the great deep burst forth." It seems that *most* of the water came from below, not from above. Few people realize what a tremendous amount of water is found in molten rock (magma) trapped beneath the earth's surface! When a hole or crack develops in the solid rock capping the more liquid magma, the pressure release causes the super-super hot water to flash into steam, and "BOOM" we have an upward-outward rush of vapor, gas, dust, and ash, producing a volcanic explosion and/or an outpouring of liquid rock on the surface (lava)! A geologist looking for a way to start a worldwide flood could hardly come up with a better mechanism than breaking up the "fountains of the great deep!"

As the volcanic fountains opened up in what is now the Grand Canyon area, the colossally stupendous force just pushed the pre-Flood rock aside and tilted it up. The Precambrian rocks in the inner gorge are indeed cracked and tilted, and igneous intrusions cut across and between them, marking, I am suggesting, the beginning of Noah's flood, recorded for our study.

The first Flood current in the area came with such tremendous force that it sheared off the tilted Precambrian rocks in virtually a straight line, producing the so-called "angular unconformity" and "great unconformity" diagrammed in Figure 34. Science tells us that the tilt-and-shear could *not* have happened slowly and gradually. One of the tilted units (the reddish Hakatai Shale) is so soft and crumbly you can dig it out with your fingernails. Another is so incredibly hard (the Shinumo Quartzite) that researchers can barely knock off a piece with a hammer. Had the rocks been tilted up slowly and eroded gradually by raindrops and rivers, the crumbly rock would be all gone, leaving valleys, and the hard unit would stick up in ridges and hillocks. *Instead,* it looks as if the Flood current that eventually deposited the Tapeats came in with such titanic force that the hard and soft rocks were sheared off almost equally in a nearly straight line.

Actually, the Shinumo Quartzite is so hard that parts of it *do* occasionally stick up into the Tapeats, but the force of the Flood was so great that it broke off huge boulders of this incredibly hard rock, picked the boulders up, and carried them miles (kilometers) away before finally dropping them! Wow! Even the Colorado River today, a classic example of strength and power, is unable to move lesser boulders downstream from the mouths of its side canyons.

Once the Flood got started, it began to deposit rock layers deep and wide and full of fossils, the "layer-cake" effect characteristic of floods — but on a scale far greater than anything recorded by human observers (except Noah and his family).

We do get some inkling of the kind of geological processes involved from the study of underwater landslides called turbidity currents. In 1929, an earthquake loosened sediment lying on the sea floor off Newfoundland near the continental slope. The loosened sediment roared down the slope at freeway speeds, up to 60 miles (100 km) per hour! How do we know? The dense, muddy slurry flowing along the bottom severed transatlantic telephone cables one after the other, so the time of travel could be calculated from the time telephone service stopped on each line. The roaring sediment spread out over the deep ocean's abyssal plain, covering an area of hundreds of square miles (kms) in a matter of *hours!* Many boulder flows, megabreccias, and other deposits which once mystified geologists are now interpreted,

Figure 34. Grand Canyon: a lot of time, or a lot of water? A record of evolution? Or of the biblical outline of history: creation, corruption, catastrophe, Christ!

even by evolutionists, as huge layers deposited rapidly by turbidity currents. Some evolutionists estimate that perhaps 40 percent of the geologic column was formed by these stupendous flows!

When biblical creationists/Flood geologists offer explanations for the rock layers in the Grand Canyon, they appeal neither to biblical authority (the Bible doesn't mention the Grand Canyon!) nor to mystical or supernatural processes. They appeal, instead, directly to the evidence we can see, touch, and measure. That evidence seems to suggest that *processes we* do *understand,* like turbidity currents, explain what we see — except that the evidence *also* tells us that the scale was regional, continental, or even global, not just local, and it was fast!

Consider this dramatic statement from the secular (evolutionary) textbook by Levine that I have used with my college earth science classes.

> Many channels on Mars dwarf our own Grand Canyon in size, and in order to form, would have required torrential floods so spectacular as to be hard to visualize by earth standards.

Note three things: First, it's normal for a scientist to interpret channels like the Grand Canyon in terms of flooding. Second, it's possible for a scientist to accept cataclysmic flooding on a planet that presently has little or no surface water. Third, a scientist can infer from the evidence left behind "torrential" and "spectacular" flooding on a scale far greater than anything ever recorded in scientific journals! Certainly there's nothing unscientific about inferring a colossal flood at the Grand Canyon from the evidence on a planet (Earth) whose surface is drenched in water!

I've mentioned that, because of the overwhelming weight of scientific evidence, many evolutionists are now calling themselves neo-catastrophists. They want nothing to do with old-fashioned catastrophism (Noah's flood!), but they agree that most layers of fossil-bearing rock were produced rapidly and broadly by flooding on a catastrophic scale, what Derek Ager compared to "short periods of terror" in the life of a soldier.

It's these short periods of terror, it seems, that caught plants and animals off guard, buried them too deeply and quickly for them to escape or to be obliterated by scavengers, and turned them into fossils. Clams and snails, for example, are not normally knocked dead and fossilized by a few sand grains or even by huge shifts of sand induced by hurricanes, but zillions were buried and fossilized, it seems, in the first overwhelming deposits of "Flood mud."

At the Grand Canyon, as around the world, the "first" or "deepest" layer to contain an abundance of fossil remains is called the Cambrian geologic system. As discussed earlier, these Cambrian "stones cry out" for creation! Instead of a few simple life forms, hard to classify and apparently thrown together by time and chance, as an evolutionist might expect, we find a dazzling variety of complex life forms, apparently well-designed to multiply after kind: clams, snails, lampshells, echinoderms, and the most complex of all invertebrates, the nautiloids ("shelled squids"), with an eye that sees the world as we do, and the trilobites, with their geometrically marvelous compound eyes.

Why should Cambrian deposits contain only (or *almost* only) the remains of sea creatures? A professor debating me in Australia put it this way: "If God created everything in six days, why don't we find mice with trilobites in Cambrian rocks?" My simple reply: "Because mice don't live on the sea floor." *Ecology, not evolution, is the key.* (He *then* said he meant his question only as a joke.)

Many people have the completely mistaken notion that the biblical flood covered the whole earth almost instantly, stirred everything up, and then suddenly dumped it all. Not at all! According to the biblical record, Noah was in the ark for over a year. It was about five months before "all the high mountains under the whole heaven" were covered, and it took several more months for the water to subside as "the mountains rose up and the valleys sank down" at the end of the Flood. As the Flood waters "slowly" rose over the earth, plants and animals were buried in a sort of ecologic series: sea-bottom creatures, near-shore forms, lowland plants and animals, then upland (with sea creatures deposited from bottom to top, as the sea eventually covered everything). Evolutionists and Flood geologists may agree that the fossil-bearing rocks were laid down in "short periods of terror," but Flood geologists see the "long periods of boredom" between layers as *minutes or months, not millions* of years!

Indeed, once the rock layers at the Grand Canyon began to stack up, it seems they "forgot" all about "evolutionary time." In one small step (especially small with a heavy backpack!), a hiker can step right across "150 million years" of "missing evolution-ary time"! I'm talking about the contact between the Muav and Redwall Limestones (Figure 34).

The Muav is Cambrian (supposedly, "evolution stage 1"), while the Redwall is Mississippian or lower Carboniferous ("evo-lution stage 5"). If the Grand Canyon is assumed to represent stages in evolution laid out for all to see, where are evolutionary stages 2, 3, and 4 (Ordovician, Silurian, and Devonian)? Evo-lutionists recognize that's a serious question. Grandparents can't have grandchildren without first having children, and plants and animals can't evolve directly from stage 1 to stage 5 without evolving through stages 2, 3, and 4 first. Everyone agrees that in any "chain of life," you can't skip generations!

Evolutionists recognize the problem of rock layers ("150 million years' worth") missing from the Grand Canyon — *but* they also have a ready solution to the problem: erosion. Stage 2, 3, and 4 rocks really were deposited, they suggest, but they were uplifted and eroded away; then stage 5 rock (Mississippian Redwall) was laid down directly on top of stage 1 rock (Cam-brian Muav). It's as if erosion tore out three chapters from the story of evolution.

That evolutionary argument is certainly logical and potentially correct. We see erosion erasing rock layers today, and we can infer that erosion also did so in the past. So evolutionists went looking for evidence of erosion, but they were honest enough to admit that they did not find it, at least not on a sufficient scale.

When a rock layer is eroded slowly and gradually by streams and rivers, as discussed earlier, an irregular surface is produced. When sediment later accumulates on this surface and hardens, the wavy contact line produced is called a *disconformity*, and often old stream beds may be identified along its surface. That's *not* what we find at the Redwall/Muav (Mississippian/Cambrian) contact. Over hundreds of miles of exposure in and out of various side canyons, the two rock layers are in smooth, horizontal contact. There are occasional small erosional dips called Temple Butte Devonian, but the regional picture is clear: it looks like one rock layer was deposited directly on top of the other with very little time break. According to the evidence, those "150 million years" never existed at all![63]

If there were strong evidence for 150 million years of erosion, geologists would call the contact a *disconformity*. Because the evidence suggests, instead, smooth, continuous deposition with little time break, the contact *should* be called a *conformity*. Admitting a 150-million-year "hole" in evolutionary theory would be far too difficult for most evolutionists, so they use the contact term we discussed earlier: *paraconformity*. Flood geologists just accept the evidence as it stands: *no* 150 million years. Evolution requires 150 million years at that point, hence, the term "paraconformity" is offered, *not* as a solution to the problem of all that missing time, but as a label for a problem to be solved by future research.

Evolutionists *believe* that *other evidence* for evolution is so strong that paraconformities can be regarded as just minor glitches in an otherwise convincing story. That's exactly how *I* dealt with "minor mysteries" when *I* believed and taught evolution. There's certainly nothing wrong with that approach, but note that it's an act of *faith,* not science. Flood geologists can simply *accept* the directly observable evidence for rapid, continuous deposition, the more scientific choice at this point.

Another scientific triumph for creationists/Flood geologists lies just above the missing "150 million years." In another research breakthrough that earned him further grudging respect from evolutionary antagonists, Dr. Steve Austin documented the rapid, catastrophic death of perhaps four billion nautiloids and other sea creatures preserved in a six-foot (2 m) bed near the base of the Redwall Limestone. In one dramatic pulse, a colossal sandy debris flow buried fossils along a path at least 135 miles (217 km) long and 30 miles (50 km) wide, stretching from the east end of the Grand Canyon westward past Las Vegas. As of this writing, multiple research papers are being prepared, as well as proposals for permits to do further research in the canyon.[64]

There's further evidence to encourage Flood geologists to think that they have made the correct scientific choice. If individual sediment layers were hardened, uplifted, eroded, then covered again with water, it's likely that the lower hardened layers would crack in a pattern different from cracks formed in layers above them, and produced and moved millions of years later. In other words, there should be "buried faults," cracks through one layer not continuing into the layer above, but there are virtually *no buried faults* above the Precambrian in the Grand Canyon. There are faults, all right, but they cut continuously through the *whole sequence* of Paleozoic layers present (Cambrian, Mississippian, Pennsylvanian, and Permian), *not just part of it.* That evidence suggests the whole "layer cake" was formed rapidly and continuously, without a major break in time — just as you would expect from understanding the Grand Canyon in terms of what the Bible says about Noah's flood.

Then we come to the Coconino Sandstone. Above the Redwall are several other major layers (Supai Group, Hermit

Shale, Coconino Sandstone, Toroweap Formation, and Kaibab Limestone, as shown in Figure 34). All these were obviously laid down as water-borne sediment (i.e., flood deposits) — except the Coconino. The Coconino is a cross-bedded sandstone usually interpreted as a huge desert dune deposit.

Why did I have to bring that up? I've been trying to encourage you to think about the horizontal bands of the Grand Canyon rock as a "layer cake" formed by global flooding. How could 400–600 feet (125–185 m) of desert dune get sandwiched between two layers of sediment deposited during the year of Noah's flood?

The first time someone asked me that question, I didn't know what to say. Admitting the problem, I sputtered something about how the Bible talks about a great wind that blew over the earth as the Flood subsided, but then I also admitted that the layers above the Coconino suggested the Flood was still depositing.

Then somebody reminded me of what I should have known already: dunes also form underwater. Ripple marks in sand at the beach are just "mini-dunes," and my students and I have actually watched much bigger dunes form and travel underwater while on scuba dives (in rough seas) to the Florida Keys. The weight of evidence now favors the formation of the Coconino as an *underwater dune deposit.* Most telling is the work by Dr. Leonard Brand on the abundant animal trackways for which the Coconino is famous.[65]

In this case, my confidence in Flood geology was confirmed by further research. It remains to be seen whether the evolutionist's confidence will *ever* be encouraged by further study of paraconformities. There are surely many other questions to be researched, but the weight of evidence we have available now (and that's as far as science can go) seems to suggest strongly that the horizontal rock layers at the Grand Canyon were formed rapidly, *not* by a lot of time, but by a *lot of water instead!*

If the rock layers got stacked up under water, we have another problem. The North Rim of the Grand Canyon is now over 8,000 feet (over 2,500 m) above sea level. How did that happen? How did the rock layers end up far above sea level, and where did that big gash, the canyon itself that cuts through all those layers, come from?

The Bible tells us that at the end of the Flood "the mountains rose up and the valleys sank down." An evolutionist friend of mine once told me that the best evidence he knew for the creation/corruption/catastrophe model was that *any land existed at all on the earth*. If our planet had spun down from a gas cloud, he said, the outer layers would consist of basaltic ocean crust (density 3.5g/cm^3), covered by a concentric layer of granite (3.0 g/cm^3), the whole thing covered by over 2 miles (3 km) of water (density 1.0 g/cm^3)! He said it looked as if "someone with big hands" (the closest he could come to saying "God") took the granite and shoved it up into a pile to form the dry land. Then he added that the "guy with big hands" was also smart enough to thin the basalt under the granite piles to maintain the earth in gravitational balance (isostasy) so that it wouldn't fracture as it rotated.

Perhaps God did use supernatural means to raise the land after the Flood as He did on the third day of the creation week. Or perhaps He used secondary means not yet discovered. A biblical creationist/Flood geologist would never want to rule out God's direct supernatural intervention (our salvation and resurrection depend on it!), but neither would he or she appeal to supernatural processes unless logic or the evidence clearly pointed in that direction. Actually, neither creationist nor evolutionist is satisfied with present models for "upwarp" and "downwarp," moving big chunks of land above and below sea level.

However the land was raised, the next question is this: Where did the canyon itself come from? The Flood may have *stacked* the rock like a giant layer cake, but what *cut* the cake?

One thing is for sure: the Colorado River did *not* do it. The Colorado River starts about 12,000 feet (ca. 3,500 m) up in the Rocky Mountains of western Colorado. By the time it gets to the Grand Canyon area, it's at about 5,000 feet (1,500 m). That's the problem. The Grand Canyon is definitely *not* a lowland valley. The North Rim of the canyon is over 8,000 feet (2,500 m) high! For the Colorado River to carve the canyon, it would first have to hack its way half a mile (over 700 m) uphill! Water just doesn't do that, especially when there's the opportunity to flow downhill in a different direction. For this and several other reasons, even evolutionary geologists *no longer believe* that the river *slowly* cut the canyon over 60 million years.

The Kaibab upwarp (monocline) through which the canyon is cut seems to have dammed up a great deal of water. It is possible to map the outlines of giant "fossil lakes" that once covered parts of Arizona, Colorado, and Utah. Since there seems to be no renewable source for such a vast amount of water, it may have been "leftover" Flood water trapped as the mountains rose and valleys sank. Post-Flood rains and snow melt would have added more water behind this "Grand Dam."

Then the dam broke! Water rushing through the breached dam formed *"cavitation bubbles"* which act like hand grenades to shatter rock on contact. When water released through spillways at a man-made Grand Canyon dam reached cavitation speed, it ate through the steel-reinforced concrete tubes in seconds. Water pouring through the breach in the natural, earthen "Grand Dam" would have cut the essential features of the canyon very rapidly indeed. The Colorado River is just a modest trickle caught in the twists and turns where the dam was breached. *The canyon came first; the river came second.*[66]

Now, if the evidence is as clear and simple as I'm suggesting it is, then even evolutionary geologists who were totally unwilling even to consider my biblical conclusions could at least accept the individual points as scientifically logical — and they do.

Consider Harlan Bretz. For years and years, he studied the "Channeled Scablands" of eastern Washington, an area of 15,000 square miles (40,000 km²). It looks as if a giant, braided stream cut channels up to 900 feet (275 m) deep in hard basaltic lava (much harder to cut than most of the Grand Canyon layers). Bretz postulated that a tongue of glacial ice blocked off what we now call the Columbia River near Spokane, damming up a huge body of water called glacial Lake Missoula. Then the ice dam broke. According to Bretz, the stupendous drainage from that lake cut the essential features of those channels 900 feet (275 m) deep over 15,000 square miles (40,000 km²) in — one or two million years? — no, in "a day or two." That's the conclusion presented by the U.S. Geological Survey (USGS) in its pamphlet[67] "The Channeled Scablands: the Story of the Great Spokane Flood."

At first, the "slow and gradual" school of evolutionary thinking (uniformitarians) laughed Bretz to scorn, but after examining his evidence, a team of geologists decided Bretz was right after all, and they gave him geology's highest award, the Penrose Medal. In accepting the award, Bretz said that his greatest contribution to geology was reviving the idea that great catastrophes have shaped the physical features of the earth (neo-catastrophism).[68]

Less dramatic in scale, but directly and awesomely visible, was the second modern eruption of Mount St. Helens in June of 1982. The heat generated from that explosion melted frozen mud, producing a mud flow that filled up the North Fork of the Toutle River. The smoke cleared five days later to reveal that the mud flow had eroded a zigzag main channel with many sharply tapered side canyons. Horizontal bands of sediment, some thick, and some exceedingly fine, lined the walls of the newly formed canyon. Right before our eyes, a small volcano (which never even produced a lava flow) had stacked up horizontal bands of sediment and cut channels, *forming a 1/40th size "scale model" of the Grand Canyon in just five days!* All sorts of features once thought to take millions of years were formed, instead, by *a lot of water* in just *five days!* My wife and I got to see it on a dizzying flight down the length of that "Little Grand Canyon." (See Morris[69] and Figure 35.)

Although very dramatic, both the Channeled Scablands and Mount St. Helens are quite modest events compared to the epic geologic work that would have been done by a global flood like that described in the Bible. The stupendous events that shaped the Grand Canyon are summarized in detail in *Grand Canyon: Monument to Catastrophe* (book and video[70]) and in a beautiful, easily readable coffee table book edited by canyon raft captain Tom Vail, *Grand Canyon: a Different View*.[71] (The latter was singled out for "negative discussion" by Dan Rather on the CBS evening news in 2004, but it's "selling like hotcakes" at the Grand Canyon bookstore!)

At least the worldwide evidence is now so clear that even evolutionists are talking about worldwide catastrophes. The most highly touted is supposed to be an asteroid impact that wiped out the dinosaurs and a host of other life forms. Scientists have calculated that if an ocean were hit by an asteroid about 6 miles (10 km) across (and several that size pass near earth's orbit!), a wave of water would slosh over all the continents and bring nearly instant destruction on an unimaginable scale!

The Bible doesn't say whether God used secondary agents, such as an asteroid impact, to trigger the Flood. Either way, it's encouraging to see that evolutionists recognize the evidence that points toward global catastrophe. Indeed, some evolutionists now believe the earth has suffered *multiple* global catastrophes, and I mentioned that others even see evidence of colossal flooding on Mars, a planet that presently has no significant surface water!

The asteroid catastrophes some evolutionists postulate are dramatic, and so is the biblical narrative, as it tells how "all the high mountains under the whole heaven" were once covered with water. If that were so, we ought to find billions of dead things buried in rock layers laid down by water all over the earth. Grab your pick and shovel and go looking, and what do you find? *Billions of dead things buried in rock layers laid down by water all over the earth!* Right up to sea creatures fossilized in the high Himalayas, it looks like the scientific evidence in God's world encourages us to trust the Bible as God's Word![72]

Washington State Dept. Natural Resources

Dr. Steve Austin

Figure 35. The eruption of Mount St. Helens in 1982 formed a 1/40 "scale model" of the Grand Canyon in just five days. Other effects observed at Mount St. Helens dramatically and visibly supported creation/Flood geologist theories about the rapid formation of coal, polystrates, and sediment banding. (There is an excellent DVD by Dr. Steven Austin available from Master Books: *Mount St. Helens: Explosive Evidence for Catastrophe.*)

Sometimes, I imagine a geologist who has spent 20 years roaming through the Grand Canyon. Finally, he decides to take a break and hike up to the rim. There, on a park bench, he finds a Bible. As he opens it and reads the first few chapters, he jumps excitedly to his feet:

> "Eureka! I've found it! That's what I've been seeing here in the Grand Canyon!
>
> "Now I know why the first forms of life to leave an abundance of fossil remains are so complex and varied, and classify into groups like we have today. They were created well-designed to multiply after their kinds.
>
> "Now I know why the 'geologic column' shows a decline in variety, even extinction, for so many groups. We're not looking at a record of evolutionary progress, but a record of death — a corruption of the world God had created all very good. The Grand Canyon is really a vast, open graveyard.
>
> "Now I know how fossils were preserved, how the Precambrian rocks were tilted up and sheared off, how the huge Tapeats boulders were moved great distances, why 150 million mythical years are missing at the great paraconformity, how trackways were preserved in the Coconino, and why the Colorado River is trapped in the sharp curves of the canyon. We're not looking at a record of a lot of time, but of a lot of water — the tremendous worldwide catastrophe of Noah's flood!
>
> "Now I know I can look to Christ to raise me to new life. Nobody could ever have survived the awesome destruction of the world we see reflected at the Grand Canyon. If Christ could save Noah from the Flood, he can save me from death, too!"

When I started working on my doctoral minor in geology, I really thought my study would make it very hard to accept the simple truths and promises in the Bible. My excellent professors all believed evolution, but what I learned about *fossils made it hard to believe evolution and very easy to believe what the Bible teaches about creation, corruption, catastrophe, and Christ!*

We find evidence of **creation** not only in the design and complexity of the "first" fossils found of each group, but also in the wonderfully constructed "language" of DNA; in the intricate way a baby develops in his or her mother's womb according to the plan fully present at conception; in the similarities that point to a "common Creator," not common ancestry, in classification; in marvelously interdependent adaptations, like those of the woodpecker; in the incredible variability, like all the human skin tones, stored in the first parents of each created kind.

We find evidence of **corruption**, the way God's creation was ruined by man's self-centered arrogance, not only in the death, decline, and extinction seen in all the fossil groups, but also in the effects of mutations producing disease, disease organisms, and other defects, and in the struggle to the death that is an essential part of Darwinian selection.

Evidence of a great **catastrophe**, like the worldwide flood described for Noah's time, is clear from the billions of dead things buried as fossils, extinction, rapid formation of huge sediment layers by turbidity currents, polystratic fossils that cut through many rock layers without evidence of falling over or rotting, paraconformities (vast amounts of supposed evolutionary time missing without evidence or erosion), the tilting and shearing and boulder flows in the Grand Canyon, etc., etc.

All the above can be inferred directly from the scientific evidence, although it's the Bible that really puts these together in a pattern of meaning. Evolution is based on genetics that have never been observed and fossils that have never been found. The Bible is supported by laws of heredity we put into practice every day and on thousands of tons of fossils buried in rock layers laid down by water all over the earth.

In short, *evolution is a faith that the facts have failed.* **Biblical Christianity is a faith that fits the facts.**[73]

As I told you in the beginning, I didn't always believe that. It took me three years of trying to *"prove"* evolution to two colleagues, professors of chemistry and biology, before I saw that the scientific evidence available *disproves* the traditional view of evolution taught as "fact" to millions of young people worldwide. Does that mean I've *proved* creation? Not at all. Contrary to a popular misconception, scientists can only *disprove* or *support* a theory, never prove it. As every working scientist knows, you can never tell when some new discovery will shift support to a competing theory. People (including scientists!) are finite, limited by space and time. As finite creatures, we must live by faith; there is no other choice.

We *can choose* the object of our faith. We can put our faith in our own opinions or the words of "experts," as I did through my first several years of teaching university biology. Or we can put our faith in the Word of the Living God, who stands outside our limits of space and time. Only God can tell us what is truly true, now and forever.

The difference between evolution and the Bible is certainly evident when we look back at where we've come from, but the difference is even *greater* when we consider where we're going! I once let my students watch two well-known evolutionists on a TV talk show that aired during class time. The audience wanted to know, "What does the future hold?" The fossil expert said the fate of essentially every species is extinction, and that mankind, too, would someday become extinct. The audience broke into applause, although I've never figured out what's so wonderful about becoming extinct! When they asked the evolutionist astronomer about the future, his reply was that one day the sun would expand and all life on earth would be burned to death, and again the audience broke into applause.

However, the Bible offers a more lively hope! The same God in Christ who created us, is the same God who did not turn away from us when we turned away from Him. Indeed, Jesus Christ paid the penalty for our rebellion, died to conquer death, and rose again to raise *those who believe* to new and eternal life in Him.

Jesus himself asked, "How can you believe me when I tell you heavenly things if you don't believe me when I tell you earthly things?" (John 3:12). Science shows us we *can* trust the Bible when it tells us earthly things about creation, corruption, and catastrophe. That encourages us to trust the "fourth C," Jesus Christ, for the promise of a new and abundant life now and forever, and of a "new heaven and new earth," where God will "wipe away every tear" and restore the creation to the way He made it for us in the beginning: a garden of Eden, a garden of delight. Then once again, "the wolf also shall dwell with the lamb . . . and a little child shall lead them. . . . They shall not hurt nor destroy in all my holy mountain, for the earth shall be full of the knowledge of the Lord as the waters cover the sea" (Isa. 11:6–9).

It's a wonderful, wonderful story, full of love and meaning for each person on earth, and *what we see in God's world encourages us to trust the Bible as God's Word.* Then those wonderful promises can be ours, *guaranteed by the power of the Lord God, maker of heaven and earth,* the God of all people, all times, and all places. If God made us, we can trust Him to make us *anew!* Won't you choose to trust Him now?

The study of science offers *more* than science lessons. There are spiritual lessons as well.

Endnotes

1. Roger Lewin, "Evolutionary Theory Under Fire," *Science* (November 21, 1980).
2. Jerry Adler and John Carey, "Is Man a Subtle Accident?" *Newsweek* (November 3, 1980).
3. David Raup, "Conflicts Between Darwin and Paleontology," *Field Museum of Natural History Bulletin* (January 1979).
4. David Raup, "Geology and Creationism," *Field Museum of Natural History Bulletin* (March 1983).

5. Walter R. Barnhart, *A Critical Evaluation of the Phylogeny of the Horse,* Master's thesis (Santee, CA: Institute for Creation Research, 1987).

6. Richard B. Bliss, Gary E. Parker, and Duane T. Gish, *Fossils: Key to the Present,* Two Models Creation-Evolution Series (Green Forest, AR: Master Books, 1980).

7. Gary and Mary Parker, *The Fossil Book* (Green Forest, AR: Master Books, 2005).

8. Niles Eldredge, as quoted in the *Sunday Mail,* Brisbane, Australia (September 14, 1986).

9. Andrew Snelling, "*Wollemia nobilis:* A Living Fossil and Evolutionary Enigma," *Acts and Facts* (Impact #394) (April 2006).

10. E.J.H. Corner, "Evolution," in A.M. MacLeod and L.S. Cobley, editors, *Contemporary Botanical Thought* (Chicago, IL: Quadrangle Books, 1961), p. 97. See also Duane T. Gish, *Creation Scientists Answer Their Critics* (Santee, CA: Institute for Creation Research, 1993).

11. Bjorn Carey, "Early Bird," *Discover* (April 2006): p. 15.

12. C.P. Sloan, "Feathers for *T. rex*," *National Geographic* (November 1999).

13. Storrs Olson, open letter, *Smithsonian* (November 1999).

14. Tim Friend, "The 'Missing Link' That Wasn't," *USA Today* (Feb. 1, 2000).

15. Parker and Parker, *The Fossil Book.*

16. Duane T. Gish, *Evolution: The Fossils Still Say No!* (Green Forest, AR: Master Books, 1995).

17. Parker and Parker, *The Fossil Book.*

18. Bliss, Parker, and Gish, *Fossils: Key to the Present.*

19. David Raup, "The Revolution in Evolution" *World Book Science Year 1980.*

20. M.A. Norell, E.S. Gaffney, and L. Dingus, *Discovering Dinosaurs in the American Museum of Natural History* (New York: Knopf, 1995).

21. Stephen Jay Gould, "The Return of Hopeful Monsters," *Natural History* (June/July 1977).

22. Stephen Jay Gould, "Is a New and General Theory of Evolution Emerging?" *Paleobiology* (Winter 1980).

23. Adler and Carey, "Is Man a Subtle Accident?"

24. Thomas Kelly, producer, *Puzzle of the Ancient Wing,* Canadian Broadcasting Corporation, "Man Alive" television series (1981).

25. Henry Osborn, "The Evolution of Human Races," *Natural History* (April, 1980); reprinted from *Natural History* (January/February 1926).

26. Stephen Jay Gould, "The Brain Appraisers," *Science Digest* (September 1981).

27. Stephen Jay Gould, "Smith Woodward's Folly," *New Scientist* (April 5, 1979).

28. Marvin Lubenow, *Bones of Contention,* revised edition (Grand Rapids, MI: Baker Books, 2004).

29. David Menton, *Inherit the Wind . . . a Hollywood History of the Scopes Trial* (Hebron, KY: Answers in Genesis, 2006).

30. Charles E. Oxnard, "Human Fossils: New View of Old Bones," *American Biology Teacher* (May 1979).

31. PBS, "In Search of Human Origins, Part One," NOVA series, aired June 3, 1997.

32. Michael Lemonick, "How Man Began," *Time,* March 14, 1994.

33. Adler and Carey, "Is Man a Subtle Accident?"

34. Stephen Jay Gould and Niles Eldredge, "Punctuated Equilibria: The Tempo and Mode of Evolution Reconsidered," *Paleobiology* (June/July 1977).

35. Steven M. Stanley, "Darwin Done Over," *The Sciences* (October 1981).

36. Lewin, "Evolutionary Theory Under Fire."

37. Michael Denton, *Evolution: A Theory in Crisis* (London: Burnett Books, 1985).

38. Richard Threlkeld, CBS Television, "Sunday Morning" (November 23, 1980).

39. Parker and Parker, *The Fossil Book.*

40. Tim Folger, "The Biggest Flood," *Discover* (January 1994): p. 36, 38.

41. T.E. Weier, C.R Stocking, and M.G. Barbour, *Botany,* 5th edition (New York: John Wiley and Sons, 1974).

42. Gould, "Is a New and General Theory of Evolution Emerging?"

43. Stuart E. Nevins, "Origin of Coal," *Acts and Facts,* "Impact" Series No. 41, Institute for Creation Research (November 1976).

44. Steven A. Austin, Depositional Environment of the Kentucky No. 12 Coal Bed (Middle Pennsylvanian) of Western Kentucky, With Special Reference to the Origin of Coal Lithotypes, dissertation, Pennsylvania State University (University Microfilms International), Ann Arbor, MI, 1979: page 390, order No. 8005972.

45. Steven A. Austin, *Mount St. Helens,* video (Santee, CA: Institute for Creation Research, 1993).

46. John Morris and Steven Austin, *Footprints in the Ash* (Green Forest, AR: Master Books, 2003).

47. Steven A. Austin, *Mount St. Helens: A Slide Collection for Educators* (Santee, CA: Geology Education Materials, 1991).

48. Derek V. Ager, "The Nature of the Fossil Record," *Proceedings of the Geological Association* 87(2), pages 131–159, 1976.

49. Stephen Jay Gould, "Evolution's Erratic Pace," *Natural History* (May 1977).

50. David Raup, "The Revolution in Evolution" *World Book Science Year 1980.*

51. Gary E. Parker, *Exploring the World Around You* (Green Forest, AR: Master Books, 2002).

52. Parker and Parker, *The Fossil Book.*

53. Parker, *Exploring the World Around You.*

54. Michael Oard, *The Weather Book* (Green Forest, AR: Master Books, 1997). Michael Oard, *Frozen in Time* (Green Forest, AR: Master Books, 2004).

55. Jachim Sheven, interviewed in "Meet Mr. Living Fossils," *Creation Ex Nihilo* (March–May 1993).

56. Barry Yeoman, "Schweitzer's Dangerous Discovery," *Discover* (April 2006).

57. Buddy Davis, Mike Liston, and John Whitmore, *The Great Alaskan Dinosaur Adventure* (Green Forest, AR: Master Books, 1998).

58. *U.S. News and World Report* (June 16, 1997).

59. John Baumgardner, Steve Austin, et al., *Catastrophic Plate Tectonics* (Santee, CA: Geology Education Materials, 1996).

60. L. Vardiman, A. Snelling, and E. Chafin, editors, *Radioisotopes and the Age of the Earth* (El Cajon, CA: Institute for Creation Research, 2000).

    L. Vardiman, A. Snelling, and E. Chafin, editors, *Radioisotopes and the Age of the Earth II* (El Cajon, CA: Institute for Creation Research, 2005).

61. Don DeYoung, *Thousands . . . Not Billions* (Green Forest, AR: Master Books, 2005).

    Thousands . . . Not Billions DVD/VHS (El Cajon, CA: Institute for Creation Research, 2005).

62. Tom Vail, *Grand Canyon: A Different View* (Green Forest, AR: Master Books, 2003).

63. Andrew Snelling, "The Case of the 'Missing' Geologic Time," *Creation Ex Nihilo* (June–August 1992).

64. Steven Austin, *Sedimentary Model for Canyon-Length Mass Kill of Large Orthocone Nautiloids: A Proposal for Research* (Santee, CA: Institute for Creation Research, 2001).

65. Andrew Snelling and Steven A. Austin, "Startling Evidence of Noah's Flood in a Grand Canyon Sandstone," *Creation Ex Nihilo* (December 1992–February 1993).

66. Steven A. Austin, editor, *Grand Canyon: Monument to Catastrophe* (Santee, CA: Institute for Creation Research, 1994).

67. U.S. Geological Survey, *The Channeled Scablands of Eastern Washington — The Geologic Story of the Great Spokane Flood* (1976).

68. Harlan Bretz, as quoted in "GSA Medals and Awards," *GSA (Geological Society of America) News and Information* (March 1980).

69. John Morris, *The Young Earth* (Green Forest, AR: Master Books, 1994).

    See also Austin, *Mount St. Helens,* video.

70. Austin, *Grand Canyon: Monument to Catastrophe,* book and video.

71. Vail, *Grand Canyon: A Different View.*

72. Henry Morris III, *After Eden: Understanding Creation, the Curse, and the Cross* (Green Forest, AR: Master Books, 2003).

73. Henry M. Morris, *The New Defender's Study Bible* (Grand Rapids, MI: World Publishing, 2005).

INDEX

1859, 8, 76, 81, 83, 189
"2% Difference, The,"
  51–52
"4 Cs of Biblical History,"
  14, 71, 139–140
"7 Cs of Biblical History,"
  14, 71
abrupt appearance/disap-
  pearance, 187–188
acquired traits, 103
activating enzyme, 30, 32
Acts 17:26, 131, 177
Adam and Eve, 13, 184
adaptable/adapted, 58, 93,
  95, 131
adaptations, 63–64, 66–67,
  70, 91, 94–99, 101, 230
AIDS, 57, 139–140
airplane, 29, 30, 34, 38
algae, 50, 165
alleles, 123–125, 131–132,
  142
amino acid, 21, 26–28,
  30–32
angular unconformity,
  215–216
animal trackways, 223
antibiotic-resistant bacteria,
  109–110
anti-knowledge, 50
anti-theory, 50
Archaeopteryx, 166–170
arrowhead, 17–20, 27–28,
  31
artificial selection, 76–78,
  110
asteroid impact, 206, 227
Austin, Steven, 203, 228,
  234–235
Australian Aborigines, 177
Australopithecus, 179–185
Author of life, 36, 144
bacteria, 48, 82, 108–110,
  115, 122, 140–141,
  149–150
bad thing/good thing, 236
base, 23, 27, 29–34, 36, 52,
  124, 222
beauty, 8, 70, 139
Behe, Michael, 67, 73, 97,
  138, 147

"Beyond the Reach of
  Chance," 110
biases of 19th century
  liberalism, 187
Bible, 7–8, 11–16, 19–20,
  38, 52, 62, 75, 127, 131,
  134, 137–144, 152, 157,
  177, 184, 192, 196, 200,
  203, 205, 214–215, 218,
  222–224, 227, 229–232
big jumpers, 173
birth defects, 139, 141
"blind," 92, 116
blind watchmaker, 76, 92,
  122–123
Blind Watchmaker, The, 41,
  72, 146
Bliss, Richard, 72–73, 233
Blyth, Edward, 81, 102
blue-green algae, 165
bombardier beetle, 63,
  99–101
bondage to decay, 13
Bones of Contention, 178,
  233
bonobo, 181
brachiopods, 156, 209
buried faults, 222
Cain and his wife, 114
Cambrian, 154–160, 197,
  199–200, 210, 219–222
Cambrian explosion, 155,
  157–158
carbon-14, 212–213
carbon-14 in coal, 212
carbon-14 in diamonds, 213
carbon dioxide, 207
catastrophe, 13–14, 71,
  140, 154, 157, 162–163,
  166, 189, 192, 196, 198,
  205–208, 217, 224, 227,
  229–230, 232
catastrophic death, 222
catastrophism, 206, 218
cave men, 176
cavitation bubbles, 225
CBS television, 191, 227,
  234
cell, 21, 29, 32–34, 54, 58,
  62, 70, 120, 123–125,
  129, 140, 150

censorship (censoring),
  70, 211
cephalopod, 47, 154, 157,
  210
change between types, 123,
  135
change through time, 80,
  82, 90
change within types, 123,
  135
change, yes; evolution, no,
  5, 80
Channeled Scablands,
  225–227
chemical evolution, 23,
  25–26, 39, 41, 72, 158
Chicago conference, 150,
  187–188
chimpanzee, 51–52, 73, 181
Christ, 3, 13–14, 38, 71,
  140, 142–145, 154,
  157, 162, 192, 196, 217,
  229–230, 232
Christian, 11–12, 41,
  143–144, 152
circular reasoning, 87
circumstantial evidence, 71
cleaner fish, 98
cleaning symbiosis, 63, 98,
  100–101
coal, 199, 203–204, 212,
  228
coccyx, 58
Coconino Sandstone,
  222–223
coelacanth, 172, 210
Colorado River, 213, 216,
  224–225, 229
common ancestor, 43–46,
  50, 157–158
common plan, 44–45
compound traits, 65,
  96–97, 100
compromise, 144
concrete/cement, 193–194,
  225
coney, 174
conflicts between Darwin
  and paleontology, 160,
  232

conformity, 201, 221
convergence, 46
corruption, 13–14, 71, 96,
    109, 112, 125, 139–142,
    144–145, 154, 157,
    162–163, 166, 189, 192,
    196, 198, 207, 217, 224,
    229–230, 232
Creator, 11, 18–19, 31,
    36–37, 43, 49, 51, 54,
    68, 75–77, 97, 123, 137,
    144, 184, 186, 230
Cretaceous explosion, 165
Crick, Francis, 39, 72, 158
crinoids, 209
cross-bedded sandstone, 223
crystal, 36–37
cyanobacteria, 165
Darwin, Charles, 7, 75,
    143, 159
Darwin's Black Box, 67, 73,
    97, 147
Darwin on Trial, 97, 137,
    147
Davis, Allen, 3, 15
Dawkins, Richard, 41, 72,
    92, 120, 146
Dawkins video, 122
death wins, 14
DDT-resistant flies, 82
decline in size, 163, 189,
    207
decline in variety, 229
Denton, Michael, 40, 67,
    72, 76, 97, 146, 234
desert dune deposit, 223
design without a Designer,
    5, 75, 82
Dickerson, Richard, 35, 48,
    72–73
differential reproduction, 87
dinosaur-bird, 169–171
dinosaur blood cell, 210
dinosaur pine, 166
disconformity, 201, 221
divergence, 47, 53
DNA, 5, 11, 16, 20–24,
    27–39, 49–52, 56–58,
    61–62, 66, 70–73, 83,
    106–109, 115, 120,
    123, 125, 138–141, 146,
    150–151, 184, 212, 230
DNA code, 21, 23, 36, 146

ecological competition,
    88–91
ecological succession, 90–91
ecology versus evolution, 91
eco-sedimentary zones,
    196–198
Ediacara (jellyfish, seg-
    mented worms), 159,
    193–194
edutainment, 151
egg cell, 54, 58, 62
embryo, 54–63
entelechy, 62, 146
Equisetum, 163–164
eternal life, 14, 232
Eve and Adam, 13, 184
evolutionary clock, 52
Evolution: A Theory in Crisis
    40, 67, 72, 97, 137, 146,
    189, 234
exherent order, 19, 31
extinct/extinction, 92–94,
    96, 133, 154, 156, 159,
    162–164, 171, 183,
    188–189, 206–207,
    209–210, 229–231
extrapolation, 82–84, 101,
    108, 134–135, 151, 188
eye of squid, 46–47, 219
faith, 12, 25, 39, 66, 158,
    169, 171, 199, 202, 211,
    222, 231
favorable mutation,
    116–117
*Fearfully and Wonderfully
    Made*, 63, 67
feather stars, 209
"Feathers for *T. rex*,"
    169–170, 233
finches, 8, 101–103
fitness, 84–89, 94–95, 98,
    100, 206
fittest, 9, 77–78, 84–86,
    87–89, 92–93, 95, 107,
    162, 206
Flood, the, 14–15, 80, 91,
    139, 144, 154, 157, 164,
    166, 192, 194–196, 198,
    203, 205, 207–209,
    214–216, 218–229
flood geology, 198, 223
flooding, 195, 203,
    218–219, 223, 227

floods form fossils fast, 194
Florida panther, 119
flour beetle, 90
flowering plant, 165
flu virus, 106
fossil, 5, 12, 47, 71, 132,
    149, 153–167, 169–175,
    183, 186–189, 192–193,
    195, 197–198, 202, 206,
    208–210, 213, 219, 225,
    229–231
Fossil Book, The, 161, 198,
    233–234
fossil graveyard, 12
fossil hat, 193
fossil jellyfish, 159, 193
fossils and flood conditions,
    192–198
Fossils: Key to the Present,
    161, 197, 233
founders, 131
fountains of the great deep,
    205, 215
"fresh-looking" dinosaur
    bones, 211
frozen mammoths, 208
fruit flies, 106–107, 115,
    132
fungi, 109
future, 65, 87, 92, 101,
    106, 142, 161, 221, 231
Galapagos, 8–9, 101–102
Garden of Eden, 184, 232
gene frequency, 133
gene pool, 95, 125,
    129–131, 133, 136, 144,
    206
gene pool depth, 125
gene pool width, 125
Genesis, 15, 38, 41, 70–71,
    103, 142, 166, 196,
    207–208
Genesis flood, (see Flood,
    the)
Genesis Flood, The, 15
genetic alphabet, 31
genetic burden, 113, 115,
    118–119, 121, 141
genetic bottleneck, 206
genetic codon, 130–132
genetic drift, 131, 144
genetic formula, 51, 136
genetic inertia, 129

genetic load, 115, 120, 130
genetic script writer, 120
genon, 124–125
geologic column, 157, 174,
    194, 196–198, 200,
    212–214, 218, 229
giants, 207, 212, 224–226
gill slits, 54–55, 57, 61
Gingko, 166
giraffe, 103–105
Gish, Duane, 43, 72, 233
global flood, 13, 227
God's handiwork, 111
gospel, 144
gradual evolution, 173,
    187, 197
Grand Canyon, 5, 16,
    152–153, 192, 213–215,
    217–220, 222–223,
    225–230
*Grand Canyon: A Different
    View*, 227, 235
*Grand Canyon: Monument
    to Catastrophe*, 227, 235
Grand Dam, 225
graptolites, 209
Great Spokane Flood, 226
great unconformity, 215
greenhouse gas, 207
Haeckel, Ernst, 61, 177
hair, 21, 51, 61–62, 114,
    123, 125, 134, 178
Hardin, Garrett, 67–69, 73
Hardy-Weinberg law, 129,
    145
hemoglobin, 21, 48,
    115–117, 123–125
hierarchical, 43, 53, 137
historical evidence, 153
Homo erectus, 178
homologous chromosomes/
    homologs, 123–124
homology, 5, 43–46, 48, 50,
    52–53, 71, 73, 152
Homo sapiens, 176–177
hope, 11, 13, 24, 26, 51,
    100, 143, 160, 232
hopeful monsters, 173
horse, 43, 110, 161,
    174–175
Hox gene error, 60
Hoyle, Fred, 39, 72
hummingbird, 173

Huxley, Julian, 81
Huxley, T. H., 81
hypercanes, 208
hyrax, 174
Ice Age, 71, 207–209
Icons of Evolution, 137, 146
ID (intelligent design), 26,
    31, 51, 67, 97, 137–138,
    140–141
imposed relationship, 27, 31
"Incredible Creatures That
    Defy Evolution," 63, 73
information, 2, 36–37,
    40, 49, 72, 110, 120,
    122–124, 133, 138–140,
    151, 161, 208
information carrier, 37
inherent order, 19
intelligent design (ID), 26,
    31, 51, 67, 97, 137–138,
    140
interbreeding, 119,
    132–134
intermediate links, 160
interspecific competition, 89
intraspecific competition,
    89–90
invertebrate, 48, 70, 154,
    157
irreducible complexity, 65,
    67, 96–97, 138
Java man, 178
jellyfish, 154, 159, 193
Johanson, Donald, 179,
    181, 234
John 1:1–3 and 14, 5
Johnson, Phillip, 97, 137,
    147
juvenile water, 205
Kaibab upwarp, 225
Kentucky-fried dinosaur,
    173
Kenyon, Dean, 42, 72
kind of design, 34–35, 37,
    47, 68–69, 123
Laetoli, 185
Lamarck, 103–104
lampshell, 209
Latimeria, 210
law of conservation of
    genetic variability, 129
Leakey, Louis or Mary
    or Richard or Meave,

179–183
left-handed, 26
Lepidodendron, 163–164
Lewontin, Richard, 63–64,
    73, 95–96, 99, 146, 162
life wins, 14
limits to mutations,
    107–125, 150–151
limits to natural selection,
    83–84, 87–105, 134, 151
Lingula, 209
Linnaeus, 137
Little Grand Canyon, 227
living fossils, 166, 210
logical inference, 16, 19–20,
    35, 40, 45, 71, 101, 121,
    134–135, 137, 173,
    186–187, 189, 195
logic and observation, 5,
    16–17, 19, 42, 190, 208
Logos, 38
long term versus short
    term, 92
lot of water versus a lot of
    time, 214, 217, 223, 226
Lucy, 179, 181–182, 185
lumper, 134
Lyell, Charles, 198
macroevolution, 82, 96,
    133, 145, 150–151, 188
malaria, 115–117
Mars' "grand canyon," 218
mathematical challenges,
    108
matrix, 49, 53
melanin, 84, 126, 128
Mendeleev, 49, 53
messenger RNA (mRNA),
    29, 31–32
microevolution, 145,
    150–151
migration versus muta-
    tion, 91
Miller, Stanley, 23–24
millions of years, 10, 12, 14,
    82, 122, 143–144, 152,
    171, 193–194, 198, 204,
    210–212, 220, 222, 226
millions of years of struggle
    and death, 10, 12, 82,
    143–144, 152, 198, 211
mischievous results, 90,
    116–117

misplaced fossils, 199–200
missing 150 million years, 222
missing link, 169–171, 187, 210
Mississippian, 197, 209, 220–222
mitochondrial Eve, 184
modular, 48–49, 136
molecular clock, 53
molecular homology, 50, 52–53, 71, 73
molecular machinery, 97, 151
Molecules to Man, 82–83, 108
Mongoloid idiocy, 61
morphologic series, 171, 174
Morris, Henry M., 3, 15, 235
mosaic, 48–50, 64, 136, 154, 168
mousetrap, 67
Mount St. Helens, 203, 205, 226–228
multiply after kind, 137, 165, 174, 213, 219
multiply and fill, 91, 93–96, 118, 130
mutational decay, 115
mutational disorders/diseases, 111–119
mutations, 10, 16, 66, 94, 105–116, 118–120, 122–124, 130, 136, 138–142, 145, 149, 173, 230
mutations, yes; evolution, no, 108
National Geographic, 169–170, 183, 233
natural selection, 5, 9–10, 66, 71, 76–84, 87–97, 100–103, 105, 110–111, 116–119, 122, 139, 141–142, 144, 157, 162, 206
natural selection, yes; evolution, no, 5, 83–84, 90
"Nature's Challenges to Evolution Theory," 67–69
nautiloid/nautilus, 154,

156, 210
Neanderthals, 176, 178, 180
Nebraska man, 178–181
Negro, 177
neo-catastrophism, 226
neo-Darwinian, 105–107, 118, 171, 173
net relative reproductive efficiency, 87
new creation, 181
new heaven and new earth, 13, 232
new life, 3, 12–14, 144, 229
Noah's ark effect, 206
Noah's flood, (see Flood, the)
non-branching traits, 50
numerical fitness, 85–89
not by a lot of time, 223
one blood, 131
one race, the human race, 131, 177
ontogeny recapitulates phylogeny, 61
Oparin, A.I., 25
ordered repeat pattern, 36
origin of life, 5, 20, 25, 30, 35, 38, 40, 43, 72–73, 76, 159
Origin of Species, 8, 76, 95, 101, 143
Oxnard, Charles, 182, 234
Paley, William, 41, 68
pangenesis, 103
paraconformity, 201, 221, 229
Patterson, Colin, 50, 73
Peking man, 178
peppered moths, 77–84, 93–94
petrified, 166, 193
Petrified Forest, 193
pharyngeal (throat) pouch, 57, 77
pigeon, 77–78
Piltdown man, 170, 177–178, 180–181
plasmids, 109
plate tectonics, 212
platypus, 64, 134, 171
polystrates/polystratic fossils, 202–204, 228
post-neo-darwinian, 132,

137, 173
Precambrian, 158–159, 165, 193, 213–215, 222, 229
Precambrian/pre-Flood rocks in Grand Canyon, 213–217
probability, 27
progress/progressive change, 9, 94, 104–105, 113, 116–117, 119, 141–143, 149, 170, 194, 229
progressive creation, 143, 152, 192
properties of matter, 18–20, 23, 28, 32, 38–40
properties of organization, 18–20, 28, 38, 71
protein, 5, 20–21, 23, 26–27, 29–35, 48, 56, 62, 70, 110, 120, 123, 126, 139–140, 212
Psalm 139, 63, 67
punctuated equilibrium, 173
race, 7, 87, 94, 131, 177
racism, 177
Raup, David, 160–162, 206, 232–233, 234
recombination, 109, 121, 129
Redwall/Muav, 221
regulator genes, 60, 173
religious implication, 81
reproductive isolation, 133, 144
reworked specimen, 200
R-group, 27–30
ribosomal RNA (rRNA), 29, 33
ribosomes, 31–32
RNA, 21, 29–33, 140
Romans 1:20, 19
Sagan, Carl, 17, 143, 147
same kind, 29, 35, 43, 48, 57, 91, 123–125, 132, 154, 162, 207
scale model of Grand Canyon, 226, 228
science classes, 70, 218
scientific application, 81
scientific evidence of creation, 15–16, 18, 20,

43, 76, 138, 208, 218, 229–231
scientific malpractice, 170
Scopes trial, 68, 178, 191
sea lilies, 154, 209
segmented worms, 159
sequential, 108, 137
serial homology, 43
sexual homology, 45
Shinumo quartzite boulder, 216
short periods of terror, 206, 219–220
sickle cell, 117, 124–125
Signorino, Charles, 5, 12
sin, 3, 13–14, 102
skin color, 20, 126–130
soft, fresh-looking tissue inside a *T. rex* femur, 210
spark chamber, 23–26
special creation, 10, 34, 162, 164, 166
speciation, yes; evolution, no, 5, 133
species, 8, 12, 48, 76, 81–83, 88–93, 95–96, 100–101, 113, 115–116, 118–119, 132–139, 142–143, 156, 160, 177, 187–188, 231
specified complexity, 36–37
spina bifida, 60
Spirit Lake, 203, 205
splitter, 134
stasis, 121, 187–188
step-by-step evolution, 67, 138
stratigraphic leak, 200
stratigraphic series, 171, 174
stromatolites, 165
struggle and death, 9–10, 12, 14, 66, 68, 75–77, 81–83, 96, 100–103, 118, 130, 143–144, 152, 174, 194, 198, 211
struggle for survival, 8–9, 77, 85, 87, 92, 142
subspeciation, 83, 134
succession, 90–91, 197
super hurricanes, 208
survival of the fittest, 9, 77–78, 87, 93, 162, 206

survival of the luckiest, 162, 206
survival of the survivors, 87–88
symbiosis, 63, 98, 100–101
"tail" of embryo, 29, 54–55, 58, 60–62, 77, 167–168
"tail bone," 58
Tapeats Sandstone, 216
tautology, 87
TCSD (time, chance, struggle, death), 10, 14, 66, 76, 149–150
territorial population control/territoriality, 92
theistic evolution, 143
"Think about it," 5, 68–69, 71, 135, 138, 146, 152, 168, 193
Thousands . . . Not Billions, 213, 235
thousands of years old, not billions, 210, 212–213
three bases, 27–28, 31
throat pouch, 57, 77
throwback, 57, 60–61
time versus evolution, 80, 82, 90, 110, 115, 119, 141, 145
tools of science, 17, 42
transatlantic telephone cable, 217
transcendent simplicity, 35
transfer RNA (tRNA), 29, 32
translase, 30, 32, 33
transspeciation, 83, 134
trilobite, 155–157, 199, 212
triplet codon, 32
turbidity currents/ turbidites, 216–218, 230
turkey, 112–113
two-model, 68, 73
typographic error, 120
typology/typological, 53, 137
underwater dune deposit, 223
underwater landslides, 89, 216–217
uniformitarianism, 198

unique combinations, 134–136
unsubstantiated, sensationalistic tabloid journalism, 169
unsurvival of the unfittest, 93–94
upward or downward, 111
use and disuse, 103–105
variation within kind, 81–82, 90, 95, 109, 118, 120, 123–125, 129, 132–135, 145, 174, 187
variation within species, 83, 118
variation, yes; evolution, no, 5, 126
varieties, 9, 77–78, 81, 85, 93, 95, 103, 109, 124–125, 131–133, 163
vertebrate, 45–47
vestigial organ, 54, 57, 141
virus, 21, 57, 106, 125, 139–141
volcano, 29, 203, 205, 226
war of nature, 9–10, 77, 83, 92, 94, 140, 143, 198
well designed, after kind, 159, 165
well designed to multiply after kind, 159, 165
Whitcomb, John C., 3, 15
wollemi pine, 165–166
woodpecker, 63, 65–67, 70, 73, 94, 98–99, 101, 230
Word of the Living God, 231
world view, 9, 14, 171
life view, 20
worldwide flood, 196, 215, 230
Y chromosome Adam, 184
yolk sac, 54–56, 58, 61